D1590053

John
Garfield

John Garfield

THE ILLUSTRATED CAREER IN FILMS AND ON STAGE

by

Patrick J. McGrath

McFarland & Company, Inc., Publishers
Jefferson, North Carolina, and London

British Library Cataloguing-in-Publication data are available

Library of Congress Cataloguing-in-Publication Data

McGrath, Patrick J., 1955–
    John Garfield : the illustrated career in films and on stage /
Patrick J. McGrath.
      p. cm.
    Includes filmographies, bibliographical references, and index. ∞
    ISBN 0-89950-867-7 (lib. bdg. : 50# alk. paper)
    1. Garfield, John—Criticism and interpretation. I. Title.
PN2287.G377M35   1993
791.43′028′092—dc20   92-56666
                                                  CIP

Manufactured in the United States of America

McFarland & Company, Inc., Publishers
  Box 611, Jefferson, North Carolina 28640

To the memory of my father,
James,
and of my brother,
Richard,
from whom I learned . . .
and am still learning

Table of Contents

Acknowledgments

I would like to express my gratitude to the following individuals and organizations for their help in the writing of this book: Dick Andersen, John Berry, Dane Clark, Bill Cramarosso, Tony Crnkovich, Ken Dumroese, Eddie Brandt's Saturday Matinee, Ernestine Hall, Film Favorites, Mike Kanter, Mary Kilburg, Otto Kremsreiter, Ann and Jim McGrath, Terry McGrath (trusty research assistant), Jim and Marge Muting, Concepcion Pagan, John, Mary, and Wayne Richards, Vincent Sherman, the staff of the Margaret Herrick Library of the Academy of Motion Picture Arts and Sciences, Brian Stagg, and Steve Woods.

I would like to extend a special thanks to my friend Ted Okuda for his sound advice throughout the project, and, finally, a very special thanks to a very nice lady, Marie Windsor, one Hollywood star who is just regular people.

Preface

John Garfield was one of the finest actors the United States has yet produced. He was a sensitive, caring man in his personal life and a determined, intense actor on stage and screen. It is unfortunate that he is all but forgotten today, for his film portrayals would have great meaning to current audiences, especially the nation's urban poor—just as they had for audiences of the 1930s and 1940s.

Garfield's films have not been shown consistently on television or in revival theatres. There were some signs of a John Garfield revival in the middle to late 1970s, when a number of fine books chronicling his life and career were published: Larry Swindell's splendid biography, *Body and Soul: The Story of John Garfield* (1975); *The Films of John Garfield* by Howard Gelman (1975); *John Garfield* by George Morris (1977); and *John Garfield—His Life and Films* by James N. Beaver, Jr. (1978). I would like to thank each of these gentlemen, first for having enough interest in John Garfield to sustain the sacrifices necessary in such projects, and second, for the wonderful works that resulted from their efforts.

All of the above titles were valuable reference sources, but with the exception of Mr. Gelman's work they are, sadly, long out of print. With this lack of current material on Garfield's life and career in mind, I felt the time had come for another look at John Garfield, the man and the actor.

I hope fervently that somehow enough interest can be generated to rekindle the spark that Messrs. Swindell, Gelman, Morris, and Beaver ignited in the 1970s, a time when it looked as though John Garfield might finally attain his rightful place in the annals of motion picture history.

Author's note: The name Julie has been used to identify John Garfield. This informality of expression certainly does not imply that I knew the man. But he was known as Julie to almost everyone he came in contact with; therefore I feel it is appropriate and expedient to refer to Garfield as Julie, and the name will appear many times throughout the text.

Chapter 1

The Wild Boy in the Streets

Projected on the screens of the world, he was the Eternal Out-sider, forced to glimpse paradise but not allowed to dwell there. Often he joked that he was playing out his own life on film. He was the first of the rebels: John Garfield, the antihero in revolt against a world he never made.[1] John Garfield's life story reads like any of his early Warner Bros. films, filled with every cliché about the poor boy from the streets of New York. But that's the way it was...

He was born Jacob Garfinkle on March 4, 1913, in a three-room flat on Rivington Street, part of New York's Lower East Side. The name Julius was added to Jacob's name during infancy, and he was known as Julie from then on. His father David was a coat presser and a cantor in the synagogue. His mother Hannah was a sickly woman, and she had a difficult second pregnancy when she gave birth to Max in 1918.

Hannah Garfinkle died in 1920, and David took his sons out of the East Side. Without a mother to watch over him, Julie became a roamer. For three years, 1920–23, he wandered the streets of East Brooklyn, which served as a natural habitat for the youth. Julie remembered: "We moved from Rivington Street to Brooklyn and then to the Bronx. I did a lot of jobs when I was a kid — paper boy, grocery boy, all those things. I guess maybe I got a point of view then. All the kids I knew were poor kids. Some turned out bad, some just ordinary, and some turned out nice."

David Garfinkle married a widow named Dinah Cohen in 1923, and they took Julie to live with them in the Bronx. Brother Max was left behind with relatives in Brooklyn. Julie quickly fell in with a gang of kids in his new neighborhood. Gang members were coached regularly on the only law of the street: Don't rat on nobody. While the gang did not necessarily terrorize the neighborhood, they were not angels, either. Years later, John Garfield often liked to tell reporters of his impoverished youth:

> I'll tell you my analysis. Not having a mother [he never recognized Dinah], I could stay out late. I didn't have to eat regularly or drink my milk at 4 o'clock. I could sleep out and run away, which I did a lot of. I wanted the attention I missed at home, so I became the leader of a gang. That way I got attention and was recognized as being important. It wasn't a bad gang — you know, in poor districts in New York there's a gang to every block. We never robbed at the point of a gun; we'd steal potatoes from a grocery store, or crackers. But that's a poor boy, not a bad boy.
>
> I was full of nerve. I remember somebody said, "I dare you to hang off the roof for a dime." The gang stayed in the street while I climbed five floors and hung off the roof for a dime, all the neighbors looking at me and shoutin'.
>
> When I think back, the neighbors were always sayin', "Oh, that poor Julie, that poor orphan." I loved it. The Italians would invite me in for dinner — it was an Italian neighborhood mostly. Oh, I loved it. Sometimes, I think those were the best days.

Another way of getting attention was reenacting the movies that the gang had seen. They staged these plays in the basement of an abandoned mill, giving Julie his first taste of acting. He had found his calling and his passion would grow with each passing year.

The Garfinkles had many confrontations with juvenile authorities, mostly over Julie's ditching school. He was expelled from schools three times before receiving the biggest break of his young life. A school official suggested that Julie should be enrolled in Angelo Patri's school for "special cases," P.S. 45.

Angelo Patri was born in Italy in 1876 and arrived in New York in 1889, unable to read or speak English. But he worked hard and graduated from City College of New York in 1896. He dedicated his life to teaching other immigrant children to seize the promise that America offered. He believed that every child had a God-given vocation, a gift that had to be discovered.

In September 1926, Julie moved in with an uncle in the East Bronx and began attending classes at P.S. 45, where he met the man who would have a profound influence on his life. More than 20 years later, John Garfield still had a vivid memory of his first meeting with Dr. Patri. Garfield wrote of this encounter:

> The slight man at the desk said quietly, "Sit down, son." I sat down, tense with defiance. I was thirteen years old and had been kicked out of schools. Now I was being entered in Angelo Patri's school for problem children. So what? Angelo Patri looked over the papers. They told my case history. I was born in the lower East Side of New York City. My mother had died when I was seven. My father was a poor tailor who couldn't earn a decent living. We froze in winter, sweated in summer. Every few months, try as he might, my father couldn't meet the rent, so we moved to another tenement. Pop would work and just when it looked as if we'd be okay, we'd be on the move again. My companions were the neighborhood toughs with whom I constantly fought in blind, speechless fury. Patri finished reading and then asked, "Why do you fight with other boys?" "I'm just as good as they are," I told him. "I can lick all of 'em—even the guys that are bigger than me." Patri was thoughtful for a few minutes. Then he said slowly, "There are two people in every one of us. One fights with his fists; the other fights with his brain. We have to decide which one will take over."
> "I'm doing all right with my fists."
> "No one does well enough with his fists alone. Even fighters in the ring, if they are smart, wait for their brains to tell them what to do. Which reminds me—how would you like to do your fighting in the ring hereafter?"
> I was dumbfounded. "You think I could become a pro?"
> "No reason why not, if you'll train and let the guy in your head take over for a change."

Angelo Patri also had memories of this first encounter with Julie: "He seemed full of antagonism, as if he believed everybody—all grown people—were against him. But there was really nothing wrong with Julie, and I liked him. But he had that bad stammer."

For this reason, Patri delivered the boy to Mrs. O'Brien's speech class. Mrs. O'Brien doubled as the dramatics coach and it was her one-act plays which reawakened Julie's love of acting. The youth, with Patri's blessing, determined that his future would be spent in the pursuit of thespian glory. Garfield recalled:

> One day Mr. Patri said, "You're doing all right as a boxer. You like it when they shout for you, don't you?"
>
> "Yeah, sure," I agreed. "It kinda makes a guy feel important."
>
> Mr. Patri smiled. "The best way to get applause is on the stage. You do well in the debating society. I've a hunch you might have acting talent. How'd you like to take part in the school play?"
>
> The guy in my head showed me that maybe it wasn't a bad idea. To my surprise, I discovered that I could act and I liked it even better than boxing.

In the fall of 1927, Julie entered and won the Bronx district championship in the annual city-wide debating contest with his speech, "Franklin, the Peace Maker of the Constitution." The competition further fueled his desire to act. John Garfield always kept a warm spot in his heart for his mentor:

> Patri's idea was that there was no bad boy — it was all environmental. He's an admirable man, an anti-fascist with liberal ideas about everything. He kept us out of trouble by getting us interested in things ... dramatics, athletics, carpentry, orchestra. I always wanted to be in the limelight and I found I could get it by being on the stage. That was the beginning of everything for me. For a lost boy to be found, someone has to do the finding. Dr. Patri found me, and for reaching into the garbage pail and pulling me out, I owe him everything. The good things that came my way would not have been possible but for that sweet, funny man.

In the summer of 1928, a chance meeting took place on a Bronx basketball court between Julie and a young actor who lived in the area. The young man was Clifford Odets, and the friendship between the two would be lifelong. Odets was a member of the Theatre Guild and his talk deepened Julie's ambition to become a professional actor.

Julie wanted to drop out of school to pursue his dream. He was selling the *Bronx Home News* and working as a sparring partner in the local gym to earn money. But Angelo Patri had different ideas.

He arranged for Julie to attend Roosevelt High School and, in addition, obtained a dramatic scholarship to the Hecksher Foundation for the boy. Although Julie did not do well in school (eventually dropping out early in his sophomore year), he thrived on the dramatics at Hecksher. His scholarship ended in the spring, but through Dr. Patri's influence he met one of the eminent Broadway actors of the time, Jacob Ben-Ami. Ben-Ami arranged for Julie's acceptance into the American Laboratory Theatre which was run by Richard Boleslavsky and Maria Ouspenskaya as a training ground for the Theatre Guild. One of Julie's fellow students was George Tobias, who would later act in many John Garfield movies.

Herbert Biberman was a stage manager and director for the Guild. He took Julie under his wing and gave the boy a job as an assistant on the Broadway production of *The Camel Through the Needle's Eye,* starring Claude Rains, Henry Travers, and Miriam Hopkins. Claude Rains would later be a major influence on John Garfield's early screen career. Another actor in the Guild company who impressed Julie was Morris Carnovsky. Their paths would cross many more times; Julie always considered Carnovsky to be the best.

The world of the New York Theatre in the late 1920s and early 1930s was a lively, effervescent place. Some of the greatest names in Broadway history graced the marquees: the Lunts, Paul Muni, Edward G. Robinson, Claude Rains, Jacob Ben-Ami, the Adlers, Eddie Cantor, James Cagney, Joan Blondell, Claudette Colbert, Miriam Hopkins, Franchot Tone, George Arliss, and many more. Other creative talent included: Elmer Rice, Maxwell Anderson, Harold Clurman, Sidney Kingsley, Richard Boleslavsky, Maria Ouspenskaya, Clifford Odets, Cheryl Crawford, Lee Strasberg, Eva LeGallienne, Moss Hart, and James Light (then the "boy wonder" of Broadway). Julie would rub elbows with many of them, and the impressions he gathered from these encounters would go a long way in shaping his ideas about the world, both on stage and off.

Around the time that *The Camel Through the Needle's Eye* was running on Broadway, there was a faction of the Theatre Guild which often practiced at the Lab (American Laboratory Theatre). Among this group were Stella Adler, Clifford Odets, Lee Strasberg, Franchot Tone, Harold Clurman, Cheryl Crawford, and Luther

Morris Carnovsky, a member of the Group Theatre whom Garfield always admired.

Adler. They envisioned a new kind of American drama, and Julie saw a bright future for their kind of acting. This splinter group staged *Red Rust* in December of 1929. Julie appeared in a small part, but more significantly, his name in the program was listed as Julian *Garfield*. The Garfield part came from a character on a radio drama which Odets had written, Garfield Grimes.

After *Red Rust*'s closing, Harold Clurman decided to move on his dream of establishing an independent permanent company of actors dedicated to performing socially relevant plays; the Group Theatre was born. Clurman, Cheryl Crawford, and Lee Strasberg were the directors. Members of the company included Odets, Stella and Luther Adler, Ruth Nelson, and Morris Carnovsky. Julie was denied admission despite the efforts of Odets and Luther Adler.

In the spring of 1930, Julie was accepted at Eva LeGallienne's
Civic Repertory Theatre, due once again to Jacob Ben-Ami's inter-
vention on his behalf. The company was shutting down for the summer, but he could start in the fall. In the meantime, Julie entered
the Golden Gloves boxing tournament. His first bout turned out to
be his last when he was knocked out in one round.

The Depression was deepening its hold on the big city, and the
summer passed very slowly. The little money that seventeen-year-
old Julie could pick up was earned by hustling pool in a hall near
the Fourteenth Street Theatre, which housed the Civic Repertory.
But with the coming of autumn, the Civic company reassembled
with Jules Garfield, as Julie was also known, as a member of the
troupe. He attended classes mornings and evenings and worked in
the garment district pushing clothes carts in the afternoons.

During that season of 1930-31, the Civic staged such plays as
Liliom, Journey's End, and *Alison's House.* Fellow struggling actors
in the Civic company included Howard DaSilva and Burgess
Meredith. Trying to make ends meet, Julie took jobs as an elevator
operator, a busboy, and a paper boy, back on his old corner selling
the *Bronx Home News.* Times were tough all over. It was around
this time that he began dating the girl who would become his wife,
Rose Seidman (aka Roberta Mann and Roberta Seidman).

Julie's apprenticeship with the Civic ended in the spring of
1931, and his father urged the boy to give up acting. John Garfield
recalled that period: "There was a revolution going on at home.
Why didn't I earn some money? Why didn't I do something prac-
tical, like chicken farming? Even Robbie's family was telling her,
'Actors are bums'."

David Garfinkle had successfully lined up a job in a factory for
his son. Julie said thanks but no thanks and took off on a trip across
the country with his friend Joe La Spina. Julie's parting scene with
Robbie did not go quite the way he would have scripted it: "I
remember saying goodbye to Robbie. She was my girlfriend even
then. We were on the roof of the tenement house where she lived;
it was a warm day, spring. I said, 'I feel this is my need.' She was
unmoved. 'Everybody knows his own need,' she said. I was shoving
off really, but she didn't give me a tumble."

The boys hitchhiked and hopped freights all the way to California. Julie and Joe worked the fruit fields in California and the wheat fields in Nebraska. In Austin, Texas, they were arrested on a vagrancy charge. They were set free after Julie gave a recitation of Edgar Allan Poe's *The Raven,* presumably because the rendition had been so eloquently done. Joe found Nebraska to his liking and decided to stay, but Julie missed both New York and Robbie (probably in that order). It was early autumn of 1931 by the time he made it back.

Upon his return to the big city, Julie was more determined than ever to establish himself on the New York stage. In January 1932, with help from Herbert Biberman, Julie made a major breakthrough when he received a strong part in James Light's production of *Lost Boy. Lost Boy* got lost after only 15 performances, but Julie cleared four hundred dollars and, more important, he now had a "credit" to his name. Thanks to James Light's strong recommendation, Julie immediately went into Elmer Rice's *Counsellor-at-Law,* but not on Broadway; it was in Chicago, with the company which was headed by Otto Kruger. The play was a huge success and settled into the Harris Theatre for twenty weeks. Julie shared a dressing room with Vincent Sherman, and they formed a lasting friendship.

> The Chicago experience impressed itself upon him in many ways. The city throbbed with rugged vitality and there was anger there: breadlines were more in evidence than in New York, and Julie came to recognize a look of hunger more cutting than any pain he'd felt in his belly. Before he left Chicago, he had the makings of a political conscience.[2]

The Chicago company of *Counsellor-at-Law* closed shop with the coming of summer. The play reopened on Broadway in the fall with Paul Muni (back from Hollywood and riding the crest of his *Scarface* triumph) in the lead and Jules Garfield given feature billing. The revival lasted 120 performances and then went on a road tour which included Washington, D.C., Baltimore, Philadelphia, Pittsburgh, and Cleveland. Garfield celebrated his twentieth birthday in Philadelphia, listened to FDR's inauguration speech, and became a staunch advocate of the new president's policies.

Universal Studios acquired the screen rights to *Counsellor-at-Law,* but Paul Muni was unable to participate because Warner Bros. refused to lend him out. The studio executives at Universal also wanted Julie to recreate his role as the office boy, but, upon Elmer Rice's advice, he refused. The fly in the ointment had been Universal's insistence on a long-term contract as part of the deal. Garfield still yearned for a spot with the Group Theatre.

Around this time, the Theatre Union was formed. Although there was no official permanent company of actors, the Theatre Union hoped someday to rival the Group. (And whereas the Group had been conceived for artistic rather than political aspiration, from the beginning the Theatre Union was committed to social crusade. It opposed racial and religious bigotry.[3]) Garfield appeared in the Theatre Union's first production, *Peace on Earth,* written by Albert Maltz and George Sklar. After the play's closing, Julie began attending classes taught by Clifford Odets at the Theatre Union. Odets and Joe Bromberg were unofficial liaisons between the Group and the Theatre Union. Through Odets's urging, Julie was finally accepted as an apprentice with the Group in April of 1934: "This was the height of my ambition. Robbie and I stayed up all night talking and weeping."

This was a transitional time for the Group, which had just escaped the throes of death with the help of Sidney Kingsley's surprise hit *Men in White.* The Group was now poised to enter its golden period. Julie's first appearance in a Group Theatre production, *Gold Eagle Guy,* came in Boston in October 1934. Joe Bromberg had the lead. Julie had a small role, but wowed audiences with a spectacular fifteen-foot leap on stage.

November was the month of two momentous occasions for Julie: the Broadway opening of *Gold Eagle Guy* and his marriage to Roberta Seidman. The Garfields moved into a small Greenwich Village flat, and, though Julie urged his new bride to quit working, she held on to her job at Macy's. *Gold Eagle Guy* was not the success that everyone had counted upon, and Lee Strasberg suggested that the Group release its actors for the balance of the season to seek

employment in outside productions. The actors' loyalty to the
Group was so great, however, that no one was willing to leave (at
least at this time).

Then, on January 5, 1935, Odets's *Waiting for Lefty* opened at
the Fourteenth Street Theatre. Julie worked backstage and appeared in the crowd scene at the finale. Elia Kazan's performance,
along with Odets's eloquence, combined to give the Group a rous-
ing success.

The enthusiastic response to *Waiting for Lefty* prompted the
Group to stage Odets's *Awake and Sing,* to be directed by Harold
Clurman. Clurman assembled a strong cast of Group veterans:
Stella Adler, Art Smith, Phoebe Brand, Joe Bromberg, Morris Carnovsky, Luther Adler, and Sanford Meisner. The only major part yet
to be filled was that of Ralph Berger, the young son pleading for
a "chance to get to first base." Clurman later recalled, "Julie was the
logical choice. The part required a certain quality and he had that
quality. If anyone doubted that he was an able actor, doubt vanished
after rehearsals began."

Awake and Sing (which would be a shining hour for the Group
and one of the great American dramas of the 1930s) opened on February 19, 1935, and continued for 185 performances. Julie infused
the part of Ralph Berger with his special brand of instinctive acting,
combining toughness and innocence. Brooks Atkinson wrote that
Jules Garfield "plays the part of the boy with a splendid sense of
character development." The critic would remain in Garfield's corner through his entire career. Fortunes ran high for the Group, and
only the coming of the hot summer months could cool the momentum.

Awake and Sing reopened on September 9, 1935, and played
New York for a month before hitting the road to Philadelphia for
several weeks. The company worked on two new plays by day while
performing *Waiting for Lefty* and *Awake and Sing* by night. The
latter was saluted by Henry Murdoch of the *Philadelphia Inquirer*
as an "American classic." Murdoch called Garfield a man who was
"modest about his work, greatly in love with the theatre and with
the Group." It was a love that would never die.

The two new Group offerings were *Weep for the Virgins* by

Nellise Child and *Paradise Lost,* which many felt would be Odets's best work. Things soon began to turn sour, however. Julie was passed over in favor of Sanford Meisner for a plum part in *Paradise Lost;* instead he was given a role in *Weep for the Virgins,* which closed after only nine performances. Strong work by Ruth Nelson, Phoebe Brand, and Garfield failed to create favorable box office results.

More cause for weeping was the lukewarm reception given to *Paradise Lost.* The play would run for two months, closing in February 1936, but by that time Odets would be in Hollywood writing the screenplay for Gary Cooper's *The General Died at Dawn.* While Odets's leave was only temporary, Joe Bromberg signed a long-term contract with 20th Century–Fox, and Alan Baxter also went to California. The studios were after Julie to sign, but he was committed to the Group and turned a deaf ear to their offers. Garfield would later state his love for the Group: "I didn't learn anything about acting until I joined the Group Theatre. They taught me an entirely new approach, an entirely new technique. Those were the days before the Group was prosperous and we used to live on potatoes." Indeed, times were tough. By this time, Robbie was out of work and the Garfields were living with another Group couple.

Financially strapped again, and reeling from the defections, the Group went on tour with *Awake and Sing* in the spring of 1936. The itinerary included several Eastern cities and Chicago. Robbie Garfield was able to accompany her husband, and the trip served as a very belated honeymoon for the young couple. The tour was a success and helped to sustain the company, but there were lingering doubts about the Group's continued existence as the 1936-37 season loomed on the horizon.

Clifford Odets returned from Hollywood, but the play he brought with him, *Silent Partner,* did not stir any noise among the Group hierarchy; it was put on the back burner. A proposed deal for John Howard Lawson's *Marching Song* fell through, leaving the Group with only the Paul Green–Kurt Weill anti-war drama *Johnny Johnson.* The production opened on November 19, 1936, at the Forty-Fourth Street Theatre and ran for sixty-eight performances. Julie played a pivotal role as a German soldier. After *Johnny*

Johnson's closing in January 1937, the Group went into a retrenchment. Clurman, Crawford, and Strasberg resigned but agreed to return for the new fall season. The actors were encouraged to take jobs elsewhere. Morris Carnovsky took a part in Paul Muni's film, *The Life of Emile Zola.* Even Clurman went to Hollywood for several months to serve as associate on *Blockade,* which Odets was writing for producer Walter Wanger.

Julie found himself besieged by offers. He hired Arthur Lyons as his agent and Lyons landed him a $300/week contract for *Having Wonderful Time,* directed by Marc Connelly. The play opened at the Lyceum Theatre on February 20, 1937, with Julie heading a cast that included Katherine Locke, Sidney Fox, Ann Thomas, and the then-unknown Sheldon Leonard. The warm comedy was a smash hit; during the run, many of Marc Connelly's friends came backstage to meet Garfield: Dorothy Parker, Moss Hart, Cole Porter, George S. Kaufman, Richard Rodgers, Lorenz Hart, George Gershwin, and a very special man who would become a friend for life, Oscar Levant.

Julie was again attracting the attention of the movie scouts, and both Paramount and Warner Bros. wanted him to take screen tests. While Julie cited his loyalty to the stage and the hoped-for revival of the Group, he did make a brief test for Warners. They liked what they saw, but when Julie insisted on a clause that would allow him time off for stage work, Warners refused.

Odets and Clurman returned from Hollywood in late summer 1937. The Group members quickly reassembled. There was talk of staging Odets's *Golden Boy* as the major fall production. Harold Clurman was installed as the company's sole managing director following the departures of Lee Strasberg and Cheryl Crawford. The previous summer at Pinebrook Camp, Odets and Garfield had whiled away the hours with talk about the boxing world. From these conversations, Odets fashioned a drama about a boy torn between two worlds—one artistic (music—the violin) and one materialistic (money—boxing). Odets had written the lead, Joe Bonaparte, for Julie. So when the call came, Garfield left the cast of *Having Wonderful Time* (and his $300/week) behind, to accept the *Golden Boy* assignment (at $75/week).

John Garfield at the start of his film career.

Julie thought that *Golden Boy* was the greatest play ever written. Then came the crushing blow. Clurman wanted Luther Adler (who would soon become Clurman's brother-in-law) to play Joe Bonaparte. Odets had already installed Frances Farmer (with whom he was having a very torrid affair) in the Lorna Moon role, thereby effectively losing control over who should play the male lead. Julie went to Clurman in an attempt to win the role that had been written for him. Morris Carnovsky, Elia Kazan, Bob Lewis, and even Luther Adler went to bat for Garfield, but Clurman was unmoved. Julie was assigned a supporting role as Siggie, the fighter's comic brother-in-law. *Golden Boy* proved to be golden indeed for the Group (it was the company's most successful production), opening in November of 1937 and continuing for 250 performances.

During the run of *Golden Boy*, Julie was introduced to Arthur
Lyons's partner, John McCormick. McCormick had been a production executive at First National Pictures before that company merged
with Warner Bros. He still knew many people at Warners, and he
was able to convince them to agree to a contract which included the
stage clause. Julie was unsure about signing, so he consulted with
Clurman, who told him not to sign; then Odets told him essentially
the same thing. Robbie, who was pregnant with the couple's first
child, made it unanimous. Julie usually listened to her advice, but
this time was different. He signed the contract in Warner Bros.'
New York office in February 1938.

Nearly ten years later, Garfield cited the disappointment of
missing out on the Bonaparte role.

> I eventually got the male lead in *Having Wonderful Time* at
> $300—more money than I expected to see—but in the middle of
> the run I gave it up for the leading role in *Golden Boy* at far less
> money. I had thought security was the aim of my life but the guy
> in my head showed me that it had changed to "integrity." That
> role would prove to the world, and to me, that I was a good actor.
>
> As things turned out, another actor played that role. I had to
> take a small part to stay with the show. Those were bitter days but
> I trusted the guy in my head. I gave the part all I had and offers
> came from Hollywood. I had turned them down before but now
> I thought, if I can be a good actor in Hollywood, the audiences will
> be in the millions instead of the hundreds. So, I tried one picture.

The Group's members were incensed by Julie's decision. Many
vowed never to forgive him. He argued that they had forgiven Franchot Tone, Alan Baxter, and others who had defected. His defense
left many unmoved. Years later, even after he helped many of them
(financially and career-wise), there were still traces of bitterness.

Elia Kazan later recalled that the Group did not fear that Julie
would fail in pictures, but that he would succeed too well:

> It all tied in with *Golden Boy*. Had he played the lead, as we
> all sooner or later realized he should, no picture company could
> have dislodged him, not at that time. We were all very upset, but

we weren't being fair to Julie. Carnovsky was full of righteous indignation, but he was making more than double Julie's salary, and wasn't half as good-looking.[4]

Garfield later said of the decision: "I just reached a point where I had to do something on my own. Other people were always making decisions about me, and for me. So I thought, it was a way of being my own man." Robbie stayed behind in New York and Julie bought a 1933 Chevrolet to make the cross-country drive. It was the spring of 1938, and the movies were about to receive the services of an interesting and original actor.

Chapter 2

They (Warner Bros.) Made Him a Criminal

John Garfield once said: "When I was cast as a leading man I thought it was ridiculous. When they saw the rushes, people began to say, 'Who is this Garfield?' I always said, 'He's from the stage and he's going right back!'" That was a reflection of his uncertainty upon his arrival in Hollywood; just as uncertain were his new employers, Warner Bros. The only thing studio chief Jack Warner was sure of was that Julie's name had to go. Jules Garfield sounded too Jewish. When Julie pointed out the fact that he was Jewish, Jack Warner remained firm. Finally, a compromise was reached and press releases went out announcing the arrival of Warners' new contract player, John Garfield.

Warner Bros.' roster of stars in the spring of 1938 included James Cagney, Errol Flynn, Paul Muni, Edward G. Robinson, Pat O'Brien, George Brent, the Dead End Kids, Bette Davis, and Olivia De Havilland. Below this stratum came the near stars Claude Rains, Humphrey Bogart, Wayne Morris, and Dick Foran. The company needed new blood, and, in addition to Garfield, hopes for the future were riding on the likes of Dennis Morgan, Eddie Albert, Ronald Reagan, Jeffrey Lynn, Priscilla and Rosemary Lane, Ann Sheridan, Gale Page, and Jane Bryan.

While Julie marked time waiting for his first part in pictures, he was very busy away from the studio. Garfield was outspoken about his liberal politics and joined many liberal groups, including the Anti-Nazi League and the Hollywood Independent Citizens Committee. As a result, his name was added to the Martin Dies Committee list (which had been formed that year by the U.S.

House of Representatives) of Hollywood names with possibly subversive politics. Of course, the list also included the names of such people as Eddie Cantor and even Shirley Temple (who was ten years old at the time).

From the very start, Garfield established a reputation as a hard worker who treated everyone on the lot with respect, especially the lowly grips, gaffers, etc. The only problem was that none of the projects the studio tried to put him in were satisfactory. Julie was scheduled for a part in a Jane Bryan picture, *Girls on Probation,* but was passed over in favor of Ronald Reagan. Then the plan was to remake the *Patent Leather Kid,* a boxing film which had been a big hit for Richard Barthelmess in 1927. While waiting for the *Patent Leather Kid* to be readied, Garfield was told to report to the set of *The Sisters,* which starred Bette Davis and Errol Flynn. But *The Sisters* was a period piece set around the 1906 San Francisco earthquake, and Julie's Bronx accent betrayed him. So he was out of *The Sisters.* Bette Davis and Paul Muni indicated their desire for Julie to play in their production of *Juarez,* but shooting was still some time away. Then Julie heard of a part in a proposed Errol Flynn vehicle titled *Because of a Man.* By the time the cameras rolled, the title would be changed, Errol Flynn would be replaced by Jeffrey Lynn, and John Garfield would be cast in his first motion picture (in the breakthrough role of Mickey Borden), the newly named *Four Daughters.*

Shooting began on *Four Daughters* in April 1938. Michael Curtiz, one of the top directors in Hollywood, was in charge of the cast, which mainly consisted of unknowns. The script was by Lenore Coffee and Julius Epstein, based on Fannie Hurst's short story, *Sister Act.* As Larry Swindell points out, Garfield also made an important acquaintance:

> An unexpected benefit was Garfield's association with Claude Rains, whose performances for the Theatre Guild Julie had admired. They were usually seen together during idle moments on the set. Rains consistently gave rich performances on film, and when he felt he had won Julie's confidence, Rains offered a tip that brought Mickey Borden's character into a better screen perspective.

Contrasting scenes from Garfield's startling screen debut (*Four Daughters*, 1938). *Top:* The rebel hero finds love for the first time in his troubled life. Pictured are John Garfield and Priscilla Lane. *Bottom:* Hard times beset Mr. & Mrs. Mickey Borden (John Garfield and Priscilla Lane).

There was a difference between acting on stage and before a movie camera. Claude Rains explained, "You were addressing May Robson as if she were seated in the last row of the balcony. The critics will like that, but if dramatic truth is your aim. . . ."

Julie muted his scene, Rains assured him it was right, adding, "and I notice it's rubbing off on Priscilla (Lane)." Julie later said, "Claude Rains taught me things some people never learn about acting in films. He warned me about Mike Curtiz and his mania for close-ups. That's when you have to underplay. No two directors are alike, so an actor must always make adjustments."[5]

Filming ended in June, and although everything had gone smoothly, nobody connected with the film (with the possible exception of Claude Rains) knew just how special a picture the finished product would be. That special quality would be in large part due to Garfield's brilliant performance as the doomed composer Mickey Borden.

Garfield was immediately put into *Blackwell's Island,* a "B" picture directed by William McGann. Rosemary Lane played the female lead. The film was shot in 16 days on a shoestring budget. There was a benefit for Julie in that some of the scenes were to be shot in New York on the actual Blackwell's Island. The only drawback was that news of his partying and carousing reached Robbie before he did. He vowed to be a good husband and was forgiven, but their marriage would be on shaky ground from that day forward. After the location shooting finished, Julie was given a vacation to spend time with his wife.

News of the *Four Daughters* premiere in Hollywood confirmed that the studio had a smash hit, with Garfield stealing the picture. He was hailed as a startling innovation in screen characters, and as the sensational new "find" — not of the year, but of the decade. Fannie Hurst told reporters: "The picture had outgrown my simple story and acquired a life of its own." She added that the Mickey Borden characterization was all John Garfield's. B. R. Crisler wrote in the *New York Times:*

> He (Garfield) bites off his lines with a delivery so eloquent that we still aren't sure whether it is the dialogue or Mr. Garfield who

is so bitterly brilliant. Our vote, though, is for Mr. Garfield and for whatever stars watch over his career on the stage and screen.

The pivotal scene centered around Borden's playing his own composition. When Ann Lemp (Priscilla Lane) urges him to complete his song, he answers, "What for? The fates are against me. They tossed a coin—heads I'm poor, tails I'm rich. But they tossed a two-headed coin." The rebel hero had been born.

The film was nominated for five Academy Awards, including Best Picture. Garfield was nominated for Best Supporting Actor but lost to Walter Brennan. Julie told the New York reporters after the Gotham premiere at Radio City Music Hall on August 9, 1938:

> When an actor doesn't face a conflict, he loses confidence in himself. I always want to have to struggle because I believe it will help me accomplish more. I believe the more successful an actor becomes, the more chances he should take. An actor never stops learning.

Four Daughters served as a career boost to virtually everyone involved. The September 10, 1938, issue of *Motion Picture Herald* carried a six page ad trumpeting the film:

> "I believe *Four Daughters* is the best picture of my career." J. L. Warner, vice president in charge of production for Warner Bros.
>
> "*Four Daughters* is one of the best pictures of anyone's career." *The New York Times*.
>
> *Four Daughters* is the triumphant beginning of a glorious career for all these brilliant personalities.... These are the Four Daughters:
>
> Rosemary Lane plays Kay:
> "Rosemary Lane is perfect!" *N.Y. Daily News*.
> "Rosemary Lane turns in an excellent performance!" *Variety Daily*.
> "Rosemary Lane is tops!" *Motion Picture Herald*.
> Priscilla Lane plays Ann:
> "Priscilla Lane's stardom is assured!" *N.Y. Daily News*.
> "Priscilla Lane is a certain bet for stardom!" *Film Daily*.
> "Priscilla Lane is on the road to stardom!" *New York Sun*.

Lola Lane plays Thea:

"Lola Lane is practically perfection!" *New York Herald Tribune.*

"Lola Lane excels anything she's done!" *Hollywood Reporter.*

"Lola Lane plays her stirring role unusually well!" *N.Y. World-Telegram.*

Gale Page plays Emma:

"Gale Page is a brilliant actress!" *Brooklyn Daily Eagle.*

"Gale Page turns in an excellent performance!" *Variety Daily.*

"Gale Page is marked for cinema greatness!" *Hollywood Reporter.*

These Are The Two Surprise Personalities:

John Garfield plays Mickey:

"John Garfield is the film find of the year!" *New York Daily Mirror.*

"John Garfield is sensational!" *Motion Picture Herald.*

"John Garfield gives a performance seldom equalled!" *N.Y. World-Telegram.*

Jeffrey Lynn plays Felix:

"Jeffrey Lynn clicks decisively!" *N.Y. Journal American.*

"Jeffrey Lynn triumphs!" *New York Times.*

"Jeffrey Lynn is outstanding!" *Showmen's Trade Review.*

Walter Winchell exalted: "The rave of the city, to read the critics, is *Four Daughters* at the Music Hall. It gives your emotions a workout. . . . Pictures like *Four Daughters* will put Bank Night out of business." The ad concluded with the following notice: "Following its remarkable holdover, *Four Daughters* is now included on the exceptional program available to the Industry Drive from Warner Bros."

Four Daughters was Warners' opening film for the 1938-39 season. Autumn 1938 saw the Garfields traveling to Hollywood as a family, including a new arrival, daughter Katherine. Robbie Garfield quickly became a fund-raiser for many liberal causes. The Garfields' social circle was dominated by writers, some directors, and a few actors. Some of Julie's oldest friends were included, the Joe Brombergs and Garfield's old mentor Herb Biberman and his wife Gale Sondergaard among them. Julie's contract was revised, giving him star, rather than feature, status. He went back to work in a name-above-the-title vehicle, *They Made Me a Criminal.*

Lobby card for *They Made Me a Criminal* (1939).

Busby Berkeley was given the directorial assignment. After years of service as choreographer on such musicals as *42nd Street, Footlight Parade, Gold Diggers of 1933, Dames,* and several others, Berkeley had been promoted by the studio to the directors' ranks. *They Made Me a Criminal* was his eleventh film as a director, but it was his first chance at a big dramatic picture. Berkeley acquitted himself nicely, but he would return to the world of musicals after completion of the film.

The cast included Claude Rains and May Robson (both fresh from *Four Daughters*), Ann Sheridan, Gloria Dickson, and the Dead End Kids, who, like Garfield, had come to Hollywood from the streets of New York via Broadway. The "Kids" had created a sensation in *Dead End* (1937), and had appeared to advantage in two 1938 films: *Crime School* (with Humphrey Bogart) and *Angels with Dirty Faces* (with James Cagney). *They Made Me a Criminal* would prove to be the last major film the boys would appear in, but they continued their careers in various guises (Dead End Kids, East Side Kids, Bowery Boys) for nearly 20 years.

While Garfield was preparing to film *Criminal,* Jack Warner was planning a sequel to *Four Daughters.* Julie went to see Warner to ask how this sequel was possible since his character had died in the original. Warner said not to worry, that Garfield should be happy with his star billing in only his second picture. Garfield made the mistake of reminding Warner of *Blackwell's Island,* which the studio head had forgotten. Warner immediately ordered new scenes to be shot for the movie, with Michael Curtiz directing, so that the company's new leading man would not be seen in a cheap picture. As a result, Julie discovered just how busy a Warner Bros. player could be, reshooting *Blackwell's Island* in the morning, and appearing in *They Made Me a Criminal* in the afternoon. And while he was still working on these pictures, *Juarez* finally began filming.

They Made Me a Criminal opened at the Strand Theatre in New York on January 20, 1939. While the filming had been done under difficult weather conditions, with temperatures often rising above 100 degrees Fahrenheit (location shooting had taken place in Palm Desert), the experience had still been very pleasurable for Garfield. This was largely attributable to the presence of the Dead End Kids, whom Julie loved working with. The feeling was mutual, and this rapport showed on screen, giving the picture a vitality that it otherwise might have lacked. Garfield became a "big brother" to the gang (Bobby Jordan, Billy Halop, Leo Gorcey, Gabriel Dell, Bernard Punsley, and Huntz Hall).

Years later, Hall remembered fondly:

> I was 18 and Julie was closer to 25. I remember we used to call him the "poet" and the "philosopher." Being New Yorkers, John understood us more. He talked to us about politics and government. We knew about Hitler before the war. John told us to look out for him, that he was a dangerous man.
>
> Julie was a guy I loved. We were all younger than he was, but when we were working with him, he would sit down with us and talk on an artist-to-artist level. He would say, "Listen, do you think this scene works better this way?"

Also helping the film was a strong performance by Gloria Dickson, a fine actress who would die tragically in a fire in 1945. She

The Dead End Kids (Huntz Hall, Gabriel Dell, Bobby Jordan, Leo Gorcey, Bernard Punsley, and Billy Halop) let their feelings be known during the big bout in *They Made Me a Criminal* (1939).

had delivered a memorable portrayal as the wife of doomed Edward Norris in 1937's *They Won't Forget*. Her films following *Criminal* would not utilize her talents to their fullest.

The masterful James Wong Howe was responsible for the cinematography. Howe had been in Hollywood since 1917 and became a director of photography in 1922. He was fresh from *The Adventures of Tom Sawyer* (1938), and he would go on to helm many classic Warner films of the 1940s: *City for Conquest, Strawberry Blonde, Kings Row, Yankee Doodle Dandy, Air Force,* and *Objective Burma,* among others. He won Academy Awards for *The Rose Tattoo* and *Hud* in a career that spanned over fifty years. Howe and Garfield became close friends and would eventually work together on eight films.

Jack Dorney (John Garfield) angers Rutchek (Frank Riggi) before the climactic fight in *They Made Me a Criminal* (1939). Pictured (left to right) are Garfield, Ward Bond, Riggi, player, and Cliff Clarke.

They Made Me a Criminal was boffo at the box office and went a long way in shaping Garfield's "young fugitive" image. The reviews were quite favorable, especially *Variety's*:

> Garfield gives a stunning performance as the cynical scrapper who's softened up by romance. Part is just right for him. His playing shows insight, study, sincerity, and restraint. Given a few more such complimentary parts, he can scarcely miss becoming a major star. Fact that he is such a distinct personality and fine actor make[s] him a screen natural [*Hobe*].

Blackwell's Island opened on March 1, 1939, at the Globe Theatre in New York. While the picture still had the look of a programmer, it was an enjoyable, fast-moving film with another strong Garfield performance at its core. The picture was evidence that Julie could carry a small picture with little or no help. The box office returns were again very strong. *Variety* said:

Tim Haydon (John Garfield) and Sunny Walsh (Rosemary Lane) in a tense scene from *Blackwell's Island* (1939).

Yarn closely follows the newspaper exposé of conditions found on Blackwell's Island in 1934. Garfield handles his part in earnest fashion, but he is much stronger than the role assigned him. His work is starting to look typed and could benefit by the producers' mixing up his roles.

This review gave the first hint that the studio might be limiting its new star. This limitation was a problem that would become more acute over the next few years, but in the two films that immediately followed *Blackwell's Island,* Garfield did play widely divergent characters.

Juarez was the picture that Julie had been waiting months for. In addition to Muni and Davis (both of whom Julie admired tremendously), the cast included Claude Rains, Joseph Calleia, Henry O'Neill, Gale Sondergaard, and Gilbert Roland. Garfield portrayed Porfirio Diaz, a rebel in fact as well as spirit. His Bronx accent was a problem, but Warners sought to capitalize on the box office strength of his name. The picture opened in late April and, although named to the *New York Times* Ten Best List, was only a moderate success. The picture never caught fire, failing to light the imagination of the public. Part of the problem was that the film was based on two sources: the play *Juarez and Maximilian*, by Franz Werfel, and the book *The Phantom Crown*, by Bertita Harding. Screenwriters John Huston, Aeneas MacKenzie, and Wolfgang Reinhardt never meshed these sources into a cohesive whole. *Motion Picture Herald* of August 12, 1939, carried this very accurate critique from exhibitor A. E. Hancock:

> No question this is a production Warners went all the way out on, so far out if it does not get a better reception than it received here they will be a long time getting their money out of it. Brian Aherne did not get top billing but the consensus of our audience is that he ran away with the picture.

Brian Aherne as Maximilian *did* give the best performance, while Garfield brought some excitement to the lumbering proceedings. Unfortunately, some of this excitement was unintentional, due to his problems in mastering a Mexican accent. Later, Julie would say that Gilbert Roland should have played Diaz. Roland, who played a smaller role as Col. Lopez, would have been a logical choice and could have brought authenticity to the part.

The *Juarez* debacle convinced the studio that Garfield should not appear in any more historical dramas. He was definitely a modern, urban actor. Actually, he was just what Warner Bros. (which specialized in big-city pictures) was looking for—a vivid slum type who could play in gangster melodramas (like Cagney, Bogart, and Robinson) and in social dramas. He was a New York street kid whose brooding sensitivity, combined with excellent acting ability, made him the studio's best representative of the alienated young man.

Jack Warner still had not given up hope for a *Four Daughters* sequel. Julius and Philip Epstein were assigned the chore of coming up with a suitable screenplay. The Epstein brothers went to Jack Warner with a compromise. They would not write a sequel; rather, they would write a script that would employ all the major players from the *Four Daughters* cast but playing different roles. The film, a successor not a sequel, would eventually be titled *Daughters Courageous*. Everyone connected with the project hated the title, but it was dictated by the front office (no doubt as an attempt by penny-pinching Jack Warner to capitalize on MGM's spectacular *Captains Courageous*).

Daughters Courageous commenced filming in April of 1939. Michael Curtiz was back as director. The *Four Daughters* cast was reassembled: Garfield, Claude Rains, Jeffrey Lynn, Dick Foran, Frank McHugh, May Robson, and the "four daughters" — Priscilla, Rosemary, and Lola Lane, and Gale Page. Added to this stellar lineup were Fay Bainter and Donald Crisp. Garfield was top-billed as Gabriel Lopez. The story was based on the play *Fly Away Home* by Dorothy Bennett and Irving White.

Claude Rains played the part of a father (Jim Masters) who abandoned his wife and four young daughters, only to return twenty years later on the eve of his wife's marriage to a leading citizen of the community (played by Donald Crisp in his best stiff-upper-lip manner). The entire cast gave inspired performances in a true ensemble effort. Fay Bainter was splendid as the put-upon wife and mother; it was one of the finest performances the actress gave in her long and distinguished career. Priscilla Lane was again effectively teamed with Garfield; their scenes together had a certain sparkle. Claude Rains etched a memorable portrayal as only he could. His scenes with Bainter were filled with melancholy, while his scenes with Garfield were reflective of the young man he had been when he sought his "rendezvous with the universe." Garfield and Rains were brilliant together in this unjustly neglected Curtiz classic.

As if the performances weren't enough, the film was greatly enhanced by James Wong Howe's customarily brilliant cinematography and by a tender Max Steiner score. Steiner was Warners' music ace for nearly thirty years and won three Academy Awards (*The Informer, Now, Voyager* and *Since You Went Away*) during his prolific career.

Even Julie liked the film. Unfortunately, as Larry Swindell says, the verdict was not unanimous:

Sam Sloane (Donald Crisp) presents flowers to Nan Masters (Fay Bainter) as Jim Masters (Claude Rains) and the courageous (?) daughters (left to right: Rosemary Lane, Gale Page, Lola Lane, and Priscilla Lane) observe the birthday proceedings (*Daughters Courageous,* 1939).

Julie rated *Daughters Courageous* as one of the half-dozen or so, among all his films, that were successfully realized, and preferred his Gabriel characterization to the Mickey Borden part because it was more varied. But the picture was not the major hit Warners had counted on. Meriting distinction as one of the American classics of the late thirties, it is all but forgotten today. Michael Curtiz liked to call *Daughters Courageous* "my obtuse master-piece," and he meant obscure; but the picture is interestingly obtuse.[6]

Daughters Courageous opened at the Strand Theatre in New York on June 23, 1939. *Daughters Courageous* did well with the audiences and critics of the major cities but went unappreciated and largely unwatched by small town patrons. This dichotomy was reflected and reported on in the pages of *Motion Picture Herald* during July and August 1939:

Portrait shot of Claude Rains, who was in five films with Garfield. The brilliant actor was a major influence on Garfield's early screen career.

After a phenomenally successful week, New York, the first city to engage it, has extended the run indefinitely of *Daughters Courageous.*

"It's superior to *Four Daughters!*" —Walter Winchell.

"Will trump *Four Daughters* for the old Box-office slam! The cast is super-super!" —*Motion Picture Daily.*

"A major film achievement. It will unquestionably draw heavily!" —*Hollywood Reporter.*

"Top flight in entertainment. Should do even better than *Four Daughters!*" —*Daily Variety.*

"Hal B. Wallis and Henry Blanke have turned out many a big picture. This rates with their best on any and every basis of comparison! Better than *Four Daughters!*" —*Motion Picture Herald.*

Gabriel Lopez (John Garfield) romances Buff Masters (Priscilla Lane) in his own unconventional fashion in *Daughters Courageous,* 1939.

> "It's really greater than *Four Daughters!" —New York Daily Mirror.*
>
> "There is only a possible margin of surprise between *Four Daughters* and this!" —*New York Times.*
>
> "If you liked *Four Daughters* you are certain to be entertained by this!" —*New York Herald Tribune.*
>
> "Warners turned out a much better picture in this than they did in *Four Daughters!" —New York Morning-Telegram.*
>
> *Daughters Courageous* —First date (New York) hits top 2 week gross of past 6 months! A Promise fulfilled! Standing room only!

The small town side was succinctly summed up by W. E. McPhee who ran the Strand Theatre (of Old Town, Maine):

Jim Masters (Claude Rains, right) gives his blessings to the upcoming nuptials of his daughter Buff (Priscilla Lane) to Gabriel Lopez (John Garfield) (*Daughters Courageous*, 1939).

> See this production by all means before you book it. The writer viewed it. My verdict is an ordinary "B" picture. No action, no entertainment. Just a review of a husband deserting his family and coming back after 20 years just as his wife was about to marry another man.... That's all. Cost very little to produce and will produce very little business and produced very little entertainment.

Things were looking great from where Julie stood. He, Robbie, and Katherine moved into a two-story house that they rented from actress Helen Mack. The white colonial was located in the San Fernando Valley, which was a long way from the Burbank studios of Warner Bros. What was new at the studio was *Each Dawn I Die*, another prison reform picture but one with a much bigger budget

IT'S ANOTHER 'FOUR DAUGHTERS' HIT!

And they're gayer than ever, sweeter than ever, better than ever before!

Daughters Courageous

JOHN GARFIELD CLAUDE RAINS·JEFFREY LYNN·FAY BAINTER·DONALD CRISP·MAY ROBSON
and THE 'FOUR DAUGHTERS'

PRISCILLA LANE·ROSEMARY LANE·LOLA LANE
GALE PAGE *Directed by* MICHAEL CURTIZ **WARNER BROS.**

Lobby card from *Daughters Courageous* (1939) with Garfield pictured prominently and given first billing.

than *Blackwell's Island*. The plan was for Garfield to play the role of the reporter who was railroaded into prison on a phony rap, and for James Cagney to play the convict who helps him uncover the corrupt politicians. But before filming began, Warner Bros. signed long-time Paramount star George Raft to a contract and, anxious to establish him at the studio, they put him into Cagney's role and switched Cagney into the reporter's role. Julie was left out in the cold and would never make a feature film with Cagney, an actor whom he admired.

In the fall of 1939, Warners' roster of stars was published by *Motion Picture Herald* in the following order:

1. Paul Muni
2. Errol Flynn
3. James Cagney
4. Bette Davis
5. Edward G. Robinson
6. Miriam Hopkins

John Garfield and wife Robbie enjoy lunch in Dodge City. Garfield was
part of the promotional tour that Warner Bros. staged for Errol Flynn's
Dodge City (1939).

7. Merle Oberon   10. George Raft   14. Humphrey Bogart
8. John Garfield   11. Pat O'Brien   15. Jeffrey Lynn
9. Olivia De   12. Priscilla Lane   16. Ann Sheridan
   Havilland   13. George Brent

Garfield's ranking was important because of the fact that
Muni, Cagney, and Robinson were all within a few years of leaving
the studio. Indeed, the studio hailed Garfield as a mixture of the
three, but Julie would have none of it: "I'm not that good. Nobody
is that good. The people are going to the theatre with chips on their
shoulders. They're going to say—'come on, show us how good you
are.'"

Daughters Courageous was Warner Bros.' last major release of

the 1938-39 season, which had been launched so successfully with
Four Daughters. Each Dawn I Die was the opening salvo for the
1939-40 season. At this time Jack L. Warner issued "A Specific
Statement Concerning the Policy of Warner Bros. Studio," which
covered four pages in the August 19 issue of *Motion Picture Herald.*
Some of the highlights included:

> The list of our 1938-39 pictures speaks for itself. For their
> devoted efforts in making them possible I want to publicly
> acknowledge my gratitude to Hal B. Wallis, Executive Producer of
> Warner Bros. Studios, and to our associate producers.
>
> Now that our company has determined for the new season to
> spend the largest sum of money ever ear-marked for film produc-
> tion, it means that the star and the story values of *this* season's suc-
> cesses will be even greater *next* season. It means that our steadfast
> policy of giving each picture individual treatment and *not*
> "assembly-line" delivery assures uninterrupted output such as
> neither we nor any others have provided.
>
> We can therefore promise the exhibitors who have so staunchly
> supported this company that they can look forward with con-
> fidence to a continued successful relationship with Warner Bros.
> Together, we of Warner Bros. and you, our customers, can look
> confidently to a greater mutual prosperity than at any time before.

The fact that Jack Warner could make a statement that his
studio did *not* deliver in assembly line fashion had to come as a surprise to many of his top players. James Cagney, Bette Davis, Olivia
De Havilland, and others had all been suspended at various times
because of Warner's demanding schedule of production.

John Garfield's first picture for the 1939-40 season was *Dust Be
My Destiny,* released in September. The story featured Garfield and
Priscilla Lane as a young married couple on the run from a false
murder charge. The cast included Frank McHugh, Alan Hale,
Stanley Ridges, Henry Armetta, and two of the Dead End Kids,
Bobby Jordan and Billy Halop. The film received some excellent
contributions from Robert Rossen (screenplay), Max Steiner
(music), and James Wong Howe (photography). At the picture's
center were the performances of Garfield and Priscilla Lane. Garfield

**John Garfield as Joe Bell, young man on the run in *Dust Be My Destiny*
(1939).**

gave one of his most impressive early screen portrayals, crackling
with energy and intensity. Miss Lane, an underrated actress, was his
equal every step of the way. *Variety* reported:

> Garfield has a role particularly tailored to general typing of re-
> cent film portrayals and will enhance his popularity. Miss Lane is
> competently sincere throughout, with several dramatic scenes ris-
> ing far above the material provided.

Frank S. Nugent cast a dissenting vote in his review for the *New
York Times:*

> John Garfield, official gall-and-wormwood taster for the
> Warners, is sipping another bitter brew at the Strand in *Dust Be
> My Destiny.* Personally, we're tired of the formula.

Mabel Bell (Priscilla Lane) and Joe Bell (John Garfield) get some timely
help from Nick (Henry Armetta) in their flight from the police in *Dust Be
My Destiny* (1939).

Dust Be My Destiny scored very well economically, and Warner
Bros. planned to continue the Garfield-Lane team in a new picture
which promised to be a blockbuster, *The Roaring Twenties*. James
Cagney and Humphrey Bogart were already assigned to the film,
and the script was another by Robert Rossen (with Richard Macaulay
and Jerry Wald). But then Garfield was pulled out of *The Roaring
Twenties* and his part was rewritten for Jeffrey Lynn. Meanwhile,
Garfield was cast as George Raft's younger brother in *Invisible
Stripes*. Julie refused to do it and went on the first of what eventually
would be eleven suspensions in his years at Warner Bros.

While serving out his suspension, Garfield missed a chance at
the Joe Bonaparte role in the screen version of *Golden Boy* when a
proper loan-out deal could not be reached with Columbia, the
studio which owned the film rights. William Holden got the role

The defense attorney (Moroni Olsen) tries vainly to get Joe Bell (John Garfield) to speak on his own behalf during the trial in this scene from *Dust Be My Destiny* (1939).

Julie coveted, and he also played the *Invisible Stripes* role Julie had not coveted. Garfield took his case to his closest friends on the Warner lot, the writers: the Epstein brothers, Casey Robinson, Jerry Wald, Norman Reilly Raine, Robert Buckner, and Robert Rossen. They were not only his confidants, but also his friendly tormentors when Julie would try to bluff them in intellectual conversations in which he was clearly overmatched. But he had a genuine thirst for knowledge in literature and the writers sensed it. They also recognized Garfield's instinctive ability to bring a character to life, infusing the part with more depth than the printed word implied.

Robert Rossen was especially close to Julie. Rossen was working on the script for *A Child Is Born;* Garfield wanted to play the male lead. Rossen talked him out of it, pointing to the fact that the girl had all the best scenes. The writer advised Julie to take the prison picture that he (Garfield) had been offered. The film was *Castle on*

Joe and Mabel (John Garfield and Priscilla Lane) embrace in the happy closing moments of *Dust Be My Destiny* (1939) as Nick (Henry Armetta) and Mike Leonard (Alan Hale) look on.

the Hudson, a remake of Spencer Tracy's 1933 picture, *20,000 Years in Sing Sing.* Julie was intrigued by the idea of playing a part that the esteemed Tracy had played.

Garfield rendered a strong performance as the guy who takes the rap for his girl. Ann Sheridan was good as the girl (and what guy wouldn't take the fall for this gorgeous lady); Burgess Meredith, Julie's old New York pal, was effective as a fellow convict; and Pat O'Brien was the warden (naturally). Rounding out the cast were Jerome Cowan, Henry O'Neill, John Litel, and Guinn "Big Boy" Williams, all under the direction of Anatole Litvak. The picture opened at the Globe Theatre in New York on March 3, 1940, to strong box office but disappointing reviews. B. R. Crisler in the *New York Times* commented:

> This is merely a routine notice that Mr. John Garfield, formerly of the Group Theatre, who was recently sentenced to a term in Warner Bros. pictures, is still in prison.

Tommy Gordon (John Garfield) and Kay (Ann Sheridan) in yet another
Warner Bros. prison yarn, *Castle on the Hudson* (1940).

Julie was disappointed that the critics did not think more
highly of the film or his performance. He was in a continual struggle
to prove that he had far more range as an actor than the studio was
willing to let him demonstrate.

> Julie desired growth as a performer above anything else, but
> with each new variation on what was essentially a single role,
> Warners seemed bent on determining the limitations of his talent
> rather than investigating its farthest horizon. Garfield was back on
> suspension after refusing to do *Flight Angels*.[7]

What he really longed to do was a comedy. "Fate's whipping
boy" was in need of a change of pace. He took his argument to
Henry Blanke, the associate producer of *Four Daughters, Juarez,
Daughters Courageous,* and *Four Wives.* This last film was the sequel that Jack Warner had longed for when *Four Daughters* had

clicked. *Four Wives* featured Garfield in flashbacks to his *Four Daughters* footage. Warners released this film on December 22, 1939, during Garfield's suspension between *Dust Be My Destiny* and *Castle on the Hudson,* creating the illusion of a working actor. J. L. Warner seldom missed a trick in the area of exploitation.

Garfield pointed out to Blanke that he had done a pretty fair job in the Broadway comedy *Having Wonderful Time.* Also, if the studio was so determined to make him into the next James Cagney or Edward G. Robinson, why couldn't he inject comedy into his pictures in the same manner as Messrs. Cagney and Robinson? Blanke pointed to the box office returns from Julie's prison/fugitive pictures in defense of the studio's position. But Henry Blanke and Jack Warner knew that an inactive Garfield was not helping the studio. In an unusual move, they invited Garfield to select a story in an effort to get him back before the cameras.

The story Julie selected was Maxwell Anderson's play *Saturday's Children* which had originally been presented on Broadway in 1927. The play had also been filmed twice previously; in 1929 under its original title and in 1935 as *Maybe It's Love,* which had starred Ross Alexander and Gloria Stuart.

The Epstein brothers were selected to do the screenplay. There was a problem in finding a leading lady. First, Jane Bryan was set, but she married and retired. Then Priscilla Lane was cast and subsequently dropped. Her star, which had been beaming brightly just a few months earlier, was in descent. She never teamed with Garfield again, which was a shame because they always worked so well together. Miss Lane did continue appearing in films until 1948; however she never quite duplicated her early success. After Lane fell out of the running, Garfield intervened on behalf of Anne Shirley. Julie got the studio to arrange for her services on loan-out from RKO, where she was one of the major leading ladies. Shirley had been in films since the age of four, first under the name Dawn O'Day, then switching to Anne Shirley due to her success in *Anne of Green Gables* in 1934.

The next step was to find a director. Julie and the Epstein brothers went to bat for Vincent Sherman, Garfield's old buddy from the Chicago company of *Counsellor-at-Law* and from their

Lobby card for *Castle on the Hudson* (1940) shows a grieving Ann Sheridan as Garfield prepares to "go up the river" yet again!

New York stage days. The timing was right, and Sherman was riding high after his first directorial effort, Humphrey Bogart's *Return of Dr. X* (1939), which was a surprise hit. With everything falling into place, *Saturday's Children* would be one of Julie's happiest experiences in his screen career.

Claude Rains took the third starring role as the girl's father; of Vincent Sherman, Rains said, "This man is precious . . . one of the best directors of actors I've worked with." Sherman went on to direct such fine films as: *All Through the Night* and *The Hard Way* (both 1942), *Mr. Skeffington* (1944) featuring Claude Rains in the title role, *The Unfaithful* (1947), *The Adventures of Don Juan* (1949), and *The Young Philadelphians* (1959). He also directed extensively for television.

Other members of the cast included Roscoe Karns, Lee Patrick, Frank Faylen, John Qualen, Elizabeth Risdon, Berton Churchill,

John Garfield, Anne Shirley, producer Hal Wallis, and "Miss Finland,"
Aune Franks, discuss plans for the great Motion Picture Finnish Relief
benefit at Grauman's Chinese Theater on February 17, 1940. This was one
of many liberal causes that would later land Garfield in trouble with the
HUAC (House Un-American Activities Committee).

Nell O'Day, and, in his first (but certainly not last) John Garfield
film, George Tobias.

Saturday's Children proved to be everything the Epsteins, Vincent Sherman, and Garfield had hoped for. Together, they delivered a sensitive and touchingly human film. Years later, Vincent
Sherman recalled his (and Garfield's) Warner Bros. days: "We saw
each other occasionally. He became like a star overnight. He started
quite young. He wasn't prepared for that kind of success so quickly,
almost meteoric." Mr. Sherman also remembered Julie's battle
against Warners' typecasting, of which *Saturday's Children* was an
attempt to break out: "Having worked together for 10 years, I was
able to capitalize on qualities I knew he had, naïveté, sweetness,
charm, vulnerability. It was a big artistic success. He was a trained
actor with many sides to his talent."

Rims Rosson (John Garfield) and wife Bobbie (Anne Shirley) share a
tender moment in the sensitive *Saturday's Children* (1940).

Ads for the picture proclaimed, "a new and lovable John
Garfield with Anne Shirley and Claude Rains. It's a prize winner!
From the Pulitzer Prize play by Maxwell Anderson." The film opened
at the Strand Theatre in New York on May 4, 1940. Garfield received
his best notices since *Four Daughters*.

> Howard Barnes (*New York Herald Tribune*): John Garfield, who
> raised our hopes too high in his first screen acting, justifies those
> hopes in this production. He plays with the sensitive, thoughtful
> authority that he knows how to muster, as the more or less beaten
> hero of the tale.
> Bosley Crowther (*New York Times*): Particular praise is in store
> for John Garfield, the sallow Romeo with the sad face and troubled
> soul, who falls into the part of the harassed young lover as though
> it had been written for him alone, and to Anne Shirley, who en-
> dows the little wife with heroic integrity and strength of character.

It is a rich and flavorsome picture of New York's subway society, this *Saturday's Children.*

The performance was one for which Garfield himself would always be proud. The only place the film fell short of expectations was at the box office. When the picture failed to generate whopping profits, Warner Bros. was more determined than ever to keep Julie in gangster roles.

After completing *Saturday's Children,* Garfield exercised his clause to do a play. The production, Albert Bein's *Heavenly Express,* had its tryout run in Washington, D.C. in late March and early April. Garfield and fellow cast members Harry Carey and Aline MacMahon were luncheon guests of Vice President John Nance Garner on March 28, 1940. The Broadway opening was held April 18, 1940, and despite the outstanding cast of Carey (making his first Broadway appearance in 27 years), MacMahon, and Nicholas (Richard) Conte, it closed after only twenty performances.

Despite the quick closing, Julie had been reinvigorated just being back on stage. Shrugging off the failure, he hoped to be back in New York soon:

> When I first went out to Hollywood everybody said I'd never go back to the theatre. But I did. I had a little extra money and some time, so I decided to do *Heavenly Express.* It was a flop and when I got back to the studio some folks gave me the "I told you so." But I did it and I didn't regret it a bit. And I'm going to get into another play as soon as I can. Some folks used to think I was being arty about the theatre. But look at it this way — there are actors who like polo ponies and actors who like yachts. Me, I like the theatre. It's that simple. That's the reason I've got those clauses in my contract.

This turned out to be the only time that he used the Broadway clause in his contract. Garfield could take pride in some of the personal notices his performance had generated. Brooks Atkinson wrote: "Mr. Garfield plays with a glow of youth and a touch of

Poverty and romance mix beautifully as this lobby card from *Saturday's Children* (1940) attests.

Ariel ... altogether the most winning angel of death in the theatre."

The *New York Daily News* said: "Young Mr. Garfield's Overland Kid is alive with enthusiasm and a complete belief in his author and himself."

Arriving back in Hollywood, Julie and wife Robbie continued to be involved in many liberal movements. Friends would say that Robbie was the one with real political savvy; Julie was emotionally involved in an effort to help the downtrodden. Around this time, the Garfields became quite close with Edward G. Robinson and his wife. Garfield and Robinson would remain friends to the end.

Julie's next picture was the Rex Beach oil story, *Flowing Gold*. Once again he portrayed a young man on the run from the law. Pat O'Brien played his boss on the drill gang. The studio had its by-now

Idealistic inventor Rims Rosson (John Garfield) draws a crowd as he demonstrates one of his gadgets to Bobbie Halevy (Anne Shirley) in this amusing moment from *Saturday's Children* (1940).

standard problem in finding a leading lady. Ann Sheridan and Olivia De Havilland both refused to appear, so Julie persuaded the studio to hire Frances Farmer. Her experience with the Group Theatre after *Golden Boy* had been anything but pleasant, and Garfield wanted to help her troubled life and career. However sincere Julie was in his efforts, *Flowing Gold* was not a good enough picture to help advance the career of anyone, and Miss Farmer's life would continue on its sad course. She would appear in only five more films before her retirement due to various alcohol and mental problems. She died in 1970 of cancer.

Flowing Gold had been rushed into release to compete with MGM's *Boom Town*, but paled in comparison. Next on the Garfield docket was *East of the River*, which had the shortest running time (73 minutes) of any Garfield picture since *Blackwell's Island*. *East of the River* was based on an original story by John Fante and Ross

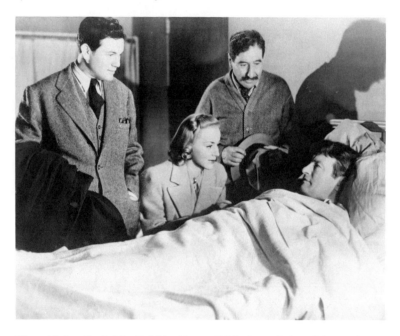

Rims (John Garfield), Bobbie (Anne Shirley), and the nightwatchman (Paul Panzer) visit Mr. Halevy (Claude Rains) in the hospital (*Saturday's Children*, 1940).

B. Wills. The studio had initially purchased the story, called *Two Sons*, for their dynamic duo of James Cagney and Pat O'Brien. Jeffrey Lynn and Priscilla Lane were also mentioned as possibilities for the parts that were eventually played by William Lundigan and Brenda Marshall.

The film, like *Flowing Gold* before it, was directed by Alfred E. Green and produced by Bryan Foy. Somehow, Julie had slipped to the "B" team. *East of the River* may well have been a programmer, but it was kept moving by the veteran Green, who had been directing since 1917. The story was set in New York (the studio's favorite locale) and featured the familiar tale of two brothers, one good (Lundigan) and the other bad (Garfield, of course). The cast, besides Brenda Marshall, included Marjorie Rambeau, Jack LaRue, Douglas Fowley, and old pal George Tobias. Theodore Strauss wrote in the *New York Times*:

John Garfield, Harry Carey, and Aline MacMahon (far right) enjoy a luncheon with Vice President John Nance Garner and Mrs. Claude Pepper (wife of the Florida Senator) during the tryout phase of *Heavenly Express* (March 28, 1940).

> The war of attrition between John Garfield and the law of the realm — or is it just the Warner Brothers? — seems perilously close to its final stages in *East of the River*.... Isn't it time that the Warners allowed Mr. Garfield really to reform — and stay that way?

Around this time, the trade papers carried the notice that Warner Bros. planned 50 features for the 1940-41 season. Noteworthy was the announcement of *The Fabulous Thirties,* an original by Mark Hellinger, the same man who had penned *The Roaring Twenties.* The plan was for Garfield to team with Priscilla Lane in a follow up to *The Roaring Twenties.* Unfortunately, the film was never made, despite the intriguing potential of the story. Garfield was also announced to star in a film version of Charles Kaufman's novel *Fiesta in Manhattan,* which never came to pass. And finally, Warners announced the purchase of Henry Bellamann's novel

Hot Rocks (Cliff Edwards) and Johnny Blake (John Garfield) try to bring
in a gusher in *Flowing Gold* (1940).

Kings Row, to star James Cagney and John Garfield. Ronald Reagan
and Robert Cummings eventually starred in the 1942 film.

Warner Bros. also announced a new line-up of stars:

1. Bette Davis	9. George Brent	16. Geraldine Fitz-
2. James Cagney	10. Olivia De	gerald
3. Paul Muni	Havilland	17. Eddie Albert
4. Merle Oberon	11. John Garfield	18. Brenda Marshall
5. Errol Flynn	12. Pat O'Brien	19. Virginia Bruce
6. Ann Sheridan	13. Miriam Hopkins	20. Jeffrey Lynn
7. Edward G.	14. George Raft	21. Ida Lupino
Robinson	15. Humphrey Bogart	22. Dennis Morgan
8. Priscilla Lane		23. Wayne Morris

Hap O'Conner (Pat O'Brien) and Johnny Blake (John Garfield) look sky-ward (possibly for divine career guidance) in another lobby card for *Flowing Gold* (1940).

Behind-the-camera people included: Jack L. Warner as vice president in charge of production and Hal B. Wallis as executive producer.

Associate producers included: Bryan Foy, Henry Blanke, William Cagney (Jimmy's brother, who would be involved in Jimmy's last five films under his current contract), Bob Fellows, Edmund Grainger, Mark Hellinger, David Lewis, Robert Lord, and Wolfgang Reinhardt. Directors included: Lloyd Bacon, Michael Curtiz, William Dieterle, Ray Enright, Alfred E. Green, Edmund Goulding, William Keighley, Anatole Litvak, William McGann, Irving Rapper, Lewis Seiler, Vincent Sherman, Raoul Walsh, and William Wyler.

After *East of the River*, Garfield was offered the Mad Dog

Johnny Blake (John Garfield) and Hap O'Conner (Pat O'Brien) eye each other warily while Linda Chalmers (Frances Farmer) seems blissfully unaware that she is in the eye of the storm (*Flowing Gold*, 1940).

Earle part in *High Sierra*. He refused it because George Raft had already turned it down, and Julie thought that he deserved more consideration than that. The film would firmly establish Humphrey Bogart as a star. Actually, Warners had originally planned the story as a Paul Muni vehicle, but once he was out, it fell to Raft then to Garfield and finally to Bogart. In any event, Julie was back on suspension.

Warner Bros. was planning a lavish production of Jack London's *The Sea Wolf*. Edward G. Robinson was set for the title role and Ida Lupino was also in the cast. Julie had great respect for both of these professionals; he came off the suspended list to enact the part of rebellious seaman George Leach. Years later, Edward G. Robinson wrote: "John Garfield was one of the best young actors I ever encountered, but his passions about the world were so intense, I feared he would soon have a heart attack."

Top: Mama Lorenzo (Marjorie Rambeau, standing) welcomes home prodigal son Joe (John Garfield, left) while Laurie (Brenda Marshall) and Tony (George Tobias) join in during this cheery breakfast reunion in *East of the River* (1940). *Bottom:* Joe (John Garfield) bids a sad farewell to Laurie (Brenda Marshall) as rival mobster Cy Turner (Douglas Fowley) lurks menacingly in the background (*East of the River,* 1940).

Top: Three highly charged performers (John Garfield, Ida Lupino, and Edward G. Robinson) threaten to melt the celluloid in *The Sea Wolf* (1941). *Bottom:* Ruth Webster (Ida Lupino) falsely accuses George Leach (John Garfield) of having revealed her shady past to the crewmen (*The Sea Wolf,* 1941).

Small-time hood Harold Goff (John Garfield) applies the pressure to the local citizenry: Olaf Knudsen (John Qualen), George Watkins (Eddie Albert), and Jonah Goodwin (Thomas Mitchell) (*Out of the Fog,* 1941).

Michael Curtiz directed with his usual care and Robert Rossen's script was interesting for, among other things, the smoldering love scenes between the Garfield and Lupino characters. Their moments crackled with electricity and the studio envisioned a whole series of films to feature the pair. Edward G. Robinson contributed one of his memorable performances and newcomer (his first U.S. film) Alexander Knox displayed sensitivity in the role of writer Humphrey van Weyden, based on Jack London himself.

The studio wasted no time in reteaming Garfield and Ida Lupino, this time for *Out of the Fog.* The film was based on Irwin Shaw's play *Gentle People.* Shaw had Garfield in mind when he wrote the story, but it was Franchot Tone who returned to the

Group to star in the Broadway production. In the film version, Thomas Mitchell and John Qualen were the two old men being terrorized by the cheap waterfront gangster Goff (Garfield). Eddie Albert, Aline MacMahon, Leo Gorcey, Bernard Gorcey, and George Tobias were also featured in the gloomy picture, which sunk at the box office. Garfield gave a disciplined performance but, for the only time in his career, his character had no redeeming values. The poor returns at the theatres and the coming of war combined to shelve any plans the studio may have had for future Garfield-Lupino teamings.

Chapter 3

Fighting the War(ners)

In 1941, John Garfield made a very significant career move when he dropped Lyons & Lyons as his agents in favor of Lew Wasserman. Julie felt that Arthur Lyons too often took the studio's position in the many battles Garfield waged with Jack Warner. Of even greater importance, Garfield put his business affairs in the hands of Bob Roberts. Roberts was an old New York friend; together they began plans to produce their own films upon completion of Julie's Warner contract. As Garfield would later relate: "All I want is more mature material. I refuse to be typed continually. My kick is purely on artistic grounds."

After completing *Out of the Fog,* Garfield went on suspension for refusing to appear in *Blues in the Night.* He came off suspension to star in *Dangerously They Live,* which ran a scant 71 minutes. Bryan Foy was back as producer, but despite the cramped budget, Robert Florey brought some excitement to the proceedings with his directorial expertise. The story was one of the studio's many Nazi-spies-in-America efforts, which was the major reason Julie had chosen it. Nancy Coleman, Raymond Massey, Lee Patrick, Moroni Olsen, and John Ridgely were featured in the film.

Off screen, John Garfield was one of the first major film stars to entertain the U.S. Armed Forces during World War Two. In fact, he led a troupe consisting of Laurel and Hardy, Ray Bolger, Mitzi Mayfair, Jane Pickens, and Chico Marx on a tour of Caribbean military bases in the fall of 1941, before America's entry into the war. This tour was the first of many trips Garfield would make over the next four years, either to entertain troops or to sell bonds. Julie remarked, "I'm glad I did it, and I want to do it again. If I can't do it as a civilian, then I'll do it the other way." The tour also served

57

John Garfield sells tickets to Julie Bishop (Warner Bros. starlet) for the grand opening of the Hollywood Canteen in 1942.

as the catalyst for the founding of one of the bright spots in the Hollywood social whirl during the war years.

The Hollywood Canteen was founded in early 1942 as a place where servicemen could rub elbows with Hollywood's elite. The stars acted as waiters and waitresses, and the famous actresses of the day became dancing partners for the GIs. Julie was aided immensely by Bette Davis in the launching of the club. It was her clout which turned Julie's idea into a reality. Davis served as president and

Garfield as vice president. The Canteen continued as a beacon for enlisted men through the duration of the war.

Meanwhile, Garfield's next film assignment promised to be something different. For one thing, it was his first film away from Warner Bros. He had been loaned out to MGM to costar with Spencer Tracy and Hedy Lamarr in that studio's adaptation of John Steinbeck's *Tortilla Flat*. Unfortunately, flat was an apt description for Victor Fleming's direction. The cast, consisting of John Qualen, Henry O'Neill, Sheldon Leonard, Akim Tamiroff, Donald Meek, and Allen Jenkins certainly was worthy of something better. *Variety* remarked: "It is Frank Morgan, as the old man with a vision of St. Francis to his credit, who virtually swipes the picture." Still, Julie enjoyed working with Tracy and there were persistent rumors that he really enjoyed "working" with Hedy Lamarr.

The Garfields returned to New York in the spring of 1942. Julie's father, David, was dying, and the family rushed to be at his side. Julie had supported his father for the last five years. After David Garfinkle's death, Julie would continue to help his stepmother Dinah financially. Ironically, David Garfinkle never saw any of his son's movies. "I used to get passes for him when I was on the stage," Garfield recalled, "but I couldn't get passes for the movies, so he didn't go. I offered to pay for them, but he wouldn't let me spend the money."

Back in his home town, Julie was swarmed by interviewers. He told reporters that he did not endorse the rumored government plan to keep actors out of the service and in the studios for morale purposes. "We'll go when we're called, just like everyone else." Julie's outspoken patriotism and his efforts on tour did not go unappreciated.

Franklin Delano Roosevelt extended an invitation to the White House. The president asked Julie to lead some bond-selling tours. Garfield agreed to help, taking an active role in the sale of war bonds as part of the Stars Over America campaign. Julie was expecting to enter the military ranks himself very soon; he was startled upon learning he had been rated 4-F. The army doctors detected a strong heart murmur, which in all probability had been with Julie since he had contracted scarlet fever as a boy.

Julie and Robbie continued their efforts in various liberal organizations and causes. Robbie and Mrs. Edward G. Robinson were involved in Russian relief work, while Julie became more active as an executive board member in the Screen Actors Guild. He also lent financial support to help establish the Actors Laboratory Theatre in Hollywood, which was largely populated by Group Theatre alumni.

In July 1942, Warners announced two John Garfield vehicles, *Dangerous Road* and *The Patent Leather Kid* (again!). Neither plan came to fruition. Evidently, the Warners never tired of announcing Garfield for *The Patent Leather Kid;* the *Motion Picture Herald* of August 18, 1945, carried this announcement: "John Garfield has been assigned the starring role in Warner Bros.' *Patent Leather Kid* which Arnold Albert is scheduled to produce."

In September 1942, Warner Bros. announced the purchase of *Deep Valley,* a novel by Dan Totheroh, for Ann Sheridan, Humphrey Bogart, and John Garfield. The story would languish on the studio's shelves until 1947, when it finally reached the screen with Ida Lupino, Wayne Morris, and Dane Clark. Also in 1942, Julie went to court to have his name legally changed from Jacob Garfinkle to John Jules Garfield. The change was done in order that daughter Katherine would have no trouble when she entered school. A second child arrived in July 1943. This time it was a son, and his arrival helped draw the Garfields close after another of their "troubled" periods. The proud parents named the boy David Patton Garfield, in honor of Julie's late father and General Patton.

Back at work, Garfield appeared in a string of films largely designed to help the war effort. Theodore Strauss in the *New York Times* reported:

> Ever since war came Mr. Garfield has been busily bounding about the country and foreign places on camp tours and bond-selling campaigns, in addition to fairly steady routine at the studio in such items as *The Fallen Sparrow,* the forthcoming *Thank Your Lucky Stars,* and *Destination Tokyo,* which was made in secrecy. He has been vice-president of the Hollywood Stage Door Canteen, which recently sold its story to Warner Brothers for $250,000,

John Garfield takes time off from filming *Air Force* to help bit players Sylvia Opert (left) and Dorothy Schoemer (right) gather presents for the Warner employees in the service.

which will be used to erect a soldier's hospital. Mr. Garfield, who feels a decent pride about the matter, likes to think that his films, no less than his war work, make a point. On the basis of the evidence one would say they did. Mr. Garfield has been speaking out for democracy for a long time.

The first film in the string was *Air Force,* directed by one of Hollywood's very best, Howard Hawks. Hawks imbued the film with his characteristic touches, focusing on the camaraderie among the men and the realistic action scenes. Garfield headed a cast that included Harry Carey, Gig Young, Arthur Kennedy, Richard Lane,

John Garfield proudly shows director Howard Hawks two that didn't get away. The men were on location in Tampa, Florida, for the filming of *Air Force* (1943).

John Ridgely, and old friend George Tobias. The film was one of the most popular war movies, not only with the public but also with the critics. *Air Force* was third in the *National Board of Review* poll and placed in the *New York Times* Ten Best Films of 1943. The film opened at the Hollywood Theatre in New York on February 4, 1943. Among the favorable reviews were the following:

> David Larner, *New Yorker:* The most irresistible personalities involved are John Garfield and Harry Carey, who appear to be perfectly content to speak when spoken to. *Air Force,* a superbly thrilling show, is easily the best aviation film to date.

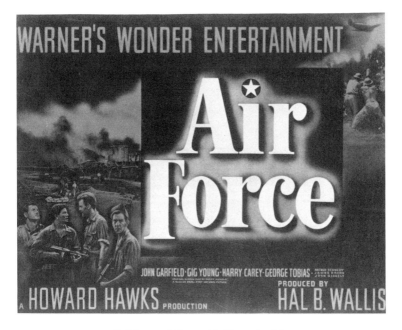

Lobby card from *Air Force* (1943).

Bosley Crowther, *New York Times:* It is . . . a continuously fascinating show, frequently thrilling and occasionally exalting. . . . John Ridgely is *a* refreshingly direct as the bomber's intrepid captain. . . . Harry Carey gives a beautiful performance as the quiet and efficient crew chief, and John Garfield's tough creation of Winocki is superior despite its brevity.

Philip T. Hartung, *Commonweal:* When Warner Brothers decided to produce *Air Force,* they must have decided to make a flying film that was bigger and better than all others. They have done just that.

Garfield's next assignment was on loan-out to RKO for *The Fallen Sparrow.* The story was close to his heart, as it dealt with the Spanish Civil War. Offscreen he had long been a Loyalist supporter, and now he was playing the part of a Loyalist survivor dogged by Nazi spies upon his return to the United States. Garfield gave a performance that foreshadowed some of his later work as a man troubled

Williams, White, and Quincannon (left to right, a young Gig Young, Harry Carey, and John Ridgely), three stalwart members of the crew of the *Mary Ann* and of the cast of *Air Force* (1943).

by some inner turmoil. This performance, combined with Richard Wallace's taut direction and Nicholas Musuraca's photography gave the film more power than the murky script (Warren Duff) suggested. The picture pleased wartime audiences and was one of RKO's biggest moneymakers in 1943.

Maureen O'Hara was the leading lady; featured in the cast were two fellows who would later become familiar faces on television, John Banner (Sgt. Schultz of *Hogan's Heroes*) and Hugh Beaumont (Ward Cleaver of *Leave It to Beaver*). Theodore Strauss stressed just how important the contributions of Garfield and Richard Wallace were in his review in the *New York Times:*

> By virtue of a taut performance by John Garfield in the central role, and the singular skill with which director Richard Wallace has highlighted the significant climaxes, *The Fallen Sparrow* emerges

Kit (John Garfield) comforts the parents of his murdered pal Louie Lepetino (Rosina Galli and William Edmunds) in *The Fallen Sparrow* (1943).

as one of the uncommon and provocatively handled melodramas of recent months.... Through these scenes Mr. Garfield remains almost constantly convincing, and, without his sure and responsive performance in a difficult role, Mr. Wallace's effects would have been lost entirely.

Garfield appeared as himself in his next two movie assignments. *Show Business at War* was a multi-studio effort which featured various stars in short subjects (usually around 17 minutes) that centered on some aspect of the war effort. Garfield, Eddie "Rochester" Anderson, Louis Armstrong, Jack Benny, Edgar Bergen, Joe E. Brown, James Cagney, Michael Curtiz, Linda Darnell, Bette Davis, Deanna Durbin, Errol Flynn, Al Jolson, Hedy Lamarr, Mickey Rooney, Frank Sinatra, Orson Welles, Eddie Cantor, and Olivia De Havilland were just some of the luminaries that donated their services to the series.

Thank Your Lucky Stars was next, a 124 minute jam-packed Warner Bros. musical comedy extravaganza. The stars of the picture were Eddie Cantor (in a dual role), Joan Leslie, and Dennis Morgan. Garfield performed a comic rendition of *Blues in the Night,* while engaging in some mayhem with Eddie Cantor. Other guest stars included: Humphrey Bogart, Bette Davis, Olivia De Havilland, Errol Flynn, Jack Carson, Alan Hale, Ann Sheridan, Dinah Shore, and (you guessed it) George Tobias. The film proved to be one of the top-grossing pictures of 1943.

Garfield's next film was a serious war drama, *Destination Tokyo.* The film was directed by Delmer Daves (who also helped with the screenplay), produced by Jerry Wald, and written by Albert Maltz. This team would later collaborate with Garfield on the *Pride of the Marines* project. Cary Grant was top-billed as the submarine U.S.S. *Copperfin*'s commander. The stellar Warner cast included Dane Clark (formerly Bernard Zanville of the Group Theatre), Alan Hale, John Ridgely, William Prince, Robert Hutton, and John Forsythe. *Destination Tokyo* was a top-grossing film for 1944 and made that year's *New York Times* Ten Best list.

> Bosley Crowther, *New York Times:* The Warners have got a pippin of a submarine action film in *Destination Tokyo....* Credit all and sundry with the first thundering war film of the year.
>
> *Newsweek:* Warner Brothers' newest tribute to the armed forces rates very near the top of the list.... Cary Grant gives one of the soundest performances of his career; and John Garfield, William Prince, and Dane Clark are always credible either as ordinary human beings or extraordinary heroes.

Following the success of *Destination Tokyo,* Julie appeared in one of his least successful pictures, *Between Two Worlds.* The film was based on the play *Outward Bound,* which Warners had previously filmed in 1930. Garfield was proud to be playing the same role that Leslie Howard had done in the earlier screen version. But despite the presence of Garfield and such other major talents as Sydney Greenstreet, Paul Henreid, Eleanor Parker, Edmund Gwenn, and (the ever present) George Tobias, the film failed to inspire audiences or critics (virtually wasting one of Erich Wolfgang Korngold's most beautiful scores). The problem was in the direction; Edward A. Blatt made his directorial debut with this film. He would go on to direct only two more films in his undistinguished career, *Escape in the Desert* (1945) and *Smart Woman* (1948). Perhaps the finest film he was associated with was Errol Flynn's excellent *They Died with Their Boots On,* on which he served as dialogue director.

Newsweek summed it up best:

> In attempting to bring Vane's (playwright Sutton Vane) spirit world up to date, Daniel Fuchs (screenplay) has merely obscured its persuasive simplicity with topical references and dialogue that is either pompous or pedestrian. The cast is left pretty much at loose ends by Edward Blatt's direction and the revised material at hand.

Exhibitors echoed these sentiments:

> Played one day only and got by due to the fact that our patrons like Garfield, George Tobias, and Sydney Greenstreet . . . must be seen from beginning, otherwise the customers would be quite muddled because of the nature of the story. A. H. Kaufman, Fountain Theatre, Terre Haute, Indiana.

Another Warner Bros. all-star bonanza served as Garfield's next screen chore. This time the film was the aptly titled *Hollywood Canteen.* Garfield and Bette Davis appeared as themselves and gave a brief rundown of the Canteen's founding. The plot, such as it was, centered around a soldier's (Robert Hutton) attempts to date Joan Leslie (playing herself). Dane Clark appeared as Hutton's best friend. The plethora of guest stars included: The Andrews Sisters, Jack Benny, Joe E. Brown, Eddie Cantor, Jack Carson, Joan Crawford, Helmut Dantine, Sydney Greenstreet and Peter Lorre in a very amusing sendup of their sinister screen images, Alan Hale, Alexis Smith, Craig Stevens, Zachary Scott, Barbara Stanwyck, Dennis Morgan, Eleanor Parker, Ida Lupino, and Roy Rogers. Practically everyone except George Tobias.

Capt. Cassidy (Cary Grant) and Wolf (John Garfield) prepare to go topside in *Destination Tokyo* **(1944).**

The many movie commitments limited Julie's overseas trips, but he did make several bond-selling tours in the East. Around this time, Garfield's marriage was again sailing in troubled waters. He and Eleanor Parker, who had appeared in *Between Two Worlds,* were rumored to be "involved." Julie wanted her in his next picture, *The Pride of the Marines.* The film would be a Garfield project from start to finish. It was the story of Philadelphia's Al Schmid, a true hero who had been blinded in the Guadalcanal battle.

Julie read a magazine account of Al Schmid and was anxious to put the story on the screen. He took the idea to Albert Maltz, an old friend who had written *Peace on Earth* for the Theatre Union in 1933. Garfield had appeared in that production and also in Maltz's *Destination Tokyo.* Maltz worked up a screenplay which won the studio's hearty approval. But shooting was not scheduled to commence until late 1944, some nine months away, and there was no guarantee it would be shot at all as audiences were turning away from war films in favor of pure escapist fare.

Henry (Paul Henreid) tries to stop Tom Prior (John Garfield) from telling the rest of the ship's passengers that they are dead while Henry's wife Ann (Eleanor Parker) anxiously looks on (*Between Two Worlds,* 1944).

The delay enabled Julie to plan an extended overseas junket. He was still very bitter about his draft classification and believed it was his duty to entertain the troops fighting the war: "I've got to get overseas to entertain troops. Nothing else seems important to me. I can't think of anything else. I've got to go." In the spring of 1944, Garfield led a troupe consisting of Eddie Foy, Jr., Sheila Rogers, Olga Klein, and Jean Darling.

The entertainers arrived in Naples with the bombs from German planes falling all around them. They did not give any shows in the city but went immediately to the front lines. While there, they honored an Army staff request to entertain Yugoslavian guerillas; this action would later be misinterpreted by the House Un-American Activities Committee, which saw it as support for

Staunch Roosevelt supporter John Garfield takes time off from his bond-selling tour to attend the President's birthday party in 1944. Others present include (left to right): Jose Iturbi, Brian Donlevy, Jinx Falkenburg, District Comissioner J. Russell Young, Red Skelton, Lucille Ball, and Walter Pidgeon.

communism. Garfield reported on the tour in the August 1944 issue of *Silver Screen:*

> You can't know unless you've been there what a sense of inner satisfaction it gives a guy to be out there . . . to have done that little bit which is so important to help things along. . . . Believe me it *is* important. After you've been there you realize it. You'll never in your life again give a performance which is as important as that one out where the G.I.s are sitting around in the mud or in the hospital where the wounded lads look up at you with that . . . that look.
>
> But you've got to do a good job—probably the best job you ever did in your life—or the whole thing's a failure. You just can't throw some stuff together any old way and expect to wow 'em because they have been away from home a long time and you think they haven't kept up with entertainment. If you don't give them

your best they'll know it. And you had better not have gone in the first place. That's one thing I brought back with me — the conviction that it won't do to underestimate G.I. Joe's intelligence or his good taste.

It isn't as tough for a genuinely funny man who is a master of the ad lib, like Foy, as it is for a straight man like me. He knows he can amuse them. But I have to work at it. I can't get up and say, "Look, fellows. I'm John Garfield!" and expect that to mean anything. I've got to have good stuff. I had to have good writers. I had to work at it. I had to be *careful.* The front is where if you make a misstep, you're in no man's land. And that's bad.

The article continued that it was when they got to the hospitals that the work became, as John put it, "really rugged." Garfield recalled:

That was hard to do. The ambulatory and convalescent cases could assemble and we could give them a show. But we had to go to the ones who were really bad . . . had to go from bed to bed. After I'd gone through my first ward of the serious cases, I wondered whether I could go on . . . whether I really knew what to do. Then someone told me that Joe E. Brown had made it a point to shake the hand of each boy and ask him where he came from. I took my cue from that and began doing it. I've trouped a lot and I've been in nearly every city and most counties . . . in the U.S., so that when one of them told me the name of his home town, the chances were that I could tell him I'd been there. I might even remember someone's name! I got so I could do it and even be almost glib about it. But I'll never forget the things I saw in those hospitals. . . .

The magazine noted that Garfield was away from Hollywood for over three months, giving his best for G.I. Joe. But he was still working at it.

There are all those messages to deliver, from the boys to their parents, their girls, their dear old grandmothers. Some of them require letters, some long-distance telephone calls. . . . They all have to be attended to, or else you have not finished the job you started out there.

Silver Screen concluded the article with this item: "John has been classified 1-A and may be a G.I. Joe himself, by the time you read this."

It was true. Garfield felt a real kinship with the soldiers and ached to get into battle. Immediately upon his arrival in New York at the close of the tour, he managed to pull enough strings to be reclassified as 1-A. He was summoned for a physical, which he passed, and awaited the call to duty. But in June of 1944, Julie suffered a mild heart attack and became an official reject.

Garfield's consolation prize for the Army's rejection was word from Warner Bros. to go ahead with *Pride of the Marines,* which the studio would not have filmed except as a John Garfield vehicle. The role of Al Schmid was the closest Julie came to playing a traditional American hero, and he found the perfect role model to peg his performance on, Schmid himself. Julie went to Philadelphia to live with the Schmids for several weeks. Not only did Julie study Schmid, but he also formed a real friendship with the blinded hero.

During the filming of *Pride of the Marines,* the Garfields bought a house on Carroll Drive in Beverly Hills. Edward G. Robinson helped Julie pick out some paintings to furnish the place, but some of the best paintings were Garfield's own drawings. Painting was one of his few hobbies, along with sports. Robbie had hired a nurse to help with the infant David, and the nurse was retained as a household helper. The nurse, Hilda Wane, would figure prominently in one of the most tragic events in Julie's life.

Kathy Garfield was allergy-prone and sometimes had trouble breathing. She attended a St. Patrick's Day picnic in 1945 at a ranch owned by a Garfield family friend. Since the ranch was 100 miles from Los Angeles, Hilda Wane accompanied Kathy and they stayed overnight. During the night, Kathy's throat became swollen, and when she was not any better in the morning, Hilda Wane drove her home. By the time they reached Beverly Hills, Kathy was in desperate trouble. She died less than an hour after reaching home. Death was attributed to a spasm of the glottis; Katherine Garfield was six years old.

Julie had been at the studio and did not reach home in time. He blamed himself, saying that he had neglected her. Friends said the loss rendered him permanently gloomy. But the tragedy did bring him and Robbie into a stronger, more stable phase of their marriage. Garfield became a much better father to his son David and to the daughter who would be born the following year. Neighbor Vincent Sherman believed the tragedy somehow made Julie a better person.

Pride of the Marines opened as World War II was closing. The film opened at the Strand Theatre in New York on August 24, 1945, but before that, there was a special World Premiere at the Mastbaum Theatre in Philadelphia on August 8, 1945. The premiere was part of Al Schmid Day in his home town and was attended by more than 1,500 veterans of Guadalcanal. Warner Bros.' ad campaign for the film proclaimed: "If you've ever run a love story more wonderful than this one — Tell it to the Marines!"

It was the biggest box office hit Garfield had at Warner Bros. Although Al Schmid was a traditional hero, he possessed rebel hero traits after becoming blind. His refusal to lean on anyone, even the woman who loves him, and his pride in himself were brilliantly conveyed by Garfield in one of his best tough-sensitive characterizations. His performance was worthy of an Academy Award, but he did not even receive a nomination. The film was named to the *New York Times* Ten Best List of 1945.

Eleanor Parker gave a fine performance as Schmid's fiancee. The scenes between Garfield and Parker carried conviction. *Pride of the Marines* would serve as a tremendous boost to her career, and she continued in movies for many more years. Some of her films include: *Never Say Good-bye* (1946), *The Woman in White* (1948), *Caged* (AA nomination, 1950), *Detective Story* (AA nomination, 1951), *Interrupted Melody* (AA nomination, 1955), *A Hole in the Head* (1959), and *Madison Avenue* (1962).

Garfield's good friend Dane Clark gave a splendid rendition as Lee Diamond, buddy to Schmid. Dane Clark was on a roll at this point in his career. Just as *Pride of the Marines* was being released, he won *Motion Picture Herald*'s poll of exhibitors as the top star of tomorrow, placing first overall in categories consisting of: combined vote of exhibitors, circuit exhibitors, and independent exhibitors. Clark had appeared in uniform in six consecutive films: *Action in the North Atlantic, Destination Tokyo, The Very Thought of You, Hollywood Canteen, God Is My Co-Pilot,* and *Pride of the Marines.*

Warner Bros. was grooming Dane as a replacement for Garfield should Julie not be signed to a new contract. The buildup continued for a few more films: *A Stolen Life* and *Her Kind of Man* (both 1946), and *That Way with Women* and *Deep Valley* (both 1947). However, shortly thereafter, Dane had a run-in with Jack Warner which led to blows, virtually ending his career at Warner Bros. With three years left on his contract, he appeared in only two more films at the studio, *Embraceable You* and *Whiplash* (both 1948). Warner also refused to lend Clark out to play the title role in Stanley Kramer's *Champion.* The 1949 film went a long way in helping Kirk Douglas achieve major stardom.

Dane was forced to scramble for roles (both here and abroad) in order to keep his career alive. He appeared in U.S. productions, including: *Moonrise* (1948), *Without Honor* (1949), *Backfire* and *Barricade* (both 1950), *Fort Defiance* (1951), *Never Trust a Gambler* (also 1951), and *Thunder Pass* and *Go, Man, Go!* (both 1954). His European films during this period included: *Highly Dangerous* (1951), *The Gambler and the Lady* (1952), *Blackout,* aka *Murder by Proxy* (1954), and *Paid to Kill,* aka *Five Days* (also 1954), all filmed in England and released in the United States by the poverty row company Lippert Films.

Dane Clark also appeared in the Broadway productions *The Number* (1951) and *Fragile Fox* (1954). His countless television appearances include the series *Wire Service* (1956–57), *Bold Venture* (1959), and later, *Perry Mason,* the revival (1973–74). Mr. Clark's determination and talent kept him active into the late 1980s.

Veterans Rosemary DeCamp, John Ridgely, and Ann Doran gave strong support to the stars. Delmer Daves directed with great skill; he would go on to direct many fine films of the fifties including: *Broken Arrow* (1950), *Drum Beat* (1954), *The Last Wagon* (1956), *3:10 to Yuma* (1957), *The Badlanders* (1958) and *The Hanging Tree* (1959). Albert Maltz's screenplay was superb; unfortunately, his career would soon be destroyed by the House Un-American Activities Committee. He would go without a screen credit for more than two decades, from *The Naked City* in 1948 until *Two Mules*

Ruth Hartley (Eleanor Parker) and Al Schmid (John Garfield) enjoy the Sunday funnies shortly before hearing the announcement about the bombing of Pearl Harbor in *Pride of the Marines* (1945).

for Sister Sara in 1970. Franz Waxman contributed a stirring score; he would later win Oscars for *Sunset Boulevard* (1950) and *A Place in the Sun* (1951).

All these elements combined to produce an exceptional motion picture. At the center was Garfield's incandescent portrayal. Bosley Crowther in the *New York Times* wrote:

> A remarkably natural production . . . gives the story integrity. . . .
> Albert Maltz took the journalistic accounts of Schmid's experience
> and translated them into a solid, credible drama, composed of taut
> situation and dialogue. . . . The performances are all unqualifiedly
> excellent. John Garfield does a brilliant job as Schmid, cocky and
> self-reliant and full of a calm, commanding pride. . . . To say that
> this picture is entertaining to a truly surprising degree is an

Top: Nurse Virginia Pfeiffer (Rosemary DeCamp) writes a letter home for blinded marine Al Schmid (John Garfield) in *Pride of the Marines* (1945). *Bottom:* Captain Burroughs (Moroni Olsen) congratulates Al Schmid (John Garfield) on winning the Navy Cross as Lee Diamond (Dane Clark) and Virginia Pfeiffer (Rosemary DeCamp) watch (*Pride of the Marines,* 1945).

Portrait shot of Dane Clark around the time that Warner Bros. was grooming him for major stardom (1947).

inadequate recommendation. It is inspiring and eloquent of a quality of human courage that millions must try to generate today.

The *New York Herald Tribune* said:

> Honesty and intensity make up for numerous cinematic faults in *Pride of the Marines*.... Thanks to John Garfield's brilliant portrayal of the central role, Schmid emerges on the screen with genuine personal authority.... Garfield's underacting keys the production to its central theme.

The film was a very personal thing to Julie and a triumph for his natural style of acting. He wrote a short article for *The Saturday Evening Post* of January 12, 1946, which is reprinted below:

The Role I Liked Best...
by
John Garfield

My favorite role was a foolproof one. I don't see how any actor could have helped responding with his best work to the challenge of portraying the real life hero, Al Schmid, in *Pride of the Marines*.

The movie told the story of the boy's struggle to adjust himself and work out a romance to a happy conclusion after returning from the war incurably blind, yet hoping to recover his sight.

In order to live the character honestly and with understanding, I stayed at Al Schmid's home for a month.

I found him the kind of kid we like to think of as the wholesome American type—brave, determined, resourceful, fun loving, but not without some of the faults that are American too.

After I got to know Al well, I felt it was not only an honor to impersonate him on the screen but was also an opportunity to be of some help to the veterans like him and to their families and their sweethearts. For the problems Al faced in real life, as well as in the movie, are the problems that thousands of men face today when they come back to civilian life. It seemed to me important, first, to make the movie-going public appreciate and remember that for disabled veterans the great struggle didn't end with the coming of peace; and second, to accent the optimistic fact that the same courage and intelligence which licked the enemy can help bring these broken heroes to the enduring happiness that they deserve.

Although Warners had given Garfield much freedom in the filming of *Pride of the Marines* as an incentive for him to sign a new contract, the experience only served to reinforce his desire to go independent. He had an idea of the kind of pictures he wanted to make; he would soon have the chance to prove himself.

Chapter 4

An Enterprising
Move to Independence

As the post-war era began, John Garfield and Humphrey Bogart were the biggest male stars on the Warner Bros. lot. With Paul Muni, James Cagney, and Edward G. Robinson all gone from the studio, and Errol Flynn beginning to slip, Warners was desperate to sign Garfield to a long-term contract. Bogart had recently signed a 15-year, one picture a year, $200,000 per picture deal with Jack Warner. The agreement also gave Bogart the freedom to make one picture a year away from the studio. Garfield was 32 years old and had only two pictures left on his contract. Warner Bros. offered him several deals, some rivaling (although none equaling) Bogart's deal.

The studio also bought the screen rights to Dorothy Baker's novel *Young Man with a Horn,* with the idea of using Garfield in the title role. The film would eventually be made in late 1949 with Kirk Douglas in the part. As great as Douglas's performance was, it was a shame that Garfield missed the opportunity, as it was a natural for him.

Julie's friends urged him to take the best contract he could get from Warner Bros. But he had lived for the day when he could make pictures his own way. It soon became apparent to Jack Warner that Garfield really meant to break free. He imparted this knowledge to Mort Blumenstock (head of publicity in New York) in the following telegram, dated September 7, 1945:

> Confidentially, Impossible sign up Garfield after he makes one more picture for us. He has forgotten days when I picked him up

> making six bits weekly. Nevertheless, we will get along without
> him and don't want slowdown on his publicity because naturally
> we have him in *Nobody Lives Forever* (1946), which is in vaults,
> plus one more to make (*Humoresque,* 1946) and don't want trou-
> ble with him when he making last one, as he no pushover. . . .[8]

Rather typically, Jack Warner had missed the point. Garfield
himself said, "My quarrels with the studio were never over money.
All I wanted was good parts."

As indicated by the above telegram, Garfield had already completed filming on *Nobody Lives Forever;* in actuality, he had completed that one before shooting *Pride of the Marines.* During the
war, studios were slower to release films, thereby creating a backlog.
Although Warner Bros. carried *Nobody Lives Forever* on its release
chart as early as January 1945, the picture would not be released until the fall of 1946.

Meanwhile, Garfield was loaned out to MGM to co-star with
Lana Turner in the film version of James M. Cain's steamy story, *The
Postman Always Rings Twice.* The chemistry between the two stars
helped charge the film with sexual tension. Turner, dressed all in
white, was effectively counterpointed by Garfield's dark, brooding
screen presence. It was quite possibly Miss Turner's finest performance, but director Tay Garnett credited Garfield's tremendous
screen persona for making the picture an unqualified success.

The Postman Always Rings Twice opened at the Capitol
Theatre in New York on May 2, 1946. The critics were divided on
the relative merits of the film. John McCarten in the *New Yorker*
wrote, "Neither Mr. Garfield nor Miss Turner succeeds entirely in
summoning up the violence of disposition called for by the leading
roles." *Newsweek* commented: "Garfield is the right man for his
role, and Miss Turner supplies the sex appeal. . . . This longshot can
be credited only as a near miss." The highest praise came (not surprisingly) from Bosley Crowther:

> *The Postman* . . . comes off a tremendously tense and dramatic
> show, and it gives Lana Turner and John Garfield the best roles of
> their careers. . . . Too much cannot be said for the principals. Mr.

Garfield reflects to the life the crude and confused young hobo who stumbles aimlessly into a fatal trap. Miss Turner is remarkably effective. . . .

Before the release of *Nobody Lives Forever,* Julie participated in a revival of Clifford Odets's *Awake and Sing,* which reunited many Group Theatre members from the original cast: Garfield, Art Smith, Joe Bromberg, Luther Adler, Morris Carnovsky, and Phoebe Brand. The production was staged at the Las Palmas Theatre in Hollywood under the auspices of the Actors Laboratory. The play had a healthy run during the summer of 1946 and helped to establish legitimate theatre in Los Angeles.

Nobody Lives Forever opened at the Strand Theatre in New York on November 1, 1946. The film was directed by Jean Negulesco, the first of his three collaborations with Garfield. Negulesco always stressed atmosphere over action, and his mastery at this method of directing was evident in *Nobody Lives Forever.* The story began in New York and then switched to California, with Negulesco highlighting the contrasts between the two.

Besides Garfield, other members of a strong cast included Geraldine Fitzgerald, Walter Brennan, Faye Emerson, George Coulouris, and (yes) George Tobias. Although dismissed by critics as just another gangster picture, the film had many things to recommend it: the early scenes with Garfield waxing poetic about New York; a good performance by Fitzgerald as the wealthy widow; and the relationship of the con men representing roughly three generations. Garfield played the young hood, Tobias (who, all kidding aside, was a splendid character actor) played a somewhat older crook, and Brennan played the over-the-hill con man. The scenes between Garfield and Tobias, Garfield and Brennan, and Garfield, Tobias, and Brennan were all played so excellently as to lift the picture well above the ordinary. But even Bosley Crowther had only mixed feelings to express in his *New York Times* review:

> Those customers—of which there are many—who have lived through such matters before are likely to find this repetition just a bit wearisome and even dull. . . . John Garfield and Geraldine

Top: Nick Smith (Cecil Kellaway) introduces Frank Chambers (John Garfield) to his beautiful young wife Cora (Lana Turner) which touches off a string of sensual but ultimately tragic events (*The Postman Always Rings Twice,* 1946). *Bottom:* Lobby card for *The Postman Always Rings Twice* (1946) emphasizes the sexual tensions of the story.

Things begin to unravel for Cora and Frank (Lana Turner and John Garfield) near the conclusion of *The Postman Always Rings Twice* (1946).

Fitzgerald turn in acting jobs which are worthy of better material, and George Tobias is genial and droll as the right-hand man to Garfield.... *Nobody Lives Forever* proves, indeed, that flesh is weak, we would say.

Garfield's last film under his Warner Bros. contract, *Humoresque,* was a sentimental occasion. Clifford Odets and Zachary Gold

Con man Nick Blake (John Garfield) falls in love with his "mark," the wealthy Gladys Halvorsen (Geraldine Fitzgerald) in *Nobody Lives Forever* (1946).

wrote the screenplay, based on a short story by Fannie Hurst. Garfield had helped bring Odets back from the brink of despair during the previous few years. It was Julie who had loaned him money when Odets was broke; Garfield also helped Odets secure a job at RKO, which resulted in Odets writing and directing *None but the Lonely Heart* in 1944. Now, Julie had persuaded Warners to hire Odets for *Humoresque*. Odets would never forget that it was Garfield who had been there when he was down and nearly out.

Jean Negulesco was the director, and he once again concentrated on the moody, introspective aspects of Garfield's acting style. As Paul Boray, the violin prodigy from the slums, Garfield delivered

Nick Blake (John Garfield) and Al Doyle (George Tobias) get some bad news near the finale of *Nobody Lives Forever* (1946).

one of his most soulful performances, biting off such lines as, "All my life I wanted to do the right thing, but it never worked out. I'm outside — always looking in." He was his most iconoclastic self since *Four Daughters.* He also learned to play the violin, and although it was Isaac Stern's music that was heard, those were Garfield's hands on screen (despite rumors to the contrary). Garfield, who believed in authenticity in all his roles, trained arduously for the film. Shooting was pushed back from December 1, 1945, to December 14, 1945, in order to allow Julie more time to learn the fingering techniques. Julie was very proud that no less an authority than Jascha Heifetz personally told him that his performance was entirely believable.

Oscar Levant, Julie's long-time friend, had a strong part as Sid Jeffers, Paul Boray's long-time friend. The rapport between Levant and Garfield was something special to see. Joan Crawford, fresh from her Oscar-winning performance as Mildred Pierce, was given

Young violin genius Paul Boray (John Garfield) toils within the restrictive confines of a studio orchestra, but not for long in *Humoresque* (1946). Pictured are Garfield (center) and players.

top billing. She and Garfield had a good working relationship during the shooting of the film. Years later Crawford would remark that Garfield really was a brilliant young actor. Ruth Nelson, who was with the Group Theatre during its entire existence, played Garfield's mother. Not surprisingly, their scenes together provided some of the film's most effective moments. Rounding out the cast were J. Carroll Naish, Tom D'Andrea, Craig Stevens, Paul Cavanaugh, Tommy Cook, Joan Chandler (who had been signed to a term contract by Warner Bros. because of her performance in the Broadway production of *The Late George Apley*), and Bobby Blake (who always remembered Garfield's kindness to him on the set).

The critics were enthusiastic in their praise, *except* Bosley Crowther, who wrote: "The music, we must say, is splendid — and if you will only shut your eyes that you don't have to watch Mr. Garfield leaning his soulful face against that violin or Miss Crawford violently emoting ... you may enjoy it."

Paul Boray (John Garfield), Sid Jeffers (Oscar Levant), and patroness of the arts (especially virile young artists) Helen Wright (Joan Crawford) talk things over in *Humoresque* (1946).

Philip T. Hartung in *Commonweal:* "John Garfield, as the violinist with the temperament of a genius, is proud, sensitive and intense — but he plays second fiddle to Miss Crawford's interesting and disturbing performance as an alcoholic nymph."

Newsweek: "If it leaves you a little confused, it isn't the fault of Miss Crawford or Garfield. And if the tragedy of it all proves overpowering, there is always Oscar Levant, who has the best lines in the script and trades each one in for a laugh."

Shirley O'Hara gave this glowing review in the *New Republic:* "The Warner Bros. version showing currently, with Joan Crawford, John Garfield, and Oscar Levant, is one of the best movies I've ever seen. . . . John Garfield again manages the touching combination of toughness and sensibility that makes him always interesting to see."

Paul Boray (John Garfield) and his beaming father Rudy (J. Carroll Naish)
read the reviews of his concert in the humble kitchen above the small Boray
grocery store as a very concerned Mrs. Boray (Ruth Nelson) broods in the
background (*Humoresque,* 1946).

One reason Jack Warner had been persuaded to give the
screenwriting job to Odets was that he did not believe that Garfield
could successfully launch his independent company. This was a last-
ditch effort to get Julie to stay. Indeed, many of Julie's friends
thought he was making a mistake. But Garfield left Warner Bros.
on schedule, with some sense of nostalgia, and on good terms with
almost everyone on the lot.

Garfield commented at the time:

> I came here to do one picture, make some money to carry me
> through bad times in the theatre. Even when you're good you don't
> make much on Broadway. But it so happened that picture was a
> hit and I became a star. I never planned all this to happen. I can
> afford to take chances now because I don't have to be a star to be
> happy.

Loneliness at the top as Paul Boray (John Garfield) and Sid Jeffers (Oscar Levant) ponder the Fates from Boray's penthouse high atop New York; the climax of *Humoresque* (1946).

What I mean is, right now I don't find all these exorbitant offers, all the security and money very exciting. I could sign another long-term contract, do whatever I was given, make faces, imitate what I've done before, have no new ideas, no point of view—and be a rich successful guy. But I've gotta look at myself in the mirror every morning. So I stare at my rich, contented puss that earns me all this money and my conscience says, "OK, kid, what have you been doing lately?"

Look, to a guy who used to work in a gas station or an insurance office, all this may be very tempting. But I've had a certain kind of background. I'm not talking about money. I've always been poor until I came to Hollywood, but I had a stimulating, exciting life.

Humoresque was Warner Bros.' 1946 Christmas release and went on to be in the top-grossing films for 1946-47. It topped off a great year for Garfield. In January 1946, Robbie had given birth to a daughter, Julie Roberta, and she would become a real joy to her father, helping to lift some of the gloom over the death of Katherine. Late in the year, Garfield recorded an album for children, *Herman Ermine in Rabbit Town,* in which he sang, narrated, and played all the characters. Around this time, Garfield's partner, Bob Roberts, closed a deal making their production company, Roberts Productions, part of a new independent organization called Enterprise Studios.

Enterprise was founded by David Loew and David Lewis, both veterans of the movie-making business. David Loew was the son of Marcus Loew who had formed MGM in 1924, with Loew's Inc. as the parent company. David's twin brother Arthur stayed with Loew's, eventually becoming president. David set out on his own as an independent producer. He produced some Joe E. Brown films in the late 1930s, then signed with United Artists beginning with the 1940-41 season. He had recently completed the Marx brothers film *A Night in Casablanca.*

David Lewis had been Irving Thalberg's personal assistant in the 1930s. He produced such MGM films as *Riffraff* (1936) and *Camille* (1937). Lewis moved to Warner Bros. in late 1937 and served as associate producer on *The Sisters* (1938), *Each Dawn I Die* (1939), *Kings Row* (1942), and several other pictures.

Lewis and Loew intended Enterprise to be more than an outlet for financial independence; it was a grouping of people who were committed to dealing with socially important themes in their pictures. Garfield was thoroughly at home in this environment. He was determined to make films that had something important to say:

> I want to make pictures with a point — I know I gotta continue to appear in commercial pictures like *Postman.* I know I gotta retain my position of value at the box office, but I also want to be available in between for the kind of picture that's harder to do but may turn out to be more interesting.
>
> It's chancy, this is a complicated business. I'm just beginning to catch on. I came here from Broadway with a lot of preconceived ideas, couldn't understand why they didn't put out better pictures. Now I understand more, feel I've come out of my apprenticeship, changed some of my preconceived ideas, hit a new period. Maybe

Portrait of John Garfield around the time he left Warner Bros. to begin making films on his own.

in the next few years I'll make so many mistakes I'll kill my career. I can afford the chance. There's fear in Hollywood about tackling dangerous subjects, difficult subjects. I feel I owe it to myself to be available when some enterprising people want to try something tough.

In retrospect, Garfield had been preparing for the move to independent film-making all his professional life. Although he still retained his great love of the stage, he became more aware of the power of films with the passing of the years. Of the seven films he would make after his break from Warner Bros., at least five dealt with socially relevant themes: race relations, corruption in prize fighting, legalization of the numbers racket, anti–Semitism, and corruption in horse racing. Garfield would give some of his most powerful performances in these pictures. Four of his films made after the move to independence rank among the best work of his career: *Body and Soul, Force of Evil, The Breaking Point* (made in a return to Warner Bros.), and *He Ran All the Way.*

As great as 1946 had been for Garfield, there were ominous signs of trouble ahead. As a board member of the Screen Actors Guild, Julie took an active role in a major labor dispute between two of Hollywood's unions. He initially supported the new group, Conference of Studio Unions (CSU), in its battle to obtain jobs which had been given exclusively to the American Federation of Labor's International Alliance of Theatrical and Stage Employees (IATSE).

The IATSE had the support of some of the Screen Actors Guild's most powerful members, including Ronald Reagan, George Murphy, and Robert Montgomery. The IATSE accused the CSU of being controlled by Communists. By the time the case went to arbitration, Garfield and most early backers of CSU had changed their position in favor of the IATSE. But the result was that members of the House Un-American Activities Committee were alerted to the possibility of communist activity in the motion picture industry.

Bob Roberts and Garfield had bought the screen rights to the life story of Barney Ross, boxing champ and Marine hero. Abraham Polonsky was hired to do the screenplay, tentatively titled "Burning Journey." Julie said: "If I can do it the way I want, show up the frauds and crooked side of boxing, also relate the story to the times that boy grew up in—I think I'll have something colorful, and with meaning, too." Roberts Productions also planned on filming an old Garfield Broadway favorite: "I'd like to do Clifford Odets's *Awake and Sing*—I played in that on Broadway, you know. There's a story about people I know about, exciting, and it says something."

As it turned out, Garfield's first project under the Enterprise banner was *Body and Soul,* which was a reworking of the Barney Ross story. The Ross revision was due to the fact that scenes depicting Ross' drug addiction could not be filmed because of code restrictions. *Body and Soul* would prove to be the biggest money-maker in Enterprise's short history.

John Garfield prepares for his upcoming role in *Body and Soul* (1947) with trainer John Indrisano.

Garfield played a role, boxer Charlie Davis, much like the ones he had played at Warners. The difference was that he plumbed the depths of the character much more; success was achieved early in the film and then the corruption followed. Charlie Davis was the darkest character Garfield had played up to this point in his career. The boxer forfeited his family, friends, and his girl in his drive to achieve success and the money that went with it. Garfield delivered his most mature performance to date, and he received his only Best Actor nomination from the Academy of Motion Picture Arts and Sciences. He also was nominated as Best Actor by the New York film critics in their annual poll. But Julie lost to Ronald Colman in the Oscar race and to William Powell in the New York critics' contest.

William R. Weaver wrote in the *Motion Picture Herald* of August 16, 1947 (after a special preview showing):

> The story of a pugilist, a slugger not bright or honest enough to care about such matters as the framing of fights and double-crossing of people so long as the money rolls in, is packaged here with other materials that combine to make a melodrama of terrific impact. It is rugged stuff, powerfully delivered, with John Garfield giving his best performance in years, and figures to open strongly and build as it plays. It's not for children, and its appeal may be more directly to men than to women, but it's sure to make an impressive mark on the box office ledgers of the period. . . . In the background of the direct-line story of the fighter are other stories. The fighter's attentions fluctuate between his sweetheart, excellently played by Lilli Palmer, and an expensive hanger-on, played with vim by Hazel Brooks. His sympathy is constant only with respect to a tragically injured ex-champion, finely portrayed by Canada Lee, and he sacrifices friends and scruples readily for money gain as he goes along. He is never shown as a noble figure, but always a forceful man, and the sequences showing fighters in the ring are perhaps the most effective of their kind ever filmed.
>
> It is a picture to stir comment, perhaps even controversy, and it makes the prize fight industry look pretty bad. But it is dynamic, powerful, and assuredly, a box office item of consequence. . . . Producer Bob Roberts, director Robert Rossen, and screen-playwright Abraham Polonsky worked together with rare unity of purpose in turning out an impressively professional job.

Body and Soul worked on many levels, as mentioned by the *Motion Picture Herald*. It was not only a personal triumph for Garfield, who demonstrated that he could succeed in his first independent venture, but the film also proved to be an indictment of the darker side of boxing, with its many underworld connections.

Ben Chaplin (Canada Lee) on the brink of losing his championship in *Body and Soul* (1947). Pictured (left to right) are James Burke, Canada Lee, and players.

**Shelton (Tim Ryan) and others watch as Charley Davis (John Garfield)
waltzes beauty queen Peg Born (Lilli Palmer) across the dance floor in *Body
and Soul* (1947).**

The picture opened in New York at the Globe Theatre on November 9, 1947, at a time when boxing and gambling were under investigation, especially in Manhattan. The lines at the theatres in Julie's home town stretched around the block.

In addition to Garfield, Palmer, Brooks, and Lee, the cast included Anne Revere, Art Smith, William Conrad, Joseph Pevney, and Lloyd Goff (Gough). The technical crew was superb. James Wong Howe was nominated for an Oscar for his realistic cinematography; Francis Lyon and Robert Parrish won the Oscar for Best Film Editing; the score by Rudolph Polk and Hugo Friedhofer featured the title tune by Johnny Green, Edward Heyman, Robert Sour, and Frank Eyton; and the contributions of Rossen and Polonsky were essential.

Rossen was directing only his second film, having advanced from the writing ranks. His career would be stalled by the House Un-American Activities Committee hearings of 1951, when he was identified as a Communist by several witnesses. He refused to name anybody as a party member but changed his mind after a few years of inactivity. He named at least 50 of his colleagues as Communists, and his career resumed in the mid-fifties and continued until his death in 1966. Polonsky had only one prior screen credit, Paramount's *Golden Earrings,* which was considered so bad that Paramount held up its release. Polonsky, though he received co-screenwriting credit, later stated that *Golden Earrings* did not contain any scenes he had written. He more than redeemed himself with his excellent work on *Body and Soul.*

Garfield was proud of *Body and Soul*'s "honesty and authenticity. Canada Lee, director Robert Rossen, cameraman James Wong Howe, and even I, all boxed, although I've got to admit I got my brains knocked out. But seriously, I have a great affection for it because it's got a good cast and the story is a little less safe than the usual."

The critics were impressed:

> Garfield as the fighter, gives a fine portrayal of a hard, arrogant youth who is almost turned into a bum by his desire for money [*Newsweek*].
>
> This is Garfield's role, not only from frequent repetition but from birth, and he plays it with a combination of cocky grace and the humorlessness of the self-made man which is more disarming than repugnant [Hermine Rich Isaacs in *Theatre Arts*].
>
> John Garfield gives a rattling good performance as the steel-trap fighter. . . . Trim, taut, and full of vitality, Mr. Garfield really acts like a fresh kid who thinks the whole world is an easy set-up. Altogether this Enterprise picture . . . hits the all-time high in throatcatching fight films [Bosley Crowther in the *New York Times*].

One discordant note was that production had to shut down for a time when Garfield suffered a "mild" heart attack, his second. He insisted on doing all his own fight scenes and took sparring lessons from Mushy Callahan and John Indrisano to sharpen his boxing skills. He was always under doctor's orders to slow down, and he was always ignoring the advice. Another sad note was that almost all of those involved with *Body and Soul* would have their lives and careers touched by the HUAC.

A central theme in *Body and Soul* was the issue of race relations, personified by the friendship between Charlie Davis (Garfield) and Ben Chaplin (Canada Lee in a moving performance). In many ways, Ben was the most noble and sympathetic person in the film. Garfield was deeply concerned about equality for all races. He wrote an article in the November 1947 issue of *Negro Digest* (which is reprinted here):

How Hollywood Can Better Race Relations by John Garfield

Once in an interview, I was asked, "What is your goal as an actor?" I said at that time, that my purpose is to make exciting, truthful, entertaining pictures and to play in a truthful theatre.

I believe that's still my aim. When I consider material for a picture, I want to make sure it rings true. I'm not always successful. Sometimes I make a mistake. Sometimes I'm just not thorough enough. But up to now I've been pretty lucky.

Now I even try to adhere to a sort of measuring stick. I ask myself, "What does it say? How well does it say it?" Maybe it's a self-imposed challenge, but it's a challenge all the same. It helps keep me out of a rut. Because becoming a recognized actor may make it easier to make a living; but not having to struggle makes it harder to hold to those ideals I had as a young actor.

And therefore it's in the light of those ideals, with a measuring stick of a truthful, entertaining theatre, that I want to examine a problem — the problem that grows out of the minority actor's participation in film, the problem that confronts him and the American cinema.

There is, of course, no patent medicine cure for the evils that exist in making films as far as the business of minorities is concerned. It's a pretty deep, tough subject. There are too many violations of dignity to try to simplify in one diagnosis, one cure.

So, I simply want to get a few things down. Those things which, from where I sit as an actor, and from the standards I set for drama, I find most important.

Everyone knows what an entertaining film is. But there's less talk, and less consciousness, of what a truthful film is. I think of a truthful film as a believable one, a film conforming to life as the people it tells about would know it, every day. And if it has nothing to do with life as the film's heroes would know it in their daily routines, then the truthful film says frankly, "Okay kids, relax, this is make-believe."

The thing I object to, though, is a film that's in one way or another untrue, but still says "believe me." A film with one or more stereotyped characters does just that. The stereotype can't be truthful. It lumps one special person with a whole group of people, and says "they're all alike." But after all, it doesn't take any unusual knowledge about either drama or people to know that there are all sorts of people in every group.

The stereotype can't be very dramatic, either. It's the special characteristics of an individual that make him interesting, not any taken-for-granted ones known in advance. Also, if you know it's not true, then you don't believe it. And that's inferior theatre. After all, you've got to believe a thing's really happening before you can get excited about it!

On this basis, an evaluation of movies today would result in a pretty big minus sign. But there have been some fine films, and I want to recall them as object lessons for the kind of drama I'm talking about.

Remember *Sahara*? Not only was it tops in craft, but the theme and the relationships rang true. The friendship, for example, between Rex Ingram, the Senegalese soldier, and Humphrey Bogart seemed so believable because it grew from the situation itself. It grew from the kind of persons they were, and from the battle circumstances in which they found themselves. Not once was the relation determined by any reason supposedly peculiar to a whole group. Ingram wasn't picked out to do a "yassuh boss" or pass out with fright, but to play a Senegalese soldier.

And what about *In This Our Life*? I remember the scene where the young Negro law student discusses his chances for a career with Olivia De Havilland. You believe the boy, the woman, and the whole scene, because you know the boy's fears are justified, and you, like the woman, desperately look for ways to assure and help him.

Those are a few of the examples of what realistic movies can mean. But there aren't enough, and that's what I'm concerned with in this article.

There are many films in which minority groups are caricatured to the point where truth is altogether lost. There are many more films, good in general, but untrue in their presentation of the Negro's life as totally divorced from the Caucasian's, or the Caucasian's from the Negro's. I often think people in other countries must have an awfully distorted idea about what goes on over here! Certain films may be fine, but the sum total of our cinema as it comes across is generally untrue and very mediocre film, though the production costs may have been large.

Just a carp, of course, is wrong. In the first place it's uncreative. And it was such griping at the constant caricature of the Negro, without a positive demand for him in decent roles, that led to film-makers taking the easy way out by elimination of Negroes from the film roles wherever they could.

So I try to take the constructive approach. The thing that hits me first is the general lack of Negroes in the production phases of film-making. Few if any Negro writers, directors, producers. No Negro story analysts or researchers to speak of. This is not a natural condition. And it's not a condition likely to bring any real Negro contribution to film-making.

A rounded creative process demands all interested people in all phases. Confining Negroes to situations in which they're needed because of their race, is taking unfair advantage, for my money. You use them where you can't do without them, and then by not allowing them any other related activities, refuse to return the favor.

A real push is needed here. A push by the Negroes themselves, and by the studios who do the hiring. It's healthy to note, by the way, that at least some other minority groups are having somewhat better luck in this regard. James Wong Howe, one of the notable exceptions, is a top flight cameraman in the industry.

Then there's the problem of being made to appear "special." This difficulty affects all minority group people. It's a matter of playing a role aimed to point up the "odd" aspects of the minority, rather than the everyday ones. Sometimes this "specialty" takes the form of caricature, more rarely that of extreme glorification. The latter is certainly preferable, and in occasional doses does not harm. But the only really healthy over-all approach is casual, routine, *accepted*. No great hullabaloo.

Again take the Negro as a case in point. He's usually seen on the screen in one of several "special" stereotyped roles: house servant, chauffeur, gardener, doorman. This has been carried to the place where introduction of a Negro character on the screen arouses no interest. You know what to expect. No curiosity. The character is wasted. Introduction of a "non-special" everyday Negro as a lawyer, nurse, doctor, businessman, teacher, secretary, actor, would raise the level of truth, interest, and consequently drama. The stereotype is the very antithesis of good drama.

Take *Pride of the Marines*. Remember the Negro porter? His gentle refusal of a tip for service to a blinded Marine hero made the Marine's condition that much more real. And Lee Diamond, Marine Al Schmid's Jewish buddy. Because he was a normal everyday good guy, his attempt to jolt Al out of self-pity by telling him his blindness wasn't the only problem in the world really hit home. And another bit, in the same film. When one of the guys in the fox-hole grumbles, "Yeah, I bet when I get home some Mex'll have my job," another soldier with as much or more service-time as the griper, says simply, "I am Mexican." Because you have accepted the Mexican as just any decent soldier, with no special realization to that point that he's Mexican or anything "special," you're that much more apt to feel like him, to sympathize with him. Why, he could be anybody! That scene put a lump in my throat when I saw it being shot.

Would *Pride of the Marines* have been half the movie it was without believable stuff like that? You bet it wouldn't!

We'd be naive, not to know very well that better film treatment of minorities would result in their greater integration in the life of America. But the whole social context is too much to tackle all at once. As an actor, I have a rooting interest in what remedy can be brought about in movies themselves. As a kid, I saw enough to know that certain things are right, others wrong. The fact that they exist isn't enough to make them right. And I'm convinced that unless the film medium has something to do with the correction of wrong things, it has no real place in our life.

Individuals can do a great deal in films. Carleton Moss, with his film *Negro Soldier*, helped forward an understanding of Negro war effort and boosted the stock of Negroes both as film makers and performers.

Working in *Body and Soul*, I was very proud. Proud, because I was actor in, and coproducer of, a well-integrated, entertaining drama. It has a climax that should have a terrific impact. But more, all its characters are people, whether they're Christian or Jewish,

Caucasians or Negroes. In fact, to read the script alone, it would be hard to tell which role Canada Lee, who's in it, would play. Actually, he's one of the prize fighters. But according to the screenplay he's simply a figure illustrating the vicious and corrupt nature of some phases of boxing. The aim was to show a victim of other people's greed. It just happened that he was a Negro. It could as easily have been any other fighter. And there are other similar victims in the film who aren't Negroes. In fact, my role, that of Charlie Davis, a Jewish boxer, is part of the same pattern of corruption.

Groups, too, can be very important in pushing Hollywood toward better films. One of the most constructive efforts to date has been that of, I'm proud to report, my own Guild, the Screen Actors.

The action arose because of the increasing unemployment suffered by Negro players, as a result of the popular pressures against the caricature of Negroes on the screen. With no creative suggestions offered, it began to seem much simpler for the movie industry to cut out Negroes altogether, than to make a constructive effort to cope with the matter. So, at the instigation of the Actors Guild, a joint committee from the Actors, Writers, and Directors guilds got together and mapped out a three point program.

The program is good. It specifies first that, if a Negro part is indicated in a script, it will be played by a Negro, and the racial character will not be changed; subject, of course, to normal judgement on story values. Second, that the Negro will be portrayed on the screen not as a caricature, but as a simple human being, a normal member of the community. Third, that some thought will be given to casting Negroes in the routine, unnamed bits in a script, as mechanics, secretaries, nurses, etc.

This program is not perfect. It depends almost entirely on individual willingness on the parts of writers, directors, and producers to cooperate. But to all of us who have a rooting interest in a better American film, and to those of us interested in truthful content, it's exciting to have such a forward step on the part of three of Hollywood's most important guilds.

The Winter Issue, 1948 (January-March) of *Opportunity Magazine* carried articles by both Garfield and Canada Lee under the umbrella title of "Our Part in *Body and Soul*" (reprinted below):

Fists, Brains, and Breaks by John Garfield

In my latest picture, *Body and Soul,* I play the part of an East Side boy who uses his fists more often than he uses his brains, when he uses the latter at all. I get to be champion, all right, but at what a cost! The price? Only the love of my mother and my girl friend, the deaths of two of my best friends (one of them is played by Canada Lee, who, incidentally does a terrific job), plus the realization that I was owned "body and soul" by crooked operators.

It's inevitable that an actor does some thinking about each of the roles he plays and what makes each character tick. As Charley Davis, the fighter, I didn't have to do too much probing into Charley's life and aims.

It was all too clear to me because my own boyhood had been so similar. I grew up on New York's lower East Side, where poverty and slum conditions created a sort of jungle, where a fellow had two choices if he wanted to survive: to fight or run. Well, I fought when I could and ran when I had to.

If I do say so myself, I became pretty handy with my fists. And for a while, I thought that made me quite a guy.

Then, one day in school, my ego was punctured. During a classroom discussion, I became involved in a verbal argument with some puny, bespectacled little guy. The teacher just sat back and let each of us speak his piece. Well, that undersized runt licked the stuffing out of me in front of the whole class. My instinctive reaction was to wait for him after school and to give him his lumps. But then, for perhaps the first time in my young and hot-headed life, I did some serious, constructive thinking.

What would I prove by beating up the little guy? That I was bigger and stronger than he was? Anybody could see that. Well, how could I get back at him? By licking him in a debate. I joined the school debating society. That decision proved to be the turning point of my whole life. Debating taught me respect for reasoning rather than brute force, an appreciation of words and how to use them, and—most important of all—how to face an audience without freezing up.

From debating I sort of gravitated naturally to acting. Here was a field where I could give vent to some of the mixed-up feelings inside me that heretofore would erupt in fisticuffs.

I really threw myself into my roles with the Group Theatre. Since many of the plays put on by that company were concerned with social problems on which I felt deeply, I managed to get a lot of passionate sincerity into my portrayals. I attracted the attention of Hollywood and in my first movie, *Four Daughters*, was given the part of a poor and savagely bitter young man. It was a natural for me.

Since then I've had some success as an actor. With *Body and Soul*, I am now engaged in independent production, gratifying a long-held ambition—which is the right of an artist to exercise a choice in selection of a story, roles, and to have a voice in all phases of production.

Body and Soul Has Heart, Too by Canada Lee

I enjoyed every minute of working in the picture *Body and Soul*. I enjoyed it as an actor and as a human being. That sounds funny, I know, as though actors aren't human beings, too. Most of them are.

This is what I mean. In the movie, I'm cast as a fighter. A fighter who happens to be a Negro. Not a "Negro fighter." In fact, nowhere in the entire film is the word "Negro" used. As a human being I liked that. Throughout the movie, John Garfield, the star, who plays the part of welterweight champion, calls me Ben and I, in turn, call him Charlie. There isn't a single "Yessuh, boss." That's the way Garfield, Bob Rossen, the director, and others making the picture wanted it. I liked that as a human being.

My role happens to be a meaty one and a sympathetic one. That I liked as an actor. Though shown as a has-been champion welterweight who has taken many a beating and sustained a head injury, Ben, the character I play, has integrity and pride, and intelligence. He can't express himself with fancy or big words, but he's aware of the trickiness of the so-called "clever" promoters who caused his downfall and now are enmeshing Garfield, the new champ. Ben will have no part of their schemes, turns down their bribe money, and sadly surmises that "the boys have got to" Garfield before the big fight. My big scene carries terrific impact. It's a death scene, in which Ben's head injury is aggravated. In a fury of frustration, I engage in a fight with an imaginary opponent in the training camp ring, until I sink to the canvas dying.

One incident in particular is typical of the fine outlook of the people I worked with on this movie.

John Garfield—who, incidentally, is called Julie by his friends—and I did a scene together. In it, by a slip of the tongue and affectionately, he called me "boy" when he should have called me Ben.

I hadn't even noticed it, because I knew Garfield didn't have a patronizing bone in his body. The director who hadn't caught the slip was satisfied with the scene and said: "Cut, print it." But not Garfield. Though Julie was a co-producer as well as star of the film, and reprinting meant added expenses, he said: "No, we can't print it. I called Canada 'boy' instead of Ben."

Garfield was constantly helpful. Though he was both star and producer and could have hogged any and every scene in which we both appeared, he insisted on subordinating himself in my scenes.

My *Body and Soul* experience was in contrast to the time I worked in *Lifeboat*. Though I had been assured the role of the Negro sailor would do much to advance the cause of colored people, production was very far along when I noticed that the script called for the Negro to be in a corner by himself, while the Nazi mingled freely—and, in fact—dominantly among the group. I didn't like it, but couldn't do anything about it.

There even was a prominent actor in the cast who repeatedly spoke of "niggers" and how he wished that they were all still slaves. These were his personal views, mind you, not speeches from the script. Of course he was unpopular with the other actors, who wondered why I didn't "sock the big ham."

Of course I was boiling all the time, but I was determined to control myself so that when I left Hollywood, people would say, "He's a fine actor and a gentleman." Fortunately, people like that actor are few and far between in Hollywood. Most folks I met out there are liberal and progressive minded.

Yes—I enjoyed working on *Body and Soul,* and all the people who made it. We need more pictures like it and I don't think the people out there can be pressured not to make them, either by Washington probes or by local witch-hunts.

Chapter 5

A Man Called Canada

In Canada Lee, John Garfield had found a kindred spirit, sharing similar beliefs in politics (liberal) and on the subject of equality for all races, in the real world as well as the theatrical. They formed a close relationship during the filming of *Body and Soul* and it was unfortunate that forces conspired to prevent them from working together again.

Canada Lee was born Lionel Canegata on March 2, 1907, in the Upper East Side of New York City. His father, James Canegata, helped to organize the Brotherhood of Pullman Car Porters and later served as a secretary for Standard Oil. Young Lionel enjoyed "stickball" (a form of baseball native to New York) and attended P.S. 5 in the Bronx, getting as far as the eighth grade.

At 14, Lionel ran away from home; eventually he landed a job as an exercise rider at Saratoga Race Track. Dissatisfied with the small pay, he became a boxer. He won the Amateur Metropolitan Championship as a lightweight, then turned pro. It was in his first professional fight that he acquired the name of Canada Lee. Joe Humphreys, the ring announcer, took one look at the name "Lionel Canegata" and decided that Canada Lee was a lot easier to pronounce. The fans liked it and eventually Lionel Canegata learned to accept the new name. Canada went on to have a fine eight year career as a professional fighter before injuries to his eyes forced his retirement. Following his retirement, he was at various times a violinist, a band leader, and a restaurant owner.

Mr. Lee's first acting job was in a Federal Theatre Project play, *Brother Mose*. He found that acting came naturally and cited his sports experience as part of the reason: "Something every actor has to have is audience sensitivity and I had learned that in the prize ring. Every fighter develops it. Then, when I went on the stage, I wasn't self-conscious like the typical novice. I could concentrate on the job I was supposed to do."

After *Brother Mose,* Canada appeared on Broadway in *Stevedore,* which opened on October 1, 1934, at the Civic Repertory Theatre. The play was written by Paul Peters and George Sklar and staged by the Theatre Union. Canada Lee played the part that Rex Ingram had played in the original run in April 1934. In May of the following year, Canada appeared in the Harlem Players' production of *Sailor, Beware!* which starred Juano Hernandez.

Next was the Federal Theatre Project's ambitious production of Shakespeare's *Macbeth* (1936), which was staged by Orson Welles and John Houseman. Lee enacted the part of Banquo. The 1937 season found Canada in *One-Act Plays of the Sea* by Eugene O'Neill, another Federal Theatre Project production. Later that same year came *Brown Sugar,* directed and produced by George Abbott and written by Mrs. Bernie Angus. The cast included such notables as Butterfly McQueen, Juano Hernandez, and Alvin Childress (later to gain fame as Amos in the *Amos 'n' Andy* television series.)

The Federal Theatre Project's 1938 offering featuring the Harlem Players was William DuBois's *Haiti* which, in addition to Mr. Lee, starred Rex Ingram, Alvin Childress, and Louis Sharp. The 1939 season witnessed Canada Lee in the role of Drayton in Dorothy and DuBose Heyward's *Mamba's Daughters,* which was noteworthy because it featured the legendary Ethel Waters in her first dramatic role. The cast included Jose Ferrer, Louis Sharp, and Fredi Washington. The play opened on January 3, 1939, at the Empire Theatre and enjoyed a healthy run before going on the road for most of the winter of 1939-40. It reopened at the Broadway Theatre on March 23, 1940.

In October 1940, the Negro Playwrights Company attempted to establish a theatre of Negro significance in Harlem. Theodore Ward's *Big White Fog* was the company's initial offering and it afforded Canada Lee his biggest and best role to date. Brooks Atkinson wrote in the *New York Times,* "Canada Lee gives an excellent performance in the leading part. He is forceful and magnetically

sincere." Lee's role in *Big White Fog,* good as it may have been, was
merely a tune-up for his part as Bigger Thomas in Richard Wright
and Paul Green's *Native Son,* staged by Orson Welles and John
Houseman.

Native Son opened at the St. James Theatre on March 24, 1941.
The outstanding cast included Everett Sloane, Paul Stewart, Ray
Collins, Frances Bavier (later "Aunt Bee" in the "Andy Griffith
Show"), and Joseph Pevney, who would appear in *Body and Soul*
with Canada. Once again, Brooks Atkinson was impressed: "As Bigger Thomas, he (Lee) gives a clean, honest, driving performance of
remarkable versatility.... As an actor he is superb."

Native Son was successful enough to be revived for the 1942
season. Critics again bestowed praise on Mr. Lee and his performance; his name on a marquee became a regular occurrence around
Broadway.

Also during 1942, Canada Lee appeared in two short William
Saroyan plays, *Across the Board on Tomorrow Morning* and *Talking
to You.* In addition to his busy theatrical schedule, Canada also
served as commentator on John Kirby and Maxine Sullivan's CBS
radio series, *Flow Gently, Sweet Rhythm.* Following the fall 1942
revival of *Native Son,* Canada journeyed to Hollywood to make his
motion picture debut. Alfred Hitchcock had been so impressed
with Canada's portrayal of Bigger Thomas that he cast Lee in the
role of the Negro sailor in *Lifeboat.* The film was produced by 20th
Century–Fox and starred Tallulah Bankhead (in one of her infre-
quent motion picture appearances), John Hodiak, William Bendix,
and Henry Hull.

After filming *Lifeboat,* Canada Lee returned to Broadway in
South Pacific, an ambitious and controversial drama about a sailor.
In discussing the play, Canada Lee told interviewers:

> *South Pacific* is a very tough play. That is, it doesn't pull any
> punches. If it doesn't turn out to be a really great play, it may not
> be able to overcome the resentment it may cause in some quarters.
> It just can't be so-so.
>   It's a great thing for a Negro actor — it is about a sailor who finds
> himself on New Georgia under Jap occupation. For the first time

A crowded lifeboat carries (standing, left to right) Rittenhouse (Henry Hull), Kovak (John Hodiak), Garrett (Hume Cronyn), and Joe (Canada Lee), (sitting) Connie Porter (Tallulah Bankhead) and Alice (Mary Anderson) (*Lifeboat,* 1944).

in his life he is the right color—he doesn't have to hide, he can pass as a native. He doesn't want to go back to a war which he doesn't think is his.... You see, it's not one of those nice, pat little war melodramas that are all sweetness and light. It poses a very real problem. It means an awful lot to me—I'll be in there fighting for my life.

The play, written by Howard Rigsby and Dorothy Heyward, directed by Lee Strasberg, and produced by David Lowe, did not quite fulfill its promise. Lewis Nichols (drama critic for the *New York Times* during World War Two) summed it up: "South Pacific deserves credit for taking up a real theme; the regret is that it did not finish the job more successfully."

Following *South Pacific,* Canada Lee took a small part in Philip Yordan's *Anna Lucasta.* Yordan, whose long career would include

screenwriting credits for such hard-hitting films as *Whistle Stop,
House of Strangers, Detective Story, Broken Lance* (story only,
Academy Award), *The Big Combo, The Harder They Fall, No
Down Payment,* and many others, had written *Anna Lucasta* as a
story about a Polish family in Pennsylvania.

The American Negro Theatre version starred Hilda Simms in
the title role in a cast that featured Alice Childress, Alvin Childress,
and Frederick O'Neal. Wrote Lewis Nichols, "Canada Lee is in the
company also, a courtesy on his part since the role is small, but a
tribute to his belief in the Negro Theatre and its current play."

Indeed, Canada Lee was rapidly becoming one of the strongest
voices in the fight to elevate the Negro's place in the dramatic arts.
He told interviewers:

> I want to help win better roles for the people of my race, and
> a better understanding of the people of my race. I want to do
> things that will give Negroes a new status, things to repair the
> wrong impressions that have grown up through the years—some of
> them fostered by some of my own people . . . certain Negro stars
> have played almost nothing but grinning, chuckle-headed irre-
> sponsible "plantation characters." There are people who refuse to
> accept the fact that any Negro could be different from an ignorant
> field hand. I want to help find a working order for black and white
> people. The two races are too closely associated here in America for
> one not to have an insight into the other.

The Tempest was Canada's Broadway appearance for 1945.
Shakespeare's play was interpreted by Margaret Webster under the
sponsorship of Cheryl Crawford. Canada Lee played Caliban, Arnold Moss was Prospero, Vera Zorina portrayed Ariel, and Frances
Heflin, Steven Elliott, George Voskovec, and Jan Werich were also
featured.

The next year saw Canada Lee starring in two noteworthy productions, *On Whitman Avenue* and *The Duchess of Malfi.* Mr. Lee
served as the coproducer as well as star in *On Whitman Avenue,* an
original by Maxine Wood.

In late 1946 it was reported that Lee and his partner Mark Marvin were trying to raise money to bring the story to the screen. Marvin told reporters:

Since the drama deals with Negro-White relations, there seems little likelihood that any major company would produce it. Because we felt it was so important a theme, it took us nearly a year to finance it and get it to the Cort Theatre, where it ran from May 8 through Sept. 14. And, on the basis of the audience's response to it, we felt we had a worthy subject for a good picture and a commercial one.

Unfortunately, the financing was not forthcoming and the project never materialized.

The *Duchess of Malfi* was significant in that it featured the first portrayal by a Negro actor of a white character on the professional stage in a show with an integrated cast. The always determined Canada said at the time:

I don't want to mess this up with a poor performance. It can open up vast new fields to the Negro actor, whose parts previously have been limited by color. Most of the time Negroes are relegated to funny parts that make fun of a whole race.

I hate that. I want to prove that it is art that counts. I expect the biggest going-over ever when I open, but I don't mind. This can open up all roads to the Negro actor if he has the ability.... I hope it will be a long step toward becoming Actor Canada Lee, not Canada Lee, Negro actor.

Elisabeth Bergner had the title role in *Duchess* and John Carradine made an impressive Cardinal. Brooks Atkinson (back on the drama beat after four years as a war correspondent) wrote:

John Carradine is excellent as the iniquitous Cardinal. His voice and speech are pleasant and articulate; and his portrait of character is complete.... People who are familiar with Canada Lee's recent performances are no doubt prepared for the marked development in his acting. But this playgoer, who has not seen him for four years, can only express delight over the way in which a good elemental actor has acquired mastery of the stage.

The New York stage was not graced by Canada Lee's presence in 1947, the only year during the 1934–48 period that this occurred.

Nonetheless, Canada had a big year due to his bravura performance in *Body and Soul*. He returned to the lights of Broadway in 1948 when he appeared in *Set My People Free,* Dorothy Heyward's powerful drama set in 1826 Charleston. Actually, Mrs. Heyward had written the play in 1941, but it remained on the shelf for seven years before reaching the boards. This had Brooks Atkinson puzzled:

> It has been on the verge of production every season; little quivers of excitement about it have been passing up and down Broadway all this long time. In view of the many worthless plays that have stumbled into limbo in the past seven years, it is odd that such an intelligent and interesting drama . . . should have to wait so long for a public hearing.

But *Set My People Free* proved well worth the wait. The Theatre Guild assembled an excellent cast that included Juano Hernandez, Mildred Smith, Louis Sharp, William Warfield, and Canada Lee. Direction was in the capable hands of Martin Ritt, who would later make his mark in Hollywood with such films as *Edge of the City, No Down Payment, The Long Hot Summer, Paris Blues, Hud, The Front,* and several others.

The highest kudos went to Hernandez and Lee. Brooks Atkinson wrote:

> As Denmark Vesey, the commanding figure in the play, Mr. Hernandez gives a genuinely heroic performance. He has a big, broad figure, but, better than that, he has the intelligence of a first-rate actor. In his dynamic acting, Denmark is not the type-part of a Negro fanatic, full of brute strength and animal emotion, but a fully wrought character aware of the world that surrounds him and conscious of the motivation that underlies Denmark's decisions.
>
> In a complex part that has to be played with discretion and balance, Mr. Lee also gives a superb performance. . . . (He) brilliantly acts the whole character, never letting the natural power of his acting crush the content of his part.

Canada Lee was one of the stars in the 1949 film *Lost Boundaries* which, like many of his stage appearances, had race relations as a central theme. The film also starred Mel Ferrer and Beatrice Pearson. It was Canada's third motion picture. Soon after completing work on *Lost Boundaries,* his career was in serious trouble, as were the careers of his *Body and Soul* co-workers: Anne Revere, Art Smith, Lloyd Gough, Robert Rossen, Abraham Polonsky, and, yes, John Garfield.

Chapter 6

Force of Evil

Following his brilliant performance in *Body and Soul*, John Garfield was hard-pressed to find a suitable follow-up. Not that he was hurting for offers. Garfield was reported to be considering such projects as *Look Homeward, Angel*, *Volpone*, *Moonrise*, and *Gentleman's Agreement*. "We're negotiating for *Look Homeward, Angel*, since David O. Selznick is no longer involved with the book, and if we can get it I'll do it right away at Enterprise," Garfield told the press.

Volpone was planned as a back-up if *Look Homeward, Angel* fell through (it did). Charles Laughton was slated for the title role, with Garfield as Mosca, the valet. Garfield planned to film this in a "new three-color process developed by Cinecolor and we intend to shoot part of the picture in Venice." (It wasn't shot in Venice or anywhere else.)

Moonrise also fell through, according to Garfield, "because I couldn't see eye to eye with the producers." (Dane Clark and Gail Russell starred in Republic's 1948 film adaptation of the Theodore Strauss novel.) Last, but not least, on the docket was *Gentleman's Agreement*, based on Laura Z. Hobson's novel: "It's not the lead but it's a character with guts and if it's right I'll do it," Garfield said.

Garfield did indeed appear in 20th Century–Fox's production of *Gentleman's Agreement*, directed by old pal Elia Kazan. It opened at the Mayfair Theatre in New York on November 11, 1947. This time the focus was on anti–Semitism. Garfield was third-billed below Gregory Peck and Dorothy McGuire. His role, though not large, was an integral part of the story. Many people were surprised that he took the relatively small part. Garfield said, "I'm doing it for Gadge (Kazan) because the picture says something I believe, and it needs to be said."

Gentleman's Agreement won the Oscar for Best Picture and Kazan won as Best Director. Celeste Holm won the Best Supporting Actress award over Anne Revere, who played Peck's mother in the film. Gregory Peck was nominated for Best Actor but lost (as Julie did) to Ronald Colman in *A Double Life*. The reviews were quite good:

> There are two performances which are outstanding. They are given by John Garfield, as a returning Jewish Army officer, and Celeste Holm, as a girl with excellent motives who can't get what she wants [*Newsweek*].
>
> Kazan's sure hand has bottled John Garfield's carbonated talents into a clear, constrained performance as the hero's Jewish friend [*Time*].
>
> Among the . . . performers, John Garfield stands out as a Jewish veteran, working up a powerful scene from a simple description of how a Jew in his company of engineers died during the war. He, at least, makes *Gentleman's Agreement* come alive, if only briefly [John McCarten, the *New Yorker*].

Surprisingly, Bosley Crowther cast a negative vote on Garfield's performance but praised the film: "It is this reviewer's opinion that John Garfield's performance of a young Jew, lifelong friend of the hero, is a bit too mechanical. The film still has abundant meaning and should be fully and widely enjoyed." Actually, with the advantage of hindsight, the performances of Garfield and Celeste Holm remain fresh and viable while the film has dated.

John Garfield's name blazed from marquees across the nation simultaneously in two of 1947-48's biggest motion pictures. There were overtures from various studios for term contracts, lavish single picture offers, and potential financial backers for planned Bob Roberts–John Garfield productions. Julie was at the peak of his powers, but there were shadows being cast by the darkening political situation.

In October 1947, Julie joined other film stars (Humphrey Bogart, Lauren Bacall, Richard Conte, Danny Kaye, and many

Dave (John Garfield) and Mrs. Green (Anne Revere) talk about her son's articles on anti-Semitism in *Gentleman's Agreement* (1947).

others) on a trip to Washington, D.C., to attend hearings of the House Un-American Activities Committee (HUAC), chaired by J. Parnell Thomas. Garfield had been mentioned as a possible Communist sympathizer by California State Senator Jack Tenney in a statement before the committee. Others that Tenney mentioned were Charlie Chaplin, Fredric March, and Frank Sinatra. Tenney cited a 1945 dinner (attended by the Garfields and the Chaplins) honoring Konstantin Simonov, a Soviet journalist visiting the United States as a guest of the State Department. Julie's reaction to Tenney's charges was: "I voted for Roosevelt and I've always been for Roosevelt and I guess Sen. Tenney doesn't like that." Asked if he also wished to make a less sweeping and more direct answer to the charge, Garfield added: "All I can say is that I have always agreed with Roosevelt's policies. I am a registered Democrat and vote the Democratic ticket all the time." Neither Frank Sinatra nor Charlie Chaplin could be reached for a statement, and Fredric March was in New York at the time.

Phil Green, Kathy, Anne, and Dave (left to right, Gregory Peck, Dorothy McGuire, Celeste Holm, and John Garfield) in the Oscar-winning *Gentleman's Agreement* (1947).

A long parade of congenial witnesses went before HUAC in the autumn of 1947: Jack Warner, L. B. Mayer, Sam Wood, Gary Cooper, Robert Taylor, Robert Montgomery, Ronald Reagan (who had been elected president of the Screen Actors Guild on March 10, 1947, the same day that Garfield and James Cagney, among others, had resigned from the executive board), George Murphy, Lela Rogers (mother of Ginger), and Adolph Menjou. Among the most outspoken were Menjou, Taylor, and Jack Warner. Menjou and Taylor indulged in hearsay, naming names of people who they had "heard" might be subversive. Taylor named Howard Da Silva and Albert Maltz; one of the names Menjou mentioned was that of Edward G. Robinson, who was cited as having backed the CSU in the labor dispute of 1946.

Jack Warner testified about "un–American" ideas submitted in the screenplays of Albert Maltz, Robert Rossen, and Irwin Shaw, all of whom were friends of John Garfield. Maltz would shortly become one of the so-called "Hollywood Ten," unfriendly witnesses at the 1947 hearings. The other nine writers and directors involved were Alvah Bessie, Edward Dmytryk, Ring Lardner, Jr., Dalton Trumbo, Herbert Biberman, Lester Cole, John Howard Lawson, Samuel Ornitz, and Adrian Scott. The ten were convicted for their courage in standing up to the committee's scare tactics. The charge was contempt of Congress and, after all appeals were exhausted, the ten served one-year prison terms beginning in 1950.

An organization called the Committee for the First Amendment, formed by John Huston, William Wyler, and Phillip Dunne, circulated a petition on behalf of the Ten, stressing the right of Americans to refuse questioning. The petition eventually caught up with Garfield at the Beverly Hills Tennis Club, where he signed it. The petition read, in part, that: "We, the undersigned as American citizens who believe in Constitutional Democratic government, are disgusted and outraged by the continuing attempts of the House Un-American Activities Committee to smear the motion picture industry." Garfield was one of many (Bogart, Bacall, Kaye, Conte, Huston, June Havoc, and more) to sign, and there was as yet no real sign that he would be singled out as a prime target of the witch hunters.

Garfield had always desired to balance his screen work with stage appearances. That had been the reason for his stage clause in the Warner Bros. contract, although he only used it once. Now he made a move, literally, to achieve this long-standing ambition. The Garfields made a decision to reside on both coasts. They retained their home in Beverly Hills, and, in December of 1947, they leased a triplex from writer Donald Ogden Stewart. The triplex was located on lower 5th Avenue. Julie said: "I'm a New Yorker and my wife is a New Yorker and we love New York."

The late 1940s were a creative time for American theatre and Julie fervently wanted to be a part of it. However, he turned down Elia Kazan's offer to appear as Stanley Kowalski in *Streetcar Named Desire*. Instead, he chose to play the lead in Jan de Hartog's *Skipper Next to God*, the story of a captain transporting Jewish refugees to safety. The play, produced by Cheryl Crawford and directed by Lee

Strasberg, was sponsored by the American National Theatre and Academy (ANTA) as "experimental theatre," i.e. noncommercial. The aims and efforts of ANTA struck a responsive chord in Garfield's heart:

> I have definite reasons for taking the job, however small the salary. In the first place, I'm a stage craftsman. I need practice at my craft to keep a firm hold on any ability I enjoy in my trade. But the legitimate stage has to have encouragement in every branch if it is to prosper.
>
> Above other considerations, I hope I'm proving to actors fortunate enough to be in well-placed financial brackets that they can do more than lip service if they will come to New York and appear in experimental plays.

Skipper opened at the Maxine Elliott Theatre on January 4, 1948. Garfield's salary during the initial four week run was $80/ week. When the play proved popular, it was moved to the Playhouse Theatre for a commercial run of an additional ten weeks. Julie's salary during this phase of the production was $300/week. He was quoted at the time as saying, "I consider it far more important than money to play a role I like and believe in."

Garfield received a special Antoinette Perry (Tony) Award for his contribution to New York Experimental Theatre for his part in *Skipper Next to God.* Julie also won the LaGuardia Award for Stage and Screen established by the non-sectarian Anti-Nazi League to champion human rights. He noted: "I wanted to do *Skipper,* because it is the story of a man and his conscience. A story of a man who has to make decisions." The *New York Times* hailed his portrayal: "Mr. Garfield fills the whole performance with vitality by the force, directness, and perception of his acting. . . . Mr. Garfield is a fiery, uncommonly enlightened actor."

Skipper closed after 97 performances because Garfield had to start work on his new film, *Force of Evil,* a probing look at the numbers racket.

The success of *Body and Soul* had confirmed Julie's view that new and untried talent was available outside the Hollywood mainstream or laboring within the studios. Robbie Garfield would later say: "He had a thing about new people, about giving them a chance in the films he made. He gambled on them and no matter what anybody said about them, he would try again . . . and most of them succeeded because he believed they could."[9]

Julie's gamble on *Force of Evil* centered on Abraham Polonsky and Beatrice Pearson. He decided on having Polonsky direct the picture. There had been friction between Polonsky and Robert Rossen about the ending of *Body and Soul*, with Polonsky emerging the victor. Now, he was being given complete freedom to guide a film. He co-wrote, with Ira Wolfert (whose 1943 novel *Tucker's People* was the original source), a screenplay filled with some of the most poetic "street" dialogue ever heard on screen. In his first film as a director, Polonsky displayed an expert touch for creating an atmosphere of impending doom. Sadly, he would not direct another film for 21 years, until 1969's *Tell Them Willie Boy Is Here*. This absence was due to Polonsky's refusal to cooperate with HUAC on the occasion of his April 1951 appearance before the committee. He had completed the screenplay for *I Can Get It for You Wholesale* (1951) and would not see his name in the credits again until he co-wrote *Madigan* (1968), the excellent police drama starring Richard Widmark and Harry Guardino. Mr. Polonsky survived financially by writing for television and films, never using his own name.

Beatrice Pearson was a newcomer to films, but Garfield and Bob Roberts signed her for the female lead in *Force of Evil*. She had appeared in three Broadway productions: *Get Away Old Man* (1943), *Over Twenty One* (1944), and *The Mermaids Singing* (1945). Her freshness added an extra dimension; she delivered a poignant performance as the seemingly innocent girl who can't help falling in love with Garfield's screen character. Surprisingly, she would appear in only one more film, *Lost Boundaries* (1949), with Mel Ferrer and Canada Lee, and one more Broadway play, *Day After Tomorrow* (1950), before her early retirement.

Other relative newcomers on the production side of *Force of Evil* included dialogue director Don Weis, who went on to direct many films (*A Slight Case of Larceny*, *The Affairs of Dobie Gillis*, *The Adventures of Haji Baba*, *The Gene Krupa Story*, etc.), and assistant director Robert Aldrich, who went on to have a distinguished career as a director and producer. Some of his films include: *The Big Leaguer, Apache, Vera Cruz, The Big Knife, Attack!, The Dirty Dozen, Ulzana's Raid,* etc. Both gentlemen also contributed extensively to television.

In addition to this young talent, there were many veterans both before and behind the camera. Thomas Gomez, late of many Universal films, and Academy Award nominee as Best Supporting Actor for *Ride a Pink Horse* (1947), gave a brilliant portrayal of Leo Morse, Garfield's older brother. His performance greatly enhanced the mood of gloom and despair. Other cast members were Roy Roberts, Marie Windsor, Tim Ryan, Howland Chamberlain, and Paul Fix. The cinematography was in the care of a master, George Barnes. The music was written by David Raksin, perhaps best known for his work on *Laura* (1944). In the center of all these parts was John Garfield's scintillating rendition of Joe Morse, the attorney from the wrong side of the tracks.

As Joe Morse, Garfield was resilient, tough, and, in a new twist, wealthy from the start of the film. He "didn't have enough strength to resist corruption, but I was strong enough to fight for a piece of it." George Barnes's expressive use of lighting and shadows added to the romantic feeling of the tender scenes between Garfield and Beatrice Pearson. Barnes also made excellent use of the New York locations. One of the most memorable scenes was of Joe Morse (Garfield) wandering Wall Street at dawn, but there was even a better one. The ultimate moment in this (and perhaps any) Garfield film occurred with the shot of Garfield on a small rise with the George Washington Bridge looming above as he rushed down to the Hudson River to find his dead brother. David Raksin's haunting music underscored the scene perfectly. Garfield, back in the city of his birth, was at the top of his game!

Marie Windsor, who played Edna Tucker, wife of mob boss Ben Tucker (Roy Roberts), shared some memories of her career, of John Garfield, and *Force of Evil:*

> I studied under Maria Ouspenskaya in the 7000 block of Sunset
> Blvd. in Hollywood around 1941. (Garfield had studied under Miss

Joe Morse (John Garfield) finds his dead brother Leo (Thomas Gomez) on the rocks along the Hudson River in *Force of Evil* (1948).

Ouspenskaya in 1929 and '30 in New York.) Actually, when I was 17 or 18, I'd gone to New York with my grandmother. She was a Postmistress and she had gone to Washington, D.C. on a Postmistress's convention; so we went on to New York to the World's Fair and to visit some old friends of hers.

While we were there, my family wanted to look up Maria Ouspenskaya's School, which they had seen advertised in the Cosmopolitan Magazine. It was at that point we discovered that she had just moved to Hollywood.

Miss Windsor had small parts in the films *Eyes in the Night, Smart Alecks,* both in 1942, and *Pilot No. 5* and *Three Hearts for Julia,* both in 1943. Miss Windsor also was a regular in the radio series *Romance of Rosy Ridge* during this period. Marie Windsor remembered:

I had a small scene with Clark Gable on the train in *The Hucksters.* I had a big part in *Song of the Thin Man* while I was working at Metro. (Both of these films were 1947). At the time, Otto Preminger and I were friends. When we became friends, I was under contract to Metro. Preminger said, "If they ever drop your contract, let me know." For my own sake, I wanted to do a test of the *Human Voice,* which is a one person play by Jean Cocteau. Eventually, Ingrid Bergman did it on television.

Anyway, Preminger wanted to see how it would work on film. He cut the play down to about thirteen minutes and took me over to Twentieth Century–Fox, where he was under contract. We shot the test there, hoping that I might get a contract out of it. At the time, none of the big shots who could make a decision were at Twentieth; Ben Lyon was in London, and Zanuck was in love with somebody, off skiing or something.

Finally, the six weeks option ran out, so my agent asked permission to take it out of the studio, and he took it over to John Garfield and Bob Roberts. Garfield, Roberts, and Abraham Polonsky saw the test and liked what they saw. I was thrilled to be cast in the film and thrilled to work with Garfield.

This was during a period when he was supposed to be having a drinking problem, but he certainly showed no evidence of this on the set. He was very professional on the set, but relaxed enough to engage in a little fooling around to ease the tension.

He was a darling man to work with. He was hyperactive, had a lot of energy, that was his personality. He was extremely cooperative and was willing to use me in the film although I was two inches taller than he was. (Garfield stood 5'7".) In fact, he taught me how to walk toward him in a scene, to bend my legs to hide the height difference in ¾ shots. Garfield and George Raft were two actors who did not care about the lady being taller; they would stand on boxes and do whatever was necessary for the film.

Abraham Polonsky was a wonderful director who exuded confidence in a performer. Both Polonsky and Garfield were pleased with my work. I guess *Force of Evil* was one of the first important things I did. It was a wonderful picture though it did not get much attention at the time. But film buffs certainly love it.

Passed over by most critics at the time, *Force of Evil* was praised by European film publications and built a cult following in the United States, due largely to Polonsky's involvement. One American reviewer who did recognize the film's worth was (characteristically) Bosley Crowther, who wrote:

> This film is a dynamic crime-and-punishment drama, brilliantly
> and broadly realized. . . . Mr. Polonsky has established himself as
> a man of imagination and unquestioned craftsmanship. True, he
> was very fortunate in having John Garfield play the young lawyer
> in the story, for Mr. Garfield is his tough guy to the life. Sentient
> underneath a steel shell, taut, articulate — he is all good men gone
> wrong. . . . A sizzling piece of work.

Actually, most New York reviewers were in agreement with
Mr. Crowther:

> The picture manages to be exciting all the way through and to
> engender a good deal of suspense toward the end. . . . John Gar-
> field . . . and Thomas Gomez . . . give impressive performances
> under Abraham Polonsky's guidance, and they are given excellent
> support by the other players [Kate Cameron, *Daily News*].
> *Force of Evil* . . . combines a good script with good performances
> to create an exciting and suspenseful film [Frank Quinn, *Daily
> Mirror*].
> It is the most important picture of the holiday crop. It has the
> most vitality and the most interesting acting, direction, and cast-
> ing and it is by far the most engrossing. . . . There is enough vigor
> and talent and freshness of approach flung about in *Force of Evil*
> to make one want to stick with it, regardless of the blank walls one
> bumps into and the fillings-in it takes. Garfield and Roberts and
> Polonsky have plenty [Cecelia Ager, *New York State*].
> Beatrice Pearson's . . . girlish sweetness is one of the most strik-
> ing talents the movies have introduced all season. Abraham Polon-
> sky . . . has built himself a minor masterpiece. . . . Some question
> has been raised about why these unpleasant pictures should be
> made. . . . Now that John Garfield has demonstrated his mastery
> in them, is it not about time for him to turn the force of his artistry
> in some other direction [Alton Cook, *World Telegram*]?

One New York critic who was not impressed was Otis L.
Guernsey, Jr., of the *Herald Tribune:*

> *Force of Evil* sometimes blows hot, but mostly it blows cold in
> a spotty, over-stated crime drama. . . . There is a hint of effective

drama underneath the attitudes in this Roberts production, but it doesn't come out from behind the screen at the State.

The Los Angeles critics echoed Mr. Guernsey's sentiments:

> *Force of Evil,* a picture based on the numbers racket, meanders haltingly and unconvincingly.... The Bob Roberts production has little punch, tension, or drama — certainly not as much as one has a right to expect from its subject matter . . . falls apart because of the script by Abraham Polonsky and Ira Wolfert and because of Polonsky's direction. Certainly both Garfield and Thomas Gomez were unable to surmount their material [Darr Smith, *L.A. Daily News*].
>
> *Force of Evil* is a posturing, overwritten screen drama whose pre-occupation with high sounding phrases mitigates against its entertainment values.... The direction of Abraham Polonsky is heavy and forced.... John Garfield gives as good a performance as is possible under the circumstances.... Roy Roberts, Marie Windsor, Howland Chamberlain, and Paul McVey register in supporting roles [*Hollywood Reporter*].
>
> *Force of Evil* is one of those shows which has all the elements of greatness yet fails to achieve that stature. Film's main weakness can be traced back to a poor job of direction . . . film still boasts certain entertainment qualities and the name of John Garfield to boost its box office potentialities [*Variety*].

Unfortunately, as great as *Force of Evil* was, it could have been even better; midway through the filming, Enterpise Productions collapsed due to the failure of the Ingrid Bergman–Charles Boyer film, *Arch of Triumph.* This forced Garfield and Roberts to scramble for financial backing, finally settling on a distribution deal with Metro Goldwyn Mayer. However, MGM lost faith in the project, cut ten minutes from the final release print, and promoted the film as a "B" movie. Undoubtedly, some of the "blank walls" and "fillings-in" that Cecelia Ager referred to in her review were caused by the cut ten minutes. Marie Windsor recalled a scene that she did with a little boy playing her son which was cut from the final print. The little boy was Beau Bridges. Miss Windsor also remembered:

Top: Lobby card from *Force of Evil* (1948) exploiting Garfield's connection to *Body and Soul* (1947). *Bottom:* This lobby card from *Force of Evil* (1948) clearly shows Sheldon Leonard in the role of Ficco, a part played by Paul Fix in the final release print. Also pictured: Roy Roberts as Ben Tucker and John Garfield as Joe Morse.

"Sheldon Leonard was in the original cast, because I remember him on the set." The pressbook and some lobby cards did advertise Mr. Leonard in the role of Ficco, which was played by Paul Fix in the final version. Suffice to say that *Force of Evil* was a confusing (and confused) masterpiece.

Abraham Polonsky would recall: "Enterprise was a great missed chance, but Hollywood is the capital of missed chances and strange victories. I imagine that they go together in the indignity of history. In any event, the Blacklist would've killed Enterprise."[10]

Chapter 7

One Man Alone
Ain't Got No Chance

Even with the demise of Enterprise Studio, Garfield and Bob
Roberts decided not to disband the Roberts Company. They needed
a picture, and the most firm offer came from Horizon Productions,
which had a distribution deal with Columbia. At this time, negotia-
tions were also under way with 20th Century–Fox for Garfield to appear in *The Eastside Story* (later retitled *House of Strangers*) with
Edward G. Robinson and Susan Hayward. It would have been great
if Robinson and Garfield had reteamed, but Fox eventually settled
on contract player Richard Conte for the part; he delivered one of
the best performances in his long and memorable career.

The film for Horizon, *We Were Strangers,* was based on
Robert Sylvester's novel *Rough Sketch.* The director was John
Huston, fresh from *The Treasure of Sierra Madre* and *Key Largo.*
Julie and Huston wanted to screen test the then-unknown Marilyn
Monroe for the female lead but were overruled by producer Sam
Spiegel who favored the more established Jennifer Jones. Pedro
Armendariz, Gilbert Roland, Ramon Novarro, and Wally Cassell
were the other principal players. Huston and Garfield believed that
the story (written by Huston and Peter Viertel) was an allegory on
the actions of the House Un-American Activities Committee,
though set in revolutionary Cuba in 1933. The message was lost on
the audience and the picture failed at the box office.

The acting honors in *We Were Strangers* belonged to Gilbert
Roland, who delivered a sensitive, thoughtful performance as one
of the rebels. Bosley Crowther (who did have his customary kind
words for Julie's performance) reserved his highest praise for

John Garfield in the late 1940s.

Roland: "And a Cuban laborer with a poet's soul is made by Gilbert Roland into the most genuine and affecting personality in the film."

Roland, a Hollywood veteran of nearly 25 years at the time of *We Were Strangers,* credited the film with helping him to regain momentum in his career. He continued to deliver eloquent portrayals in films and on television for the next 30 years. But Roland's presence and a strong Garfield showing were not enough to make the film wholly effective.

We Were Strangers finished shooting in late 1948, and it was at this time that the Garfields decided to make the move to New York permanent. They retained their home in Beverly Hills, but found a nice apartment on Central Park West. Both Robbie and Julie wanted the children to be raised in New York, and Julie found renewed vigor now that he was back "home."

Toto (Jose Perez), China Valdes (Jennifer Jones), Tony Fenner (John Garfield), Guillermo (Gilbert Roland), and Miguel (Wally Cassell) plan some strategy in *We Were Strangers* (1949).

Upon the return to New York, Garfield teamed with Clifford Odets, polishing a new Odets story called *The Big Knife*. The plot concerned an actor who had sold his talent to the Hollywood studios and now longed to break free. The play opened at the National Theatre on February 24, 1949, and ran for 108 performances. Lee Strasberg directed a cast that included J. Edward Bromberg, Nancy Kelly, and Joan McCracken. The production was a huge hit with audiences but received a lukewarm reception from the critics. Garfield's performance as Charlie Castle was hailed by Howard Barnes in the *New York Herald Tribune* as "genuine artistry." The *New York Sun* commented: "John Garfield with his intense and resourceful playing, does more for the character . . . than the author did."

The reviews for Odets were not nearly as kind. Old Group boss Harold Clurman wrote: "*The Big Knife* is a mess made by a great

Rare rehearsal shot from *We Were Strangers* (1949). Pictured clockwise are:
John Huston (back to camera), David Bond, Jose Perez, John Garfield, and
Ramon Novarro.

talent. It is neither the true story of Odets nor the clear account of
a freely conceived Charlie Castle." Brooks Atkinson of the *New
York Times* commented that, "To Odets this Hollywood jungle is
a great moral tragedy and he quotes one or two fancy phrases to prove
it. But his characters are a singularly undistinguished and unattrac-
tive society of egotists, racketeers, cheats, and dimwits."

During the run of the play, Julie joined other stars (Henry

Fonda, Marlene Dietrich, Marsha Hunt, and Burgess Meredith) in unbilled cameo roles in Fletcher Markle's independent film *Jigsaw*, starring Franchot Tone and Jean Wallace. On Father's Day in June 1949, Julie received recognition as a "Father of the Year" at a luncheon at the Waldorf-Astoria.

The Big Knife closed when Julie went to work on *Under My Skin* for 20th Century–Fox. He was enthused about the film, which was based on Ernest Hemingway's story *My Old Man*. Garfield played a jockey mixed up with gamblers. Micheline Presle (or Prelle) played the love interest and there were rumors that this carried over into after-work hours. However, shortly after the film wrapped, she married William Marshall, a Hollywood actor-producer. Luther Adler, Noel Drayton, and Orley Lindgren played the other major parts. This was Garfield's third (and last) collaboration with director Jean Negulesco, who managed to evoke some of the atmosphere of Paris, where most of the film was set. The screenplay by Casey Robinson, who also produced the picture, was sort of a *Body and Soul* of horse racing.

Under My Skin opened on St. Patrick's Day, 1950, at the Roxy Theatre in New York. The mixed reviews of the critics paralleled the audience reaction; the box office returns proved to be a minor disappointment for Fox. Actually, the film was far better than some people gave it credit. This was the first film in which Garfield played a father; the chemistry between him and Orley Lindgren as his son helped lift the story to notable heights. A perceptive reviewer from *Newsweek* wrote: "When left to themselves, Garfield and Lindgren are every bit the father and son Hemingway intended."

There was a major setback during the filming of *Under My Skin* when Julie suffered another heart attack, after having participated in a grueling tennis match at the Beverly Hills Tennis Club. The news wires of September 26, 1949, carried this notice: "Actor John Garfield was admitted to Cedars of Lebanon Hospital yesterday for a physical checkup after he complained of dizziness. He was reported resting easily." He was diagnosed as having heart muscle strain by Dr. Lee Siegel, who advised Garfield to avoid any exertion for the rest of his life. Julie did not slow down much (if at all), but he did devote more time to his painting.

Gangster great Edward G. Robinson displays his sense of humor as he pays a surprise visit to the set of *We Were Strangers* (1949). Held at gunpoint are a terrified (!) John Garfield and Jennifer Jones.

Julie's next film assignment was easy enough. He served as English narrator for the Italian film *Anni difficili (The Difficult Years)*. The English narrative was written by Arthur Miller. The story concerned Italy during the Fascist years. Garfield's next film work would be much more taxing, but worth every ounce of the effort that was expended on it. *The Breaking Point* served as Julie's sentimental return to Warner Bros.

Upon the occasion of his return to the old home lot, Garfield took the time to tell reporters about his leaving Warner Bros. some four years earlier:

> Nothing personal, I stayed here for all of seven years, or till *Humoresque* in 1945–46. I served my time—was suspended only 11 times—and I took it like a sport. Warners taught me the business and made me a star. I appreciate all that. But you grow up, you go on.

The winning combination of John Garfield and Orley Lindgren as father and son in *Under My Skin* (1950).

As a free lance, Garfield's arrangement with Roberts Productions called for him to receive his share of any loan-out money spread out proportionately with a 52 week guarantee. Garfield was thus in the peculiar and enviable position of being able to loan himself out. He said: "I like to be flexible. I don't want to be a movie actor only. This way I can go anywhere and do anything. I also have script and director approval on any outside picture I accept."

Michael Curtiz was set to direct *The Breaking Point*, and that was fine with Julie:

> Mike discovered me. He had wanted Burgess Meredith for the part of Mickey Borden, but Meredith was going to Europe. Mike saw a test I made and said, "That's the boy!" Among the first words I spoke on the screen were, "It stinks." I've never repeated it till now. I say, "it stinks," again in this picture, for Mike and Warner Bros.

Dan Butler (John Garfield) and Paule Manet (Micheline Prelle) enjoy a romantic interlude in *Under My Skin* (1950).

Michael Curtiz did not want to settle for an ordinary picture. Curtiz's fervor for the project was matched (if not exceeded) by Garfield's. Julie outlined his ideas for the film in a letter to the director:

From: John Garfield
To: Mr. Michael Curtiz
    Warner Bros. Studios
    Burbank, California

January 16, 1950

Dear Mike:

I am most happy to have heard from you. The only reason I didn't answer sooner was because I wanted to re-read the Hemingway book (*To Have and Have Not*), which I did.

I quite agree with you about doing it very realistically without the phony glamor, so that there is a real quality of honesty and

Jockey Dan Butler (John Garfield), his son Joe (Orley Lindgren), and Paule Manet (Micheline Prelle) attend the horse races in *Under My Skin* (1950).

truthfulness which, by the way, I feel (screenwriter) Randy Mac-Dougall captured from the book (in his screenplay).

He has followed the book quite honestly, I think, and some of the questions I would like to kind of throw out for consideration or discussion are:

The deepening of the relationship with the wife (Phyllis Thaxter), so that you get a sense of a man who although he is married for many years has a real kind of yen for her, which is usually very rarely shown in films. As Randy indicates, very warm love scenes are played with the man and his wife. I feel, however, that these scenes can be still deeper without making it too slick.

The other girl (Patricia Neal), I feel has to be carefully gone over in the sense that Harry (Garfield) should be tempted, as most men are, and almost goes through with it, but in the end kind of gets cold feet. I feel this relationship can be a little clearer.

Since Eddie (Juano Hernandez) is to be a Negro, I am of the opinion that the relationship between Eddie and Harry can also be gone into in a little more detail to show that Eddie has similar problems to Harry's, which Randy also indicated in the script, but not with enough detail. Their regard for each other, without being too sentimental, can be kicked up a bit more.

One of the interesting features of the book is that Harry loses his arm. That might be a little too morbid, but it has a wonderful quality, particularly later on in the book where he makes love to his wife. This kind of relationship, if you want to include the loss of the arm, has never been shown. It might seem a little grotesque talking about it, but I certainly think it's worth considering, as it will kick up the whole latter part of the script, purely from a characterization point of view. Of course, Mr. Warner might think it's a little too morbid. However, I feel as long as Randy has stuck so close to the original story in many respects, there is no reason why this couldn't be included. . . .

The main theme which seems to be quite simple and direct is: the struggle of a man who tries to make a living for his family and to discharge his responsibilities and finds it tough. . . .

I, too, am anxiously looking forward to working with you again and I think with Randy and Jerry (Wald) we might come up with something which will be a little off the beaten path, but also excellent entertainment and a real joy to do.

With much love and regards,

Johnny G.[11]

Michael Curtiz, who was not usually known to take kindly to suggestions from actors, not only welcomed Garfield's suggestions but he also invited Julie and Ranald MacDougall to his ranch for preproduction conferences that lasted a week. Garfield said:

I acted it all out. Randy was there, of course, and we'd talk out a sequence and then he'd write or rewrite it. I do it with my own shows, but it was nice of Mike to ask me, just the same. . . . Mike sometimes has to remind me that he *is* the director. "When you make your own productions," he'll say, "you do it that way. For me, you do it this way."

Before filming began on *The Breaking Point,* but fortunately after Julie had signed for the film, an article made the papers which would prove to be a devastating blow to Garfield. John J. Huber, a former FBI agent, accused Garfield and Edward G. Robinson of having been used as drawing cards by Communist organizations. Julie told the press:

> I made several trips during the war to entertain our armed forces, at which time I was thoroughly investigated by the FBI on all counts. The results of those investigations surely should be available now and I stand on them. If they want to string up a man for being liberal, let them bring on their ropes.

Edward G. Robinson's succinct squelcher was, "perhaps it would be a good idea to have an investigation of the persons who make such charges. They seem as un–American as anything I know."

Warner Bros., which had renewed talks with Garfield about a long-term contract, now stopped thinking along those lines. Scripts no longer found their way to Julie's door. Even close friend Jerry Wald did not want to take a chance on him, although Wald had long sought to have Garfield in a film biography of Sime Silverman, the founder of *Variety.* Julie felt "like I was a member of your baseball team but you knew I was going to get traded." By the time *The Breaking Point* went into release in September of 1950, the political turmoil was such that Warner Bros. did not promote the film to the extent that it certainly deserved.

The Breaking Point was the fourth film on which Michael Curtiz and Garfield had officially worked together. Curtiz had been at the helm for *Four Daughters, Daughters Courageous,* and *The Sea Wolf.* (He had also been called in for the additional scenes to "punch up" *Blackwell's Island.*) Curtiz was one of the elite directors in Hollywood and always brought out the best in Garfield's acting style. Garfield once commented: "I'm not the kind of actor that becomes a star in Hollywood. I would normally have been a character actor but Mike Curtiz gave me the screen personality that carried me to stardom." In many ways, *The Breaking Point* was their finest collaboration, helped greatly by Ranald MacDougall's realistic screenplay—the kind which Garfield worked best at.

The entire cast of *The Breaking Point* blended together to create a memorable film: Phyllis Thaxter, Patricia Neal, Wallace Ford, William Campbell, Sherry Jackson and Donna Jo Boyce (who played Garfield's daughters), Victor Sen Yung, and especially Juano Hernandez.

The relationship expressed by the Garfield and Hernandez characters was credited with fostering Negro-White brotherhood. Bosley Crowther wrote of Hernandez's part: "the suggestion of comradeship and trust that is achieved through the character . . . is not only a fine evidence of racial feeling, but is one of the most moving factors in the film."

Crowther continued:

> Warner Bros., which has already taken one feeble swing and a cut at Ernest Hemingway's memorable story of a tough guy, *To Have and Have Not,* finally has got hold of that fable and socked it for a four-base hit in a film called *The Breaking Point.* . . . All the character, color, and cynicism of Mr. Hemingway's lean and hungry tale are wrapped up in the realistic picture, and John Garfield is tops in the principal role—all through his playing of Harry Morgan is the shrewdest, hardest acting in the show. . . . What we have here is a good, taut adventure story.

Other reviewers joined the chorus of praise. William Pfaff in *Commonweal:* "Garfield gives an extremely good performance as a man who has made out for himself all his life; finding out in the end the price of having others than himself to make out for."

John McCarten in the *New Yorker* was similarly complimentary: "As the boatman, John Garfield is excellent, and he gets fine support from the others in the cast. Michael Curtiz is to be commended for his direction."

Ernest Hemingway considered it to be the best screen adaptation of any of his works. He sent notes to Jerry Wald (producer) and Garfield commending them on a worthy film. Garfield said, "I think it's the best I've done since *Body and Soul.* . . . Better than that."

At the end of *The Breaking Point,* Harry Morgan (Garfield)

John Garfield (as Harry Morgan) and Patricia Neal (as seductress Leona Charles) in *The Breaking Point* (1950).

had uttered "one man alone ain't got no chance," and Julie could have adopted these words as his own anthem. Having just completed one of the finest pictures of his career, in which he had delivered his most mature performance to date, he was left with no offers.

Garfield had read Nelson Algren's story *The Man with the*

Harry Morgan (John Garfield) tries to get his friend Wesley Park (Juano Hernandez) to safety in *The Breaking Point* (1950).

Golden Arm, and he purchased both the stage and screen rights to it. But Hollywood movies could not depict narcotics addiction on the screen. To produce a film and release it without a Production Code seal was too big a risk at that particular time. Julie said he'd be willing to gamble if the odds improved in his favor; he decided to retain the rights to the story. He sadly noted: "The Breen Office nixed it. Can't show drug addiction, so I can't make it, I can't defy the Breen Office. But I love it (the script). I love it so much it just gives me pleasure to own it."

From the time Garfield had moved back to New York, he had worked with growing intensity at developing his craft. He would show up at Actors Studio and work on all phases of acting, saying: "A lot of actors have hobbies, like boats and horses, but not me. The stage is mine. I much prefer it to owning a ranch. And I can't play tennis as often as I'd like to. Just doubles, now and then."

Unable to get work, Garfield found solace in his children. On

Harry Morgan (John Garfield) embraces his daughters Amelia (Sherry Jackson, left) and Connie (Donna Jo Boyce, right) as wife Lucy (Phyllis Thaxter) watches the proceedings, in *The Breaking Point* (1950).

weekends, he would take them to Fire Island. Years later, daughter Julie remembered:

> He was always quick to give of his energy. I was so young, but I remember I was always wanting him to carry me piggy-back into the ocean. I only learned later that these were sad days for him, because Hollywood wasn't giving him a chance to work.

David Garfield recalled: "I was very young when he was alive, and the few moments between us that I can remember I keep to myself because they were so few, but they all count."[12]

Among those few moments that David Garfield remembered was probably the fishing contest that was waged between the father and son in the summer of 1950. Michael Curtiz said, "He'd rather go fishing with his son, David, than be an honored guest at a swank party." *Motion Picture Magazine* (December 1950) reported:

> Call on Garfield at his (rented) summer home in Malibu and you're likely to find him surf fishing with his young son. There is terrific competition between them. This has been going on for months, but so far, David is ahead by one rock cod. When he isn't vying with his son in fishing, a visitor may come upon him surrounded by half the kids in the neighborhood, demonstrating how to fly five kites on one string. For he's not John Garfield, the motion picture star, to them. He's just a good Joe to have fun with.

This was all part of the private John Garfield, far away from the footlights.

In the fall of 1950, Bob Roberts worked out a deal with United Artists to distribute a Garfield film. The drawback was that there would be no financial backers; Julie and Roberts would have to use their own money to produce the picture. Garfield had received $135,000 from Warner Bros. for *The Breaking Point*, which he now put into producing the new project. They needed a story, hopefully one that would not only convey a strong social statement but also be commercially viable. The partners chose *He Ran All the Way*, based on the best-selling novel by Sam Ross. The story was about a small-time hood who becomes involved in a hold-up and killing. Bob Roberts had purchased the rights to Ross's novel from Liberty Films for $50,000 cash. Liberty had originally bought the story in 1947 as a directorial vehicle for George Stevens.

The next step was to assemble a cast and crew, which would not be easy considering the limited budget. Garfield decided to take a chance on John Berry as the director. Berry, born in New York in 1917, had a handful of credits including: *Seeds of Freedom* (a 1943 USSR film), *Miss Susie Slagle's*, and *Casbah*. Berry, already in hot water for his political views, would soon become even more of a target after being identified as a Communist by Edward Dmytryk. Shortly after completing *He Ran All the Way*, John Berry was blacklisted. He directed a 16mm documentary, *The Hollywood Ten,* in an effort to raise funds for the defense of the hearings' victims. Berry then went to France, where he directed a number of films through the 1950s, including Laurel and Hardy's *Utopia (Atoll K).* In 1964, Berry directed the Broadway production *The Blood Knot.* It would be 1966 before he was able to return to American filmmaking with the picture *Maya* (shot in India, but with American financing); his career would be revitalized with the critically acclaimed *Claudine* in 1974.

Veteran writers Hugo Butler and Guy Endore adapted Ross's novel into a literate screen treatment. Butler was soon to become another victim of HUAC. He would also flee to Europe before returning in 1963 with his screenplay for *A Face in the Rain.* The names of both John Berry and Hugo Butler were eliminated from the official advertising of *He Ran All the Way.*

The editor was Francis Lyon, who had won the Academy Award for his work on *Body and Soul.* Old friend Franz Waxman (his sixth Garfield film) contributed a strong music score. The redoubtable James Wong Howe, who had been friends with Julie since their work on *They Made Me a Criminal,* was behind the camera for the eighth time on a Garfield film.

Garfield and Roberts were able to sign some talented people for in front of the camera, too. The female lead was played by Shelley Winters who was establishing herself as a fine actress by this phase of her career. Wallace Ford, who had been in *The Breaking Point,* returned to deliver a thoughtful performance as Winters's father. Selena Royle, who specialized in mother roles, played the mother of the family that Nick (Garfield) holds hostage. Bobby Hyatt, a talented child actor, played the young son in a convincing manner. Gladys George as Garfield's mother and Norman Lloyd as his partner rounded out the cast. The picture was filmed on both coasts in late 1950. By the time of its release in June of 1951, John Garfield's career was in deep trouble.

After finishing filming on *He Ran All the Way,* and with no further picture offers, Garfield once again turned his attention to the stage. Selena Royle suggested that he should tackle Henrik Ibsen's *Peer Gynt,* which had not been done on Broadway since the

Fleeing hoodlum Nick (John Garfield) keeps Peg (Shelley Winters) afloat in *He Ran All the Way* (1951).

1923 production, which had starred Joseph Schildkraut and Edward G. Robinson. Paul Green, who had written *Johnny Johnson* for the Group Theatre in 1936, adapted a new version of *Peer Gynt* for this production. The play was staged under the auspices of ANTA, with Cheryl Crawford as producer and Lee Strasberg as director for his third consecutive Garfield Broadway excursion.

Julie was delighted to be doing *Peer Gynt*. He commented:

> Our plans are wonderfully shaped, for in its scenery we will have the spirit of the Pieter Bureghel allegorical works of art. I think this will add greatly to the revival of Ibsen's play. It was performed in this country by Richard Mansfield in 1894 and in 1923 by Joseph Schildkraut, with Edward G. Robinson and Selena Royle.
> I am taking a minimum salary, as I did for *Skipper Next to God,*

Nick (John Garfield), fleeing the authorities, seeks safety in numbers in the locker room of a municipal swimming pool, in *He Ran All the Way* (1951).

the last play for ANTA. Frankly, the way one must approach theatre, in my opinion, is to do the best that one can conceive for the least amount of compensation. Thus only can we keep the better literature of the stage alive.

For my part, doing *Peer Gynt* in a modern adaptation is the realization of a lifetime's ambition. I've talked about it for long enough. Now it's a pleasure to see it in motion.

Actually, Garfield had hoped to be doing a film as well as a play in New York. The planned project would have been a departure in more ways than one. The title was *Mr. Brooklyn*, an original screen comedy by Arnold Manoff. Garfield told an interviewer:

We haven't talked about this, because it is not entirely set but if things work out, it will be shot here (New York) in its entirety, and I'll not only star in it but also direct, something I've been waiting years to do. Actually, *Mr. Brooklyn*—it's all about a Brooklyn streetcar conductor and how he manages to lose his streetcar—is solid comedy, the kind of comedy we used to do here in plays like *Golden Boy.* Anyway, I've got a lot of faith in it and even if it doesn't come off it's something worth failing with.

The article also contained a notice that Otto Preminger had discussed the possibility of Garfield appearing in *Candle for Ruth,* a film Preminger was planning to make in Israel. "We haven't done any more than talk about it," Garfield admitted. "Right now, *Peer Gynt* is a challenge and something I want to do. If it goes, maybe I'll not only be able to appear on Broadway but also make *Mr. Brooklyn* at the same time. It might be a turning point in my career and other actors' careers, who knows?"

Peer Gynt opened at the ANTA Playhouse on January 28, 1951, and closed after 32 performances. The cast included such fine players as Karl Malden, Mildred Dunnock, Nehemiah Persoff, and John Randolph. The reviews were a mixed bag. Harold Clurman said:

> John Garfield, one of the actors who has had a successful Hollywood career and still loves acting for its own sake . . . is only partly equipped for the title role. His opening scenes have a certain vigorous charm, but the later Peer . . . is at the moment definitely beyond him.

Brooks Atkinson wrote:

> Mr. Garfield is an admirable and likeable realistic actor. He has a magnetic personality and a warm voice; and he is winningly sincere. But he never gets Peer Gynt off the ground. His performance is literal and casual, and is completely lacking in poetic animation.

Atkinson had made a valid point; Garfield was a realistic actor who was somewhat outside his element in a fantasy setting. This distinction had been true in *Heavenly Express* and again in *Between Two Worlds*. He worked best in a trenchant, socially relevant milieu. Late in the run of the play, Julie heard that HUAC was sending subpoenas and that its target would be movie stars.

As disturbing as the 1947 HUAC session had been (most of the Hollywood Ten were serving their prison terms) even more tragic was Chairman John S. Wood's marathon ten-part 1951–52 investigation of communism in the entertainment field. Wood was the new chairman, having succeeded J. Parnell Thomas, who was in prison himself on an income tax evasion conviction. These sessions were marked by the committee's insistence that the witnesses name names. Lifelong friendships and long-time partnerships came to an end as a result of this practice. The HUAC already knew the names of the people it sought. And, of course, the targets from the entertainment business had committed no crime; whistle-blowing in this context injured only the innocent.

> When actor Larry Parks came before the committee on March 21, 1951 to testify, he was being called upon not to provide information that would lead to acquittal or conviction, but rather to play a symbolic role in a surrealistic morality play.
>
> Congressman Walter of Pennsylvania, one of the few moderates on the committee, said: "How can it be material to the purpose of this inquiry to have the names of people when we already know them?" Unfortunately, he was overruled by the more maniacal members of the committee, chief among them Harold Velde of Illinois and Donald Jackson of California, who had succeeded Richard Nixon on the committee.
>
> Larry Parks pleaded: "I would prefer, if you would allow me, not to mention other people's names.... This is not the American way.... To force a man to do this is not American justice."
>
> "Don't present me with the choice of either being in contempt of this committee and going to jail or forcing me to crawl through the mud to be an informer, I beg you not to force me to do this."[13]

But Parks eventually capitulated and named names of those who had been members of the Communist Party. The longer he talked, the more obvious it became that the committee already knew everything he could tell it. When specifically asked, Parks said no, he did not recall having ever seen John Garfield at a Communist meeting.

The forced testimony was clearly punitive, a public humiliation of the individual. Larry Parks's only crime was that he had become a star through his success in *The Jolson Story*. Had he remained a relative unknown, the committee may not have gone after him. But John Garfield had been a major star for a dozen years, and the committee needed a victim. Julie had received his subpoena on March 6, 1951, and was scheduled to testify in April. Old friends Elia Kazan, Clifford Odets, and Lee J. Cobb (all of whom eventually named names) accused Garfield of selling out.

Bygone incidents of apparent harmlessness were recalled by the committee and came back to haunt him: the wartime tour of Yugoslavia during which he had been decorated by Tito's guards and his sponsorship of the American Committee for Yugoslav Relief; the State Department dinner honoring Russian novelist Konstantin Simonov; and membership in many liberal organizations, such as the Theatre Arts Committee, the Hollywood Democratic Committee, and the National Council of Arts, Sciences, and Professions. All these activities were described as subversive by HUAC despite their humane missions, or maybe because of them!

Accompanied by Louis Nizer and Sidney Davis as counsel, Julie arrived in Washington, D.C., to testify on April 23, 1951. Technically a friendly witness, Garfield did not name any names. He attempted to feint and weave his way through the questions without bringing harm to anyone. Some excerpts of his testimony follow:

> *Frank Tavenner, Jr.* (counsel for the committee): Have you ever been a member of the Communist Party?
> *Garfield:* I have never been a member of the Communist Party.
> *Tavenner:* While you were a member of the Group Theatre, did anything lead you to believe that there was communist activity within the Group in the form of an effort to influence its actions or the way in which it was operated?
> *Garfield:* You mean in the actual functioning of the organization or the plays that were done?

Tavenner: In the functioning of the organization or the adoption of the policies which it followed.

Garfield: I don't think so. As I said, it was purely run on an artistic basis. It was not a political organization. Of course the actors on Broadway used to call us peculiar because we didn't accept employment on the outside, and took much less money than we usually would get, because we wanted to work together. And we worked in a certain way. We had a technical craft and worked in a certain way, and they thought that was kind of strange.

Tavenner: Were you acquainted with Harold Clurman? C-l-u-r-m-a-n?

Garfield: He was one of the directors of the Group Theatre.

Tavenner: What part did he play in your going to Hollywood?

Garfield: He was against my going to Hollywood. He wanted me to stay with the Group Theatre.

Tavenner: Are you acquainted with Herbert Biberman?

Garfield: I know him casually. I didn't socialize with him.

Tavenner: Did he at one time endeavor to get you to endorse an advertisement. "Open the New Front Now"—that program?

Garfield: Can you tell me what year that was?

Tavenner: I should have said Second Front instead of New Front. It was the period along the latter part of 1942.

Garfield: In other words, you mean the Russians! In other words, the period we were allies with the Russians?

Tavenner: Yes.

Garfield: I don't specifically remember it, but I certainly felt, as everyone felt, that the Russians were our allies, and therefore we tried to help as much as possible.

Tavenner: I'm not asking about your views. I am asking about what Biberman did, if you recall.

Garfield: I don't know. I couldn't answer that.

Tavenner: Were you acquainted with Hanns Eisler?

Garfield: I knew him, yes.

Tavenner: What was the occasion of your knowing him?

Garfield: He worked in Hollywood as a musician. I met him at cocktail parties, as I met many other people. That is my acquaintance with him. He never scored any picture I was in.

Tavenner: Did you have any occasion to believe he was a member of the Communist Party?

Garfield: None whatsoever. As a matter of fact, these people . . . we never discussed politics. They never did trust me. I was a liberal, and I don't think the communists like liberals, and I was quite outspoken about my liberalism.

Tavenner: Were you associated in a business way with Hugo Butler?

Garfield: He was a writer.

Tavenner: Were you associated with him at any time in the production of a picture?

Garfield: Yes, yes, yes.

Tavenner: What picture was that?

Garfield: A picture called *He Ran All the Way,* just recently, six or eight months ago.

Tavenner: When did he write that script?

Garfield: This past summer, because we shot the picture in October.

Tavenner: Do you have any knowledge or information to cause you to believe that he was a member of the Communist Party?

Garfield: None whatsoever. The only relationship I had with him was purely on a craft basis, the picture and the writing of the script.

Tavenner: Is Mr. Butler still associated with you in a business way?

Garfield: No, sir; absolutely not. He hasn't been for the last four months.

Tavenner: You spoke of Jack Berry.

Garfield: He was the director.

Tavenner: Yes, of your picture. Do you know where he is now?

Garfield: No. The picture was completed in November. I went to New York to do a play, *Peer Gynt.*

Tavenner: We have been unsuccessful in locating either Hugo Butler or Jack Berry. We have subpoenas for them.

Tavenner: As an actor it was necessary for you to become a member of the Actors' Guild, was it not?

Garfield: Yes, sir.

Tavenner: In 1945, during the period of the strike in the moving picture industry, the Communist Party is alleged to have been interested in influencing various groups in connection with that strike. Do you have any knowledge on your own part regarding that effort?

Garfield: Well, I have no knowledge of what the Communist Party was doing because I had no association with anybody like that, but I was on the executive board of the Screen Actors' Guild for six years, and during the period of this strike, and I know pretty well what went on in terms of the strike, in terms of the guild's position, and in terms of the general atmosphere at that time.... As a matter of fact, some of us were accused of being sympathetic to the Conference of Studio Unions, which was the other side, at the beginning. Then we proceeded to get all the information we could, and we discovered the CSU didn't want to settle the strike.... The membership of the Screen Actors' Guild voted 98.9 per cent against supporting this strike, eventually.

Tavenner: Was Anne Revere one of those who voted on that same resolution?

Garfield: I am sure she did. She was a member of the Screen Actors' Guild.

Tavenner: Do you know how Anne Revere voted?

Garfield: Well, it is pretty difficult to remember. I know how I voted.

Tavenner: Mr. Garfield, the committee is in possession of considerable information relating to various Communist front organizations with which you are alleged to have affiliated in one way or another, or sponsored, ... It appears that you sponsored a dinner at the Ambassador Hotel in Los Angeles on February 4, 1945, under auspices of the joint Anti-Fascist Refugee Committee, for the purpose of raising funds.

Garfield: I have no knowledge of being a member of that organization, and I don't have any recollection of sponsoring that dinner.

Tavenner: Let me ask you that if you recall at such a meeting that you introduced Paul Robeson?

Garfield: I don't have any recollection. I possibly could have gone to it, but I was never a member of it.

Tavenner: You would recall if you introduced Paul Robeson, wouldn't you?

Garfield: I certainly would.

Tavenner: Do you recall?

Garfield: I don't recall it. If it was during the war, then it is possible it might have happened.

Tavenner: The *New York Times* of March 3, 1945, contained an advertisement paid for by the Veterans of the Abraham Lincoln Brigade advocating a break with Franco Spain. Among those listed as sponsoring the Veterans of the Abraham Lincoln Brigade is your name.

Garfield: Again let me say to the committee and to you that I was for Spain because I felt it was a democratically elected government. I was against the Communists in there as much as I was against the Fascists. However, on this particular point that you mention, I have no knowledge of ever giving permission to them to use my name. The only organization that I worked with about Spain was an organization called the Theatre Arts Committee.

Tavenner: Were you a member of or associated with Veterans of the Abraham Lincoln Brigade?

Garfield: No, sir.

Tavenner: Did you know at the time that the Abraham Lincoln Brigade was a Communist sponsored group?

Garfield: No, sir; I didn't know it. Had I known it—although I don't remember having sponsored this particular event—I would have had nothing to do with it. But I still feel the same way about Spain.

Velde (Rep. Illinois): You had no reason to believe that group was Communist sponsored?

Garfield: No, sir.

Tavenner: You mentioned earlier you were a member of the Committee for the First Amendment?

Garfield: Yes, sir. . . .

Potter: You stated you wanted to make sure there were no communists identified with this movement, Committee for the First Amendment. You must have known of a certain movement, or of certain communist activity, in Hollywood, or you would not have been suspicious of it?

Garfield: That was because of the hearing, you know.

Potter: If you were so cautious as to make sure no communist was identified with your group, certainly you knew of communist activity in Hollywood, or you would not have been so cautious?

Garfield: No, not necessarily; not necessarily.

Potter: All right.

Garfield: We had, as a matter of fact, on that committee, very strong liberals and very strong conservatives.

Potter: You don't believe there were any communists identified with the group?

Garfield: I made the point very clear. "If we are going to fight on that issue, we must be sure there is nobody in the organization with a left tinge." If you will look at the list of people who came here in 1947, the list will speak for itself, I am sure.

Potter: That was in protest to the hearings in 1947?

Garfield: Exactly.

Potter: If I remember, at that time ten Hollywood people were cited for contempt who refused to cooperate with the committee, and some of those, I am sure, were known communists.

Garfield: But they were not on the Committee for the First Amendment. We were fighting on general principles. It had nothing to do with these people. That is the whole point. It has nothing to do with these individuals, believe me. It had to do with the two basic principles. It had nothing to do with the individuals.

Wood: What you mean is that was your conception of it?

Garfield: Yes. As I have said, I wasn't in on the organization of it. I wasn't in California. Some two or three months later I did a play, *Skipper Next to God,* and the *Daily Worker* panned me and said I was a little punch-drunk for playing in a religious play like *Skipper Next to God.*

Velde: How did you know about the *Daily Worker* saying that?

Garfield: I look in all papers and try to find out all information about myself.

Velde: I was interested in how you happened to see it.

Garfield: Would you like to see the copy?

Velde: No. I have seen many copies of the *Daily Worker.* I asked how you happened to look at the *Daily Worker.*

Garfield: They review all plays.

Velde: There is nothing sinister in my question.

Garfield: Most actors, if they are actors at all, like to see all the reviews, regardless of what paper publishes them. That was a review of the play I was in.

Velde: You still haven't answered my question, Mr. Garfield. How did you happen to get a hold of a copy of the *Daily Worker?*

Garfield: It was a review in the *Daily Worker.*

Velde: I realize that. Do you remember where you obtained the copy?

Garfield: Yes. I got a copy by buying a copy. They have a dramatic critic and they review plays just like the *New York Times,* or the *Herald Tribune.*

Moulder: We subscribe to the *Daily Worker* here.

Jackson: And the witness should know that this committee also shared the criticism of the *Daily Worker.* . . .

Wood: You had been affiliated with the Progressive Party?

Garfield: I was not a member of it. The only party I was ever a member of was the Democratic Party, but I contributed money to the Progressive Citizens of America because they were an arm of the Democratic Party on some issues. For instance, they backed Mrs. Douglas in California. I supported her.

Wood: Let me ask you categorically, have you any knowledge of the identity of a single individual who was a member of the Communist Party during the time you were in Hollywood?

Garfield: No, sir.

Tavenner: I believe your name appears on a brief *amicus curiae* filed in the case of the Hollywood Ten before the Supreme Court?

Garfield: Yes.

Tavenner: Will you tell us the circumstances under which you signed the brief?

Garfield: Well, I was asked to sign it, and I said I wouldn't sign unless many other people signed it who were not in any way leftist, because I felt that I wouldn't want to lend my name to anything like that unless other people in the industry did: and they did.

Tavenner: How were arrangements made for you to join in?

Garfield: It was not joining in. . . . I thought I was being on the court's side when I signed this document, a friend of the court. I thought it was important that a man is never guilty until proven so, and it was on that principle and that alone that I signed the document, but I certainly was not the only one.

Wood: Do you recall who first approached you on that subject?

Garfield: Well, as I explained to Mr. Russell or Mr. Wheeler (Investigators for HUAC) —

Wood: We were not there at the time.

Garfield: I vaguely remember being approached at the Beverly Hills Tennis Club.

Wood: And you can't recall who brought the conversation up?

Garfield: They asked if it wasn't a person named Wilner, and I said I wasn't sure if it was or wasn't. But this particular person, Mr. Chairman, was a member of that club, so it is possible that he was the one who asked me. I am not sure on that.

Tavenner: Do you remember whether it was a man or a woman?

Garfield: I can't remember if it was a man or a woman, but it is possible it might have been a woman. I can't honestly remember.

But I know that is where I was asked, at the Beverly Hills Tennis Club.

Wood: But would you have signed it if just anybody had walked up and asked you to?

Garfield: Not if it was any stranger, no.

Wood: And you can't give the committee any further identification of the person who approached you on that subject than what you have given?

Garfield: I tried to recall, as I said. If I knew it I would really gladly tell it, but I know I was approached at the Beverly Hills Tennis Club.

Wood: All right...

Jackson: Mr. Garfield, I am still afraid that I am not entirely convinced of the entire accuracy and entire cooperation you are giving this committee. It is your contention you did not know, during the time you were in New York affiliated with the Group Theatre, which for all its artistry was pretty well shot through with the philosophy of communism—

Garfield: That is not true.

Jackson: That is a matter of opinion. You contend that during all that time in New York you did not know a communist?

Garfield: That is right.

Jackson: And you contend that during the seven and one-half years or more that you were in Hollywood and in close contact with a situation in which a number of communist cells were operating on a week-to-week basis, with electricians, actors, and every class represented, that during the entire period you were in Hollywood, you did not know of your own personal knowledge a member of the Communist Party?

Garfield: That is absolutely correct, because I was not a party member or associated in any shape, way, or form.

Jackson: During that period it might interest you to know attempts were made to recruit me into the Communist Party and I was making $32.50 a week.

Garfield: They certainly stayed away from me, sir.

Jackson: Perhaps I looked like better material. This picture, *He Ran All the Way*—who produced it?

Garfield: I did.

Jackson: You produced it?

Garfield: I didn't have any screen credit for producing it, but I always work as a coproducer.

Jackson: The script was by whom?

Garfield: Guy Endore and Hugo Butler.

Jackson: Who directed it?

Garfield: Jack Berry.

Jackson: You have never been approached at any time to join the Communist Party?

Garfield: Never.

Jackson: Nor have you been approached to assist at Communist Party functions or functions of Communist-front organizations when you knew they were front organizations?

Garfield: That is right, Mr. Jackson. I might say, if at any time that had happened, I would have run like hell.

Jackson: I must say, Mr. Chairman, in conclusion, that I am still not satisfied. . . .

Wood: Mr. Moulder, did you have additional questions?

Moulder: No questions; but, to answer Mr. Jackson's statement, I am convinced that no man should be convicted nor condemned on pure hearsay, rumor, or gossip. I sympathize with your position. Being one of the outstanding actors in this country, naturally you are going to be the subject of such rumor and gossip. I don't think any man should be criticized because he is a liberal Republican or a liberal Democrat. The statement I made to you reminds me of an experience in my last campaign when my opponent accused me of being a "pink."

Jackson: The Democrats made similar charges.

Moulder: He also accused me of making statements against this committee, which was not true. I wish to reiterate my statement that your appearance before this committee does not of itself mean you are accused of being a communist. I am clearly convinced from all the testimony adduced that you were never associated with the Communist Party or any Communist activity or subversive activity, and that you are a loyal American; and I compliment you on your vigilant fight against communism and your cooperation with this committee.

Jackson: Mr. Chairman, so long as my name has been brought into this discussion, I would like to say I do not believe any man is guilty by association or anything of that sort. I am sure the gentleman from Missouri had no intention of accusing me of anything like that. I do say that, for one who is as intelligent as this witness has proven himself to be, it shows a naive or unintelligent approach to this problem for him to have lived with this activity 10, 11, or 15 years and not know more about it than the witness knows.

Garfield: Mr. Jackson, may I answer that? I went overseas twice. I was too busy with war work. I am now conscious of what you are saying, more conscious than I ever was, but in that time I was more conscious of my bigger duty, which was to my country, and where I as an artist could contribute.

Jackson: Unfortunately, the work in which you were engaged became more suspect than the work of those overseas. . . .

Moulder: The statement was made that you belonged to organizations the purpose of which was the overthrow of our Government by force and violence. As I understand your testimony, you have emphatically denied that you belonged to such organizations?

Garfield: Yes, sir. Thank you.

Jackson: Actors' Laboratory is listed as a subversive organization.

Garfield: I was never a member of that organization.

Jackson: The witness appeared on behalf of Actors' Laboratory. I would correct my statement from "membership in" to "activity on behalf of" organizations that have been cited as subversive.

Garfield: When I was originally requested to appear before the committee, I said that I would answer all questions fully and without any reservations, and that is what I have done. I have nothing to be ashamed of and nothing to hide. My life is an open book. I was glad to appear before you and talk with you. I am no Red. I am no "pink." I am no fellow traveler. I am a Democrat by politics, a liberal by inclination, and a loyal citizen of this country by every act of my life.

After the ordeal, Julie was ecstatic; they had not broken him. But over the next few weeks, he took a thrashing in some sectors of the press. *Variety,* in the May 23, 1951, issue, revealed that Congressman Jackson had convinced HUAC to turn Garfield's testimony over to the FBI. Jackson was hoping that the records already in the FBI files would lead to the building of a perjury case against Garfield. It must be remembered that Jackson had succeeded Richard M. Nixon as a representative from California; his line of questioning and his request to the FBI reflected that he had learned the art of "red-baiting" that his predecessor had mastered.

The major trouble spots in Garfield's testimony in the eyes of

John Garfield near the end of his career.

the committee were his insistence that he had never known any communists and that he could not remember who had approached him to sign the *amicus curiae* brief. The fact that his testimony would be sent to the FBI was a major jolt to Garfield's career. What saddened him even more was the cold shoulder he received from his friends. Julie had kept them in the clear, but his sin was in having testified at all.

He Ran All the Way opened at the Paramount Theatre in New York on June 20, 1951, to lukewarm box office results. However, most critics were enthused and rated the picture a powerful drama. Robert Hatch was a dissenting voice in the *New Republic:*

Not as much was made of the possibilities in *He Ran All the Way*
as could have been and, with John Garfield and Shelley Winters
in the leads, certainly should have been. The picture skims the sur-
face.

But Philip T. Hartung wrote for *Commonweal:*

Garfield has played the unhappy, chip-on-the-shoulder young
man many times before, but this time when he loses his partner,
he's more confused than ever. Actually, *He Ran All the Way* is a
pretty good thriller.

And *Variety* added:

He Ran All the Way is a taut gangster pic. Good production
values keep a routine yarn fresh and appealing. Film is scripted,
played, and directed with little wasted motion, so that the sus-
pense is steady and interest constantly sustained.... Garfield is
highly effective as a harshly-raised hoodlum filled with some decent emotions, confused by the affection the invaded family has for
each other.

The highest praise came from (surprise!) Bosley Crowther (*New
York Times*):

Beyond any question, Hugo Butler and Guy Endore have penned
a shock-crammed script from Sam Ross's mordant novel upon
which the picture is based. John Berry's driving direction is designed
to further punctuation of shock, with Franz Waxman's music and
sound tricks adding an apt cacophony. Further, John Garfield's
stark performance as the fugitive . . . is full of startling glints from
start to end.... And in Mr. Garfield's performance, vis-à-vis the
rest of the cast, is conveyed a small measure of the irony and pity
that was in the book.

Despite the favorable notices, it soon became apparent that the
film would not do well enough for Julie or Roberts to recover their
investment. So, it was time to get back to work; but there was none
available, at least not for someone who was under such a dark cloud.

Even old friends, handcuffed by fear, were unable or unwilling to help. Julie offered his services to the various studios, but could find no takers. He learned of a western that was looking for a "John Garfield–type" and applied for the job. The response was, "Yes, we need a Garfield *type* but we can't use Garfield." Hildegarde Knef, in her autobiography *The Gift Horse,* told of an incident at Tyrone Power's house: "When someone said, 'Garfield's finished,' Marlene Dietrich said, 'Yes, because he refused to give names'; then she added, 'We're all whispering as though we were living under Hitler!'"

In the summer of 1951, Elmer Rice was busy writing a treatment of his play, *Counsellor-at-Law,* for television. The proposed series was to air on ABC, with Garfield in the Paul Muni role of George Simon. A year earlier, Julie had appeared in a ten-minute scene from *Golden Boy* on the *Cavalcade of Stars.* He became tremendously excited about the prospects of television: "Live television is just like the theatre. You've got an audience. It's also motion picture technique. You're acting in front of cameras, but you've got an audience that reacts to what you do. This is an actor's dream." The executives at ABC decided to step on Garfield's dream by refusing to allow him to appear in the series, despite Elmer Rice's protestations. To his everlasting credit, Rice resigned from the project, and the proposed series never got off the ground.

After the *Counsellor-at-Law* disappointment, Julie wandered around desperately seeking a job. Even Milton Berle, Mr. Television himself, could not get approval to have Garfield make a guest appearance on his series. Further trouble occurred in late January 1952, when Bob Roberts and Garfield broke up their partnership. "Roberts didn't pay the salary due me and thereby breached our contract," Garfield said. The parting was said to have been amicable. Garfield told reporters, "I'll probably stay in the theatre."

Bob Roberts apparently had run into some real financial troubles. In October of 1953, the Bank of America would foreclose on *Body and Soul* and *Force of Evil. Variety* reported that the bank had loaned Roberts $1,610,000 for *Force of Evil* and $1,000,000 for *Body and Soul.* There was still outstanding against both pictures $187,588 principal, $27,442 interest, and $2,470 attorney's fees.

Garfield's statement about staying in the theatre was about to come to fulfillment. First, Clifford Odets told Julie about a young writer named Norman Brooks who had written a stage play called *Fragile Fox.* Julie took an option on the play, but could not find a producer, nor could he raise the necessary funds on his own. Next, Odets and Robert Whitehead (managing director of ANTA) suggested a revival of *Golden Boy* for the American National Theatre and Academy, which had staged *Skipper Next to God* and *Peer Gynt.*

Elia Kazan was set to direct the revival but he received his subpoena from HUAC and was forced to withdraw. Odets then took over the director's role himself. Garfield was determined to prove that Harold Clurman had made a mistake in having refused him the role of Joe Bonaparte. Odets's wife, Bette Grayson, played the Lorna Moon role. She was the only weak spot in a cast that included such talented people as: Art Smith, Lee J. Cobb, Jack Warden, Jack Klugman, Norman Brooks, Tony Kraber, and Joseph Wiseman. The play began its tryout phase in Hartford in early 1952. This was Garfield's first professional appearance since his testimony before HUAC some nine months earlier. The crowds in Hartford gave a hearty stamp of approval, and the advance sale in New York insured the revival's success.

Golden Boy opened on Broadway at the ANTA Playhouse on March 12, 1952, for a limited engagement of four weeks. The run would be extended another three weeks (for a total of 55 performances) by popular demand. Garfield's Joe Bonaparte was fierce yet sensitive; he infused the role with everything he had. Now 39 years old, he still managed to project a youthfulness on stage that was necessary for the part. Brooks Atkinson wrote:

> As the prizefighter in the current performance, Mr. Garfield is giving one of his most eloquent performances. Apart from its fervor, his acting now is candid and forceful and more fluent than the part. Much of the writing is overwrought, but Mr. Garfield's fiery acting is wholly malleable.

And Richard Watts, Jr., of the *New York Post,* raved:

Luther Adler, in the original company, wasn't nearly as real, incisive, or moving as John Garfield in the present production. Indeed, this strikes me as one of the finest performances that I have ever seen Mr. Garfield give, and it serves to remind us once more that, provided with the proper sort of role, he is one of the most brilliant and satisfying of American actors.

Garfield had found vindication in the role he was born to play. Of course, Garfield wasn't the only member of the cast who had appeared in the 1937-38 version. Both Art Smith and Lee J. Cobb were playing more important parts than they had in the earlier version. Smith moved up to the part of fight manager Tom Moody (played by Roman Bohnen in the original) from his original part of Tokio the trainer. Cobb assumed the role of Mr. Bonaparte, father of the fighter. Mr. Cobb had played this part in the film version, but had played Mr. Carp in the original stage version while Morris Carnovsky portrayed Papa Bonaparte.

Wrote Brooks Atkinson:

> Mr. Cobb's thoughtful, modest, implacably honest acting gives the part real stature and compassion and helps to keep all the values of the play in order.
> Mr. Smith . . . gives a sensitive performance that catches both the decency and cheapness of the character.
> Lee J. Cobb, John Garfield, and Art Smith, who play the leading roles, give the performance the inner truth that the high-strung Group Theatre was always trying to discover in the characters it put on the stage.

Julie's happiness over the play's success did not last long. Elia Kazan rendered testimony before HUAC that was damaging to several members of the Group Theatre, including Art Smith and Tony Kraber. Further, Clifford Odets was scheduled to testify on May 19. *Golden Boy* closed on April 27, and shortly thereafter (sometime between May 9 and May 14), Garfield moved out of the family apartment and checked into the Warwick Hotel. The mounting political hysteria was partly responsible for the separation from his family. Robbie Garfield did not approve of Julie's decision to write an article for *Look* magazine in an effort to get his life and career back on track.

On May 9, 1952, Canada Lee died at the age of 45. His death was a severe blow to Garfield, who had become close to Lee during the production of *Body and Soul*. Death was attributed to natural causes, but the noble actor had been under the dark cloud cast by HUAC. Newspapers carried the following account:

> Canada Lee, 45, famous Negro actor who gave up the violin to become first a jockey, then a boxer, and who became a great success on the stage, died last night of a heart attack at his home, 235 West Fourth Street.
>
> Lee had been preparing to go to Europe to play in a movie, *Destiny of a Negro*. The actor, who had been in failing health for two years, caught a cold ten days ago and had been bedridden for that period. A spokesman said he had uremic poisoning.
>
> Friends recalled that Mr. Lee had collapsed in Africa after completing *Cry, the Beloved Country*, a film which costarred Sidney Poitier. In London in May, 1951, Lee underwent an operation which involved the cutting of nerves to relieve hypertension. Canada Lee had also suffered a slight heart attack in January, 1950, upon learning of his father's death.
>
> Mr. Lee's last entertainment job was doing special monologues in a Greenwich Village nightclub, the Village Vanguard. One of his last public appearances occurred on March 6, when he and other stage and screen personalities entertained 15,000 people at a fund-raising show of the National Association for the Advancement of Colored People in Madison Square Garden.
>
> Surviving are his widow, Frances; a son, Carl Vincent, an actor; a brother, Casper; and an uncle, Dr. David Canegata, administrator of the Virgin Islands.

Canada Lee had had trouble finding work the last few years of his life, at one point threatening to take a shoeshine box in front of the Broadway theatres which had carried his name in lights only a short time earlier. His last major work was in the Korda Brothers film, *Cry, the Beloved Country*. He told his wife he made the picture because "I wanted to show the necessity of love for other human beings."

Canada Lee once said: "All my life I've been on the verge of being something. I'm almost becoming a concert violinist, and I run away to the races. I'm almost a good jockey, and I go overweight. I'm almost a champion prize fighter, and my eyes go bad." There was no "almost" involved in his acting career. His record on stage and screen speaks for itself. His fight off stage for the rights of his people is part of his legacy: Canada Lee, a fine actor and a gentleman.

On Sunday, May 18, Garfield emerged from the Warwick. The final three days of his life would be a strange odyssey:

> People reported that they saw Garfield Sunday night wandering the streets of his old neighborhood in the Bronx. On Monday, he played tennis in the morning at Columbia University and went to a baseball game in the afternoon. Monday evening was spent playing poker with Howard Lindsay, Russell Crouse, and Oscar Levant. (Levant would say that, toward the end, Julie talked as one who doubted his own existence.)[14]

Robert Whitehead would later tell reporters that he understood Garfield sat up late playing cards with friends in a hotel Monday night and had attended to personal affairs on Tuesday, without getting much sleep.

> Art Smith had an early afternoon drink with Garfield in the bar of the Astor Hotel and later said that Julie had skipped both breakfast and lunch. Garfield told Smith that he had changed his mind about "spillling the soup" to *Look*.[15]

In the early evening, Garfield called on Iris Whitney, an ex-actress whom he had been introduced to by Robert Whitehead during the run of *Golden Boy*. Miss Whitney later gave this account: She and Garfield had dinner at Luchow's restaurant, and, after dinner, they stopped to sit in Gramercy Park. They arrived at her apartment around 9 P.M. and Garfield remarked: "I feel awful." She said that she offered to call a doctor but that he declined saying, "I'll feel better if I can get some rest."

He went to the bedroom, removed his clothing except for his

shorts and T-shirt, and got into bed. Miss Whitney said she decided to let him stay for the night, and she went to sleep on a couch in the living room. She awoke at 8 A.M. and took some orange juice to Garfield. After trying vainly to awaken him, she telephoned Dr. Charles H. Nammack, who pronounced John Garfield dead at 9 A.M. The Medical Examiner's office attributed death to a cardiac condition and said there was nothing suspicious about it.

On May 21, 1952, America lost one of its most gifted actors when John Garfield suffered his fatal heart attack, another victim of the ever-mounting paranoia that held this nation in its vise-like grip.

Chapter 8

A Man of Ideals

John Garfield gave a speech before the 1939 graduating class of P.S. 45, which included the following: "I must be in the theatre, otherwise I'd die. I'm young and the theatre is a place to learn things, a place where the actor is sometimes allowed to take a chance. If it hadn't been for this school, I would never have found out. No matter where I am or where I live, I will always act. Acting is my life."

Sadly, this speech proved to be prophetic, for acting really was Garfield's life. Once he was cut off from the thing he loved so deeply, he wandered around in an aimless manner, unsure of which way to turn. His only assignment in his chosen profession the last 15 months of his life was the personally satisfying revival of *Golden Boy*. His death followed on the heels of the play's closing.

Robbie Garfield has said, "I believe in fate, and he might have died anyway. But he wouldn't have died so angry. He was so angry."[16] Yes, maybe the fates were against John Garfield, as they had been against Mickey Borden. Garfield had a history of heart trouble, yet he never really slowed down. It was not in his nature. He had been a smoker and a drinker since his youth. He participated in many athletic activities: boxing, tennis, handball, and baseball.

Julie also worked very hard at his craft and gave of himself not only professionally but also privately. He was troubled by the inequities he saw all around him and worked hard on many fronts to make the idea of equality that his country was founded upon a reality for all people. When he did have a project, he worked at a frantic pace, like a man who sensed that time might be running out.

All of these things took a heavy toll on the man. Maybe John Garfield was destined to die young.

Abraham Polonsky wrote of Garfield in his introduction to Howard Gelman's fine book *The Films of John Garfield:* "The Group Theatre trained him, the movies made him, and the Blacklist killed him." Certainly the Blacklist contributed to John Garfield's death and was the major cause of the bitterness which engulfed him near the end. Many of his friends and associates either died during this dark period of American history (Canada Lee and J. Edward Bromberg) or had their careers curtailed or interrupted (Edward G. Robinson, Anne Revere, Gale Sondergaard, Herbert Biberman, Art Smith, Jane Wyatt, Lee J. Cobb, Robert Rossen, Albert Maltz, John Berry, Lionel Stander, Abraham Polonsky, and many others).

Through thousands of investigations over a twenty-year period, in and out of the entertainment world, no law or laws remotely essential to the security of the nation ever resulted from the House Un-American Activities Committee's work. This never was the goal of the politicians. Their goal was to gain power and to build reputations that would serve to propel them to the top, no matter how many innocent people were necessarily used as rungs on the ladder. Of course, Richard M. Nixon from the House of Representatives and Joseph R. McCarthy from the Senate used the fear generated from the Cold War to further their careers to dizzying heights.

Other factors of the hearings were that the witnesses were not allowed the right of cross-examination; there was no impartial judge or jury; and none of the exclusionary rules about hearsay or other evidence applied. This procedure was something that suited Nazi Germany better than it suited the greatest democracy in the world. As Dalton Trumbo put it, "This is the beginning of an American concentration camp."

So why was John Garfield chosen to be a victim? As an independent filmmaker during the period of the tribunals, he was out on a limb, without the protection a major studio *might* have been able to give him. His life and career made him a ripe choice as a fall guy for the committee. As early as 1939 he had said, "If an actor doesn't have a point of view, he doesn't make a dent. And I mean to make a dent." This philosophy was to remain with him throughout his career, sometimes as a hazard to that career. His "point of view" did not coincide with that of the Hollywood Establishment. Certainly his efforts in the area of race relations most assuredly were not designed to endear himself to the motion picture executives (or many other people) of the 1940s.

Huntz Hall stated that, despite governmental investigations and newspaper stories to the contrary, Garfield was never a Communist:

> Julie comes from a background of poverty. He didn't like to see the little guy pushed around.
>
> The Committee was a terrible thing. John was persecuted. I don't think John's family ever recovered from it. I know this, John loved the American people like I do. He didn't like discrimination. He was brought up with black actors. There is no color on the stage.

In a 1947 interview, Garfield told Louella Parsons (speaking about Angelo Patri):

> It sounds like everything always goes back to him, but I do know if it hadn't have been for his influence on my life, I probably would have wound up in jail with others of my gang who weren't fortunate enough to go to P.S. 45. . . . Maybe that's why I'm always for the underdog.
>
> If I can help other boys who are off on the wrong track, I feel I'm doing it for Mr. Patri.
>
> *Parsons:* Tell me, John, do you think that's the reason you have been accused of being a Communist? I mean, because you always champion the "little fellow" and work so hard in his behalf?
>
> *Garfield:* I don't know. I certainly am not a "Red." But I do want to make it my life work to try to help others. In that way I can repay in a small way the debt I owe Mr. Patri and the others who did so much for me. Remember, I was the underdog once.

Going back to the Depression years, many people joined organizations that were to be listed later as red-tinged. Many people of the New York theatrical scene were involved in this movement in the hope of bettering the human condition, not as advocates of the violent dismantling of the American system. The Group Theatre produced plays which echoed the sentiments of the dispossessed people of the 1930s, and John Garfield eventually became the best known of the Group's alumni.

Throughout his life, Garfield and his wife Robbie lent their names and support to many liberal organizations and causes. Many of Garfield's friends and associates were at one time members of the Communist Party. Unfortunately, the fact that the Communist Party was (and is) a legal political party in the United States of America was lost on HUAC. Some of the incidents that were mentioned by the committee in its case against Garfield were so misconstrued that they became implausible. Rep. Jackson's statement that Garfield's overseas work was "suspect" is incredible in light of the fact that Garfield was doing his best to serve America and boost the morale of the troops fighting the war. Also, the fact that he supported the Loyalists in Spain is something that anybody who believes in Democracy should be proud of, not condemned for. Likewise, Garfield's being a member of the Citizens Committee to End Discrimination in Baseball merits honor. Garfield's record speaks for itself. No witness, friendly, unfriendly, or anywhere in between ever named John Garfield as a member of the Communist Party, the obvious reason being that he never was a member. Indeed, both HUAC and the FBI had closed their files on John Garfield just before the actor's death. But the action had come too late.

What the committee had expected of Garfield in his 1951 testimony was the naming of names. He had been technically listed as a "friendly" witness, but he was anything but friendly to the committee. A contemporary commented that Garfield "was not protecting himself, but old friends whose names had been mentioned dozens of times. He wasn't keeping a secret. Just an idea of himself. That he collapsed before it did is a victory."[17]

Many right-wing columnists published reports that Garfield had met with three leading anti–Communists on May 16, 1952, in an attempt to clear himself. No record of any such meeting has ever been uncovered. *New York Daily Mirror* labor columnist Victor Riesel said that Garfield had completed a full statement describing how Hollywood Communists enmeshed him in their web. This was in reference to the proposed *Look* article "I Was a Sucker for a Left Hook"; but again, no record of any such document was ever uncovered. Garfield's attorney, Louis Nizer, denied that any such document was written or ever had been contemplated: "Garfield was frank and told all he knew when he went before the committee."

Howard Gelman wrote:

> It is still a fact that Garfield's name does not appear on any document disavowing his past, and he made no public confession or second appearance before the House Un-American Activities Committee. Even in his last hours, he was still resisting that final act of capitulation.[18]

The late Art Smith's recollection regarding Garfield's change of mind about the article for *Look* proves that point. Abraham Polonsky eloquently summed up Garfield's refusal to name names:

> He said he hated communists, he hated communism, he was an American. He told the committee what it wanted to hear. But he wouldn't say the one thing that would keep him from walking down his old neighborhood block. Nobody could say, "Hey, there's the stool pigeon." You see that's what he was fighting against: He should be a stool pigeon because he can only gain from it, yet he can't do it because in his mind he lives in the street where he comes from and in the street he comes from you're not a stool pigeon. That's the ultimate horror.
>
> In the end, Garfield was right to do as he did, right to act as he acted, true not only to his generation but to the country that spawned him.[19]

John Garfield was true to his country in a way that the political demagogues who attacked him could never understand. He was endowed with a poor boy's sense of fair play, believing in the ideals that the founding fathers had written into the Constitution. Clifford Odets captured the essence of his friend in his eulogy, which appeared in the May 25, 1952, edition of the *New York Times* (excerpts of which follow):

These past two years he was tired, no doubt. He had had his share of career troubles — financial projects gone wrong, witch-hunters searching his closets, attacks in part of the press for alleged impolitic activities, and sometimes bad health to boot. But Garfield's abundant and energetic nature did not flag in its outpouring of plans and work.

In these keen and bitter times, highly placed and so open to any wild attacks, Garfield remained free of malice and meanness — they were nowhere in his nature. Despite any and all gossip to the contrary, I, who was in a position to know, state without equivocation that of all his possessions Garfield was proudest of his American heritage, even rudely so. In all ways he was as pure an American product as can be seen these days. . . . His feelings never changed that he had been mandated by the American people to go in there and "keep punching" for them.

Few actors on our stage throw themselves into their work with the zest displayed by Garfield. . . . Many believed, and among them such critics as Brooks Atkinson and Richard Watts, Jr., in their last reviews, that John Garfield at 39 was just beginning to reveal himself as an actor, in terms of wider range, new sensitivity and maturity.

There is no doubt that John Garfield's death deprived motion pictures (and the stage) of an original and distinctly American actor. There are some people who believe his best work was behind him. These dissenters cite the argument that the rebel hero is best presented in a youthful light. Yet, as Clifford Odets pointed out, many critics believed Garfield was getting better. Certainly, the latter part of his motion picture and stage career contained some of his most varied, riveting, and intense performances. He had convincingly portrayed a father in two of his last films, *Under My Skin* and *The Breaking Point*. His characterizations were becoming more and more sure and mature. This evolving maturity was the result of a master working to perfect his craft.

The films and stage productions Garfield planned for the future followed the general pattern he had established over the last five years of his career. At the time of his death, he still owned the rights to Nelson Algren's *The Man with the Golden Arm*. He loved the book so much that he probably would have eventually done the film version, with or without the approval of the Breen Office. In *Conversations with Nelson Algren,* the author recalled:

> I was edified that Garfield was so personal about it. He liked the guy, Frankie Machine. He wanted to be Frankie Machine. He genuinely liked this guy and the part. I was influenced by that. I mean I was very gratified that a good actor should want to be the guy that I created.

In 1955, Otto Preminger defied the Breen Office and filmed *The Man with the Golden Arm.* Frank Sinatra gave a strong rendition of Frankie Machine, but Algren was not happy, saying that only Garfield should have played the part. (Sinatra also starred in Warner Bros.' 1954 musical remake of *Four Daughters, Young at Heart.*)

Garfield was going to make another attempt to bring Norman Brooks's *Fragile Fox* to Broadway in late 1952. His good friend and Warner Bros. costar Dane Clark eventually would star in the 1954 Broadway production. Robert Aldrich, assistant director of *Body and Soul,* directed the film version, which was retitled *Attack!* Aldrich also directed the film version of *The Big Knife,* made in 1955, with Jack Palance in the role of Charlie Castle which Garfield had originated. Commented Aldrich: "The original play had been done on Broadway with John Garfield. If you'd had an electric, charming guy like Garfield in the lead you'd have solved half the problem, but I don't think you'd have ever solved the other half."[20] The "other half" Mr. Aldrich referred to was the overblown writing (according to many) of Clifford Odets.

There were not many people (critics or otherwise) who found fault with Odets's *Sweet Smell of Success,* which was originally conceived with Garfield in the part that Tony Curtis played in the 1957 movie. Also, at the time of Garfield's death, Odets was working on a play for Julie titled *By the Sea.* Odets never returned to writing this script after his friend's passing.

Other planned projects were: a film of the life of Angelo Patri, with Garfield portraying his old mentor; *The Italian Story,* a cinematic treatment of Guido Cantelli, the composer-conductor protege of Arturo Toscanini, to be directed by Fred Zinneman; *Port Afrique,* a French African whodunit; *The Wildcatter and the Lady,* a comedy about an oil driller; *Mr. Brooklyn,* the streetcar film; and *Taxi,* with Garfield playing an iconoclastic hackie, a perfect role for him. Dan Dailey played in the 1953 film.

One reason that two comedies appear on the list is that after completing *The Breaking Point* and *He Ran All the Way,* Garfield felt the time had come for a change of pace. He was looking forward to the opportunity to do a comedy: "Not just a straight funny piece, but something delicately balanced between humor and realism."

So the cupboard was definitely not barren of ideas. How many of these would have come to fruition is questionable due to the political turmoil and the general cowardice that was sweeping the entertainment industry as a result of these "politics of fear." Also, the break with Bob Roberts may have thrown a monkey wrench into some of the plans. Of course, the break might not have occurred had the Blacklist not halted the flow of the team's plans. Yet, the potential was there, not only in the projects but also in the man himself.

Of course, the 35 films (including cameos, narrator duties, and one short) and 16 Broadway plays in which Garfield *did* appear are a rich legacy of the actor. Many of his biographers and chroniclers agree on this point. Larry Swindell (*Body and Soul: The Story of John Garfield*):

> As the forerunner of Brando, Clift, and Newman, John Garfield is a special image of the movies, and was a prophet of the New Actor on film. . . . He liked to say he was just a dumb kid from the Bronx, but that was what made him special. His approach to a role was instinctive, irreverent, amoral; and, nourished by those qualities, each Garfield characterization assumed a life of its own with more dimension than the dramatist envisioned.
>
> There is no doubting that he conveyed a magic from the stage; but present and future generations will measure him, finally, by the unique legacy that is the living screen.
>
> Surely, though, he was a product of his times. He was Depression's child, hungry for the promise of democracy, seeking only what Ralph Berger sought in *Awake and Sing:* a chance to get to

first base. He did not express the American dream, but the hopeful idealism of the underprivileged.

And while he lived, Julie obeyed the only law of the street: Don't rat on nobody.[21]

An example of Garfield's obeying the law of the street occurred in 1947, in an incident involving boxer Rocky Graziano. Graziano, who had been barred from New York rings for failing to report a bribe offer, told Garfield: "Those guys that got me barred for not reporting a bribe, they're a bunch of rats. They made me lose so much money. I coulda retired! I wanta get a couple more billings before I finish."

"I understand you refusing to rat on anybody," Garfield said. And he *did* understand.

Howard Gelman (*The Films of John Garfield*):

> Garfield was essentially an authentic representative of the people he characterized on the screen. Garfield understood his parts with an unconscious ease — it is there in his walk, his flippancy, and his immense energy. That energy could be a powerful force when controlled by a director — then Garfield could give the kind of realistic performance that few actors could equal.
>
> From his very first screen portrayal, John Garfield was a symbol for a large segment of the American population, but especially for the immigrant urban poor . . . and in film after film that followed he was that same slum kid fighting to get from the outside to the inside . . . that screen personality — the outsider — would be his mark on the American cinema. The way that character developed in his various films would prove in some ways a measure of the immigrant American's full view of himself and his success.
>
> As an actor, he was always interesting, sometimes deeply moving, and throughout his career of real importance to his audience. As a person, he was intense, deeply attached to people, and very human.[22]

James N. Beaver, Jr. (*John Garfield: His Life and Films*):

> John Garfield epitomized the ideology of the common man for Depression and post-Depression America. . . . In the weaknesses

of his characters, he showed us our own faults, and in the strengths of his characters, he gave us a road out of our faults. His films often were depressing in nature, but they also often gave us a hope of triumph, which in actuality is the triumph itself. He was the loser who, in his final understanding, won out after all.[23]

As early as 1939, Ruth Waterbury, in her *Close-Up of John Garfield* for *Liberty* magazine, wrote:

> He possesses a thing which can't be faked, a gift that puts him well ahead of any number of the film pretty boys. That is an apparently God-given ability to understand how average people think and feel — plus the ability to reproduce those moods so that, watching him, audiences feel deeply in response.

So what plays and films did Garfield consider to be among his best work? On stage, there was the revival of *Golden Boy* — a richly rewarding experience for him; also, *Skipper Next to God*, which he felt very deeply about; and, in the early years, *Awake and Sing*, which served as his breakthrough role with the Group Theatre in a play that truly is an American classic.

Of his films, there were seven of which he was proudest (listed in chronological order): *Four Daughters*, the electrifying debut as Mickey Borden and Academy Award nomination for Best Supporting Actor; *Daughters Courageous*, the successor (not a sequel) to *Four Daughters*, featuring the marvelous playing of Garfield and Claude Rains; *Saturday's Children*, a departure for Garfield in a role in which he was able to display his sense of humor, and a film which he, the Epstein brothers, and Vincent Sherman were justifiably proud of; *Pride of the Marines*, Garfield's "baby" from start to finish — evident in one of the finest and most heartfelt portrayals of his career; *Body and Soul*, the first independent film, the only Best Actor nomination, the race relations issue, and the corruption in boxing; *Force of Evil*, Polonsky's triumph, New York locations, exposé of numbers racket, powerful performance as Joe Morse; and *The Breaking Point*, which Garfield felt was "the best I've done since *Body and Soul*, better than that," the brotherhood conveyed in the characters played by Garfield and Juano Hernandez, and the intense portrayal of a "man alone."

John Garfield once described what was necessary to make a film his way:

> Harsh reality is what makes a good movie. People like to look at life on the screen the way it really is. They can identify themselves among the actors that way.
>
> It used to be that some producers thought movies had to be made to lift people out of their own lives into a kind of misty dream world filled with beautiful women, handsome men, golden chariots, and buckets of money. But that time is gone. People like honest things.
>
> As an actor, it gives me a great deal more satisfaction to play the role of a real man on the screen than to fool around with phony heroes.

His performances do stand as a legacy for future generations. In spite of all the troubles, the films John Garfield did complete in those last years were made the way he wanted to make them. They contained messages that he felt were important and needed to be said. His appearances on Broadway mirrored this feeling, as did the projects he had planned for the future. He had a genuine love of people which was reflected in his passion for acting.

Garfield was called the sincerest actor in Hollywood, intense in his work, exacting of himself. He explained his love for his craft thusly:

> I like the feel of an audience. I'd act, and go on acting, as long as even as little as 200 people would get together in a barn and want to see and hear me.
>
> Acting before a live audience is a busman's holiday for me. I did it several years ago when I played *Awake and Sing* at the Las Palmas. I did it again a couple of years ago for the American National Theatre and Academy in *Skipper Next to God*.
>
> I don't want to be a "sometime" actor. I'll act on the radio, on television, in pictures, on the stage, anywhere if anybody wants me.
>
> Friendly or hostile, a live audience provides an invigorating atmosphere for the stage actor. It's a challenge, and if you win, your reward is very direct. And there are no retakes on a bad

performance. You find out — right now. Stage acting makes acting for the movies much easier. You've felt that audience out there and you know it's alive.

Rights and privileges, that's what's important — not so much the dough. So you get to the place where you make $150,000 a picture — where do you go from there?

I know successful actors who appear in hit after hit and worry all the time whether their next picture is going to be a flop. But to me heaven is just a place where you sit down with a couple of other guys and an idea and not too much dough and you work it over and finally you say "let's do it." Maybe it clicks, maybe it doesn't, but you've had the fun and you've had the experience.

Garfield's fervor was communicated through the moving performances he contributed to American film and theatre. That was his gift and nobody (not even the House Un-American Activities Committee) could ever take that away from him. They, the powers-that-be, could deprive him of the opportunity to display his unique talents, but they could not deny him his soul. And oh, the man had soul. Yes, he did!

John Garfield Filmography

1. **Four Daughters** (1938, Warner Bros.–First National). *Directed by* Michael Curtiz. *Produced by* Hal B. Wallis. *Associate Producers:* Benjamin Glazer and Henry Blanke. *Screenplay by* Julius J. Epstein and Lenore Coffee. *Based on a story by* Fannie Hurst. *Director of Photography:* Ernest Haller. *Music by* Max Steiner. *Film Editor:* Ralph Dawson. *Dialogue Director:* Irving Rapper. *Assistant Director:* Sherry Shourds. *Art Director:* John Hughes. *Gowns by* Orry-Kelly. *Sound Recorder:* Stanley Jones. *Music Director:* Leo F. Forbstein. *Unit Manager:* Al Alleborn. *Running time:* 90 minutes.

Cast

Adam Lemp	Claude Rains
Ann Lemp	Priscilla Lane
Kay Lemp	Rosemary Lane
Thea Lemp	Lola Lane
Emma Lemp	Gale Page
Mickey Borden	John Garfield
Felix Deitz	Jeffrey Lynn
Ben Crowley	Frank McHugh
Aunt Etta	May Robson
Ernest Talbot	Dick Foran
Mrs. Ridgefield	Vera Lewis
Jake	Tom Dugan
Sam	Eddie Acuff
Earl	Donald Kerr

2. **They Made Me a Criminal** (1939, Warner Bros.–First National). *Directed by* Busby Berkeley. *Produced by* Jack L. Warner and Hal B. Wallis. *Associate Producer:* Benjamin Glazer. *Screenplay by* Sig Herzig. *Based on a novel by* Bertram Millhauser and Beulah Marie Dix. *Director of Photography:* James Wong Howe. *Music by* Max Steiner. *Film Editor:* Jack Killefer. *Assistant Director:* Russ Saunders. *Art Director:* Anton Grot. *Costumes by* Milo Anderson. *Sound Recorder:* Oliver S. Garretson. *Orchestrations by* Leo F. Forbstein. *Running time:* 92 minutes.

Cast

Johnnie	John Garfield
Tommy	Billy Halop
Angel	Bobby Jordan
Spit	Leo Gorcey
Dippy	Huntz Hall
T. B.	Gabriel Dell
Milt	Bernard Punsley
Detective Phelan	Claude Rains
Goldie	Ann Sheridan
Grandma	May Robson
Peggy	Gloria Dickson
Doc Ward	Robert Gleckler
Magee	John Ridgely
Budgie	Barbara Pepper
Ennis	William Davidson
Lenihan	Ward Bond
Malvin	Robert Strange
Smith	Louis Jean Heydt
J. Douglas Williamson	Ronald Sinclair
Rutchek	Frank Riggi
Manager	Cliff Clarke
Colucci	Dick Wessel
Sheriff	Raymond Brown
Speed	Irving Bacon
Splash	Sam McDaniel

3. *Blackwell's Island* (1939, Warner Bros.–First National). *Directed by* William McGann. *Produced by* Hal B. Wallis and Jack L. Warner. *Associate Producer:* Bryan Foy. *Screenplay by* Crane Wilbur. *Based on a story by* Crane Wilbur and Lee Katz. *Director of Photography:* Sid Hickox. *Film Editor:* Doug Gould. *Dialogue Director:* Harry Seymour. *Assistant Director:* Elmer Decker. *Art Director:* Stanley Fleischer. *Gowns by* Howard Shoup. *Sound Recorder:* Leslie G. Hewitt. *Musical Director:* Leo F. Forbstein. *Running time:* 71 minutes.

Cast

Tim Haydon	John Garfield
Sunny Walsh	Rosemary Lane
Terry Walsh	Dick Purcell
Thomas McNair	Victor Jory
Bull Bransom	Stanley Fields
Steve Cardigan	Morgan Conway

Warden Stuart Granger	Granville Bates
Brower	Anthony Averill
Pearl Murray	Peggy Shannon
Benny	Charley Foy
Mike Garth	Norman Willis
Rawden	Joe Cunningham
Deputy Commissioner	Milburn Stone
Deputy Warden Michaels	William Gould
Headkeeper Jameson	Eddy Chandler
Captain Pederson	Wade Boteler
Hempel	William Davidson
Judge	Walter Young
Ballinger	Leon Ames
Garner	James Spottswood
Mrs. Walsh	Lottie Williams
Cash Sutton	Raymond Bailey
Rico Ide	Jimmy O'Gatty
Nurse	Vera Lewis
Guard	John Hamilton

4. *Juarez* (1939, Warner Bros.–First National). *Directed by* William Dieterle. *Produced by* Hal B. Wallis. *Associate Producer:* Henry Blanke. *Screenplay by* John Huston, Aeneas MacKenzie, and Wolfgang Reinhardt. *Based in part on the play* Juarez and Maximilian *by* Franz Werfel *and the book* The Phantom Crown *by* Bertita Harding. *Director of Photography:* Tony Gaudio. *Music by* Erich Wolfgang Korngold. *Film Editor:* Warren Low. *Art Director:* Anton Grot. *Costumes by* Orry-Kelly. *Orchestrations by* Leo F. Forbstein. *Running time:* 125 minutes.

Cast

Benito Juarez	Paul Muni
Carlotta	Bette Davis
Maximilian Von Hapsburg	Brian Aherne
Napoleon III	Claude Rains
Porfirio Diaz	John Garfield
Empress Eugenie	Gale Sondergaard
Marechal Bazaine	Donald Crisp
Col. Miguel Lopez	Gilbert Roland
Miguel Miramon	Henry O'Neill
Alejandro Uradi	Joseph Calleia
Riva Palacio	Pedro de Cordoba
Jose de Montares	Montagu Love
Dr. Samuel Basch	Harry Davenport
Achille Fould	Walter Fenner

Drouyn de Lhuys	Alexander Leftwich
Countess Battenberg	Georgia Caine
Major Du Pont	Robert Warwick
Senor de Leon	Gennaro Curci
Tomas Mejia	William Wilkerson
Mariano Escobedo	John Miljan
John Bigelow	Hugh Sothern
Carabajal	Irving Pichel
Duc de Morny	Frank Reicher
Marshal Randon	Holmes Herbert
Prince Metternich	Walter Kingsford
Baron von Magnus	Egon Brecher
Lerdo de Tajada	Monte Blue
LeMarc	Louis Calhern
Pepe	Manuel Diaz
Augustin Iturbide	Mickey Kuhn
Camilo	Vladimir Sokoloff
Senor Salas	Fred Malatesta
Tailor	Carlos de Valdez
Coachman	Frank Lackteen
Senator del Valle	Walter O. Stahl
Regules	Noble Johnson

5. **Daughters Courageous** (1939, Warner Bros.–First National). *Directed by* Michael Curtiz. *Produced by* Hal B. Wallis. *Associate Producer:* Henry Blanke. *Screenplay by* Julius J. and Philip G. Epstein. *Suggested by a play by* Dorothy Bennett and Irving White. *Director of Photography:* James Wong Howe. *Music by* Max Steiner. *Film Editor:* Ralph Dawson. *Dialogue Director:* Irving Rapper. *Assistant Director:* Sherry Shourds. *Art Director:* John Hughes. *Gowns by* Howard Shoup. *Makeup by* Perc Westmore. *Sound Recorders:* C. A. Riggs and Oliver S. Garretson. *Orchestrations by* Ray Heindorf. *Musical Director:* Leo F. Forbstein. *Running time:* 107 minutes.

Cast

Gabriel Lopez	John Garfield
Jim Masters	Claude Rains
Buff Masters	Priscilla Lane
Tinka Masters	Rosemary Lane
Linda Masters	Lola Lane
Cora Masters	Gale Page
Johnny Heming	Jeffrey Lynn
Nan Masters	Fay Bainter
Sam Sloane	Donald Crisp

Penny	May Robson
George	Frank McHugh
Eddie Moore	Dick Foran
Manuel Lopez	George Humbert
Judge Hornsby	Berton Churchill

6. ***Dust Be My Destiny*** (1939, Warner Bros.–First National). *Directed by* Lewis Seiler. *Produced by* Louis F. Edelman. *Screenplay by* Robert Rossen. *Based on the novel by* Jerome Odlum. *Director of Photography:* James Wong Howe. *Music by* Max Steiner. *Film Editor:* Warren Low. *Dialogue Director:* Irving Rapper. *Assistant Director:* William Kissel. *Art Director:* Hugh Reticker. *Costumes by* Milo Anderson. *Makeup by* Perc Westmore. *Special Effects by* Byron Haskin. *Sound Recorder:* Robert B. Lee. *Orchestrations by* Hugo Friedhofer. *Musical Director:* Leo F. Forbstein. *Running time:* 88 minutes.

Cast

Joe Bell	John Garfield
Mabel	Priscilla Lane
Mike Leonard	Alan Hale
Caruthers	Frank McHugh
Hank	Billy Halop
Jimmy	Bobby Jordan
Pop	Charlie Grapewin
Nick	Henry Armetta
Charlie	Stanley Ridges
Prosecutor	John Litel
Warden	John Hamilton
Thug	Ward Bond
Defense Attorney	Moroni Olsen
Doc Saunders	Victor Kilian
Abe Connors	Frank Jaquet
Shopkeeper	Ferike Boros
Venetti	Marc Lawrence
Magistrate	Arthur Aylesworth
Warden	William Davidson
Judge	George Irving
Pawnshop Owner	Charles Halton

7. ***Four Wives*** (1939, Warner Bros.–First National). *Directed by* Michael Curtiz. *Produced by* Hal B. Wallis. *Associate Producer:* Henry Blanke. *Screenplay by* Julius J. and Philip G. Epstein and Maurice Hanline. *Based on the book* Sister Act *by* Fannie Hurst. *Director of*

Photography: Sol Polito. *Music by* Max Steiner. *Film Editor:* Ralph Dawson. *Dialogue Director:* Jo Graham. *Assistant Director:* Sherry Shourds. *Art Director:* John Hughes. *Costumes by* Howard Shoup. *Makeup by* Perc Westmore. *Sound Recorder:* Oliver S. Garretson. *Orchestrations by* Hugo Friedhofer and Ray Heindorf. *Musical Director:* Leo F. Forbstein. *Mickey Borden's Theme by* Max Rabinowitsh. *Running time:* 110 minutes.

Cast

Adam Lemp	Claude Rains
Ann Lemp	Priscilla Lane
Kay Lemp	Rosemary Lane
Thea Lemp Crowley	Lola Lane
Emma Lemp Talbot	Gale Page
Felix Deitz	Jeffrey Lynn
Dr. Clinton Forrest, Jr.	Eddie Albert
Aunt Etta	May Robson
Ben Crowley	Frank McHugh
Ernest Talbot	Dick Foran
Dr. Clinton Forrest, Sr.	Henry O'Neill
Mrs. Ridgefield	Vera Lewis
Frank	John Qualen
Mathilde	Ruth Tobey
Joe	Olin Howland
Laboratory Man	George Reeves
Mickey Borden	John Garfield

Garfield was unbilled and appeared in flashback.

8. ***Castle on the Hudson*** (1940, Warner Bros.). *Directed by* Anatole Litvak. *Produced by* Hal B. Wallis. *Associate Producer:* Samuel Bischoff. *Screenplay by* Seton I. Miller, Brown Holmes, and Cortney Terrett. *Based on the book* 20,000 Years in Sing Sing *by* Warden Lewis E. Lawes. *Director of Photography:* Arthur Edeson. *Music by* Adolph Deutsch. *Film Editor:* Thomas Richards. *Dialogue Director:* Irving Rapper. *Assistant Director:* Chuck Hansen. *Art Director:* John Hughes. *Costumes by* Howard Shoup. *Makeup by* Perc Westmore. *Special Effects by* Byron Haskin. *Sound Recorder:* Robert B. Lee. *Orchestrations by* Ray Heindorf. *Musical Director:* Leo F. Forbstein. *Running time:* 77 minutes.

Cast

Tommy Gordon	John Garfield
Kay	Ann Sheridan

Warden Long	Pat O'Brien
Steven Rockford	Burgess Meredith
District Attorney	Henry O'Neill
Ed Crowley	Jerome Cowan
Mike Cagle	Guinn "Big Boy" Williams
Chaplain	John Litel
Ann Rockford	Margot Stevenson
Ragan	Willard Robertson
Black Jack	Edward Pawley
Pete	Billy Wayne
Mrs. Long	Nedda Harrington
Principal Keeper	Wade Boteler
Goldie	Barbara Pepper
Joe Morris	Robert Strange
Clerk	John Ridgely
Clerk	Frank Faylen
Guard	James Flavin
Detective	Robert Homans
Detective	Emmett Vogan

9. **Saturday's Children** (1940, Warner Bros.). *Directed by* Vincent Sherman. *Produced by* Jack L. Warner and Hal B. Wallis. *Associate Producer:* Henry Blanke. *Screenplay by* Julius J. and Philip G. Epstein. *Based on the play by* Maxwell Anderson. *Director of Photography:* James Wong Howe. *Film Editor:* Owen Marks. *Running time:* 101 minutes.

Cast

Rims Rosson	John Garfield
Bobbie Halevy	Anne Shirley
Mr. Halevy	Claude Rains
Florrie Sands	Lee Patrick
Herbie Smith	George Tobias
Willie Sands	Roscoe Karns
Gertrude Mills	Dennie Moore
Mrs. Halevy	Elizabeth Risdon
Mr. Norman	Berton Churchill
1st carpenter	John Qualen
2nd carpenter	Tom Dugan
Mr. MacReady	John Ridgely
Mrs. MacReady	Margot Stevenson
Boy	Claudo Wisberg
Mac	Jack Mower
Elevator Operator	Glen Cavender
Joe	Gus Glassmire

Cabby	Frank Faylen
Girl	Nell O'Day
Mailman	Creighton Hale
Nurse	Maris Wrixon
Nurse	Lucille Fairbanks
Nightwatchman	Paul Panzer
Doctor	Sam Flint

10. ***Flowing Gold*** (1940, Warner Bros.). *Directed by* Alfred E. Green. *Produced by* Bryan Foy. *Associate Producer:* William Jacobs. *Screenplay by* Kenneth Gamet. *Based on the novel by* Rex Beach. *Director of Photography:* Sid Hickox. *Music by* Adolph Deutsch. *Film Editor:* James Gibbon. *Dialogue Director:* Hugh MacMullan. *Assistant Director:* Jesse Hibbs. *Art Director:* Hugh Reticker. *Special Effects by* Byron Haskin and Willard Van Enger. *Orchestrations by* Leo F. Forbstein. *Running time:* 82 minutes.

Cast

Johnny Blake	John Garfield
Linda Chalmers	Frances Farmer
Hap O'Conner	Pat O'Brien
Wildcat Chalmers	Raymond Walburn
Hot Rocks	Cliff Edwards
Petunia	Tom Kennedy
Charles Hammond	Granville Bates
Tillie	Jody Gilbert
Collins	Edward Pawley
Mike Brannigan	Frank Mayo
Joe	William Marshall
Luke	Sol Gorss
Nurse	Virginia Sale
Sheriff	John Alexander

11. ***East of the River*** (1940, Warner Bros.–First National). *Directed by* Alfred E. Green. *Produced by* Bryan Foy. *Associate Producer:* Harland Thompson. *Screenplay by* Fred Niblo, Jr. *Based on a story by* John Fante and Ross B. Wills. *Director of Photography:* Sid Hickox. *Music by* Adolph Deutsch. *Film Editor:* Thomas Pratt. *Dialogue Director:* Hugh Mac-mullan. *Assistant Director:* Les Guthrie. *Art Director:* Hugh Reticker. *Gowns by* Howard Shoup. *Makeup by* Perc Westmore. *Sound Recorder:* Stanley Jones. *Musical Director:* Leo F. Forbstein. *Technical Advisor:* Marie Jenardi. *Running time:* 73 minutes.

Cast

Joe Lorenzo	John Garfield
Laurie Romayne	Brenda Marshall
Teresa Lorenzo	Marjorie Rambeau
Tony	George Tobias
Nick Lorenzo	William Lundigan
Judge Davis	Moroni Olsen
Cy Turner	Douglas Fowley
Scarfi	Jack LaRue
"No Neck" Griswold	Jack Carr
Balmy	Paul Guilfoyle
Warden	Russell Hicks
Customer	Charles Foy
Henchman	Ralph Volkie
Henchman	Jimmy O'Gatty
Patrolman Shanahan	Robert Homans
Joe (as a boy)	Joe Conti
Nick (as a boy)	O'Neill Nolan
Guide	Frank Faylen
Usher	William Marshall
Dink Rogers	Murray Alper
Cop	Roy Barcroft
Railroad guard	Eddy Chandler

12. **The Sea Wolf** (1941, Warner Bros.–First National). *Directed by* Michael Curtiz. *Produced by* Jack L. Warner and Hal B. Wallis. *Associate Producer:* Henry Blanke. *Screenplay by* Robert Rossen. *Based on the novel by* Jack London. *Director of Photography:* Sol Polito. *Music by* Erich Wolfgang Korngold. *Film Editor:* George Amy. *Art Director:* Anton Grot. *Special Effects by* Byron Haskin and H. F. Koenekamp. *Running time:* 100 minutes.

Cast

Wolf Larsen	Edward G. Robinson
George Leach	John Garfield
Ruth Webster	Ida Lupino
Humphrey van Weyden	Alexander Knox
Dr. Louie Prescott	Gene Lockhart
Cooky	Barry Fitzgerald
Johnson	Stanley Ridges
Svenson	Francis McDonald
Harrison	Howard da Silva
Smoke	Frank Lackteen

Young Sailor	David Bruce
Helmsman	Wilfrid Lucas
Sailor	Louis Mason
Agent	Ralf Harolde
Crewman	Dutch Hendrian
1st detective	Cliff Clark
2nd detective	William Gould
First mate	Charles Sullivan
Pickpocket	Ernie Adams
Singer	Jeane Cowan
Crewman	Ethan Laidlaw

13. *Out of the Fog* (1941, Warner Bros.). *Directed by* Anatole Litvak. *Produced by* Hal B. Wallis. *Associate Producer:* Henry Blanke. *Screenplay by* Robert Rossen, Jerry Wald, and Richard Macauley. *Based on the play* The Gentle People *by* Irwin Shaw. *Director of Photography:* James Wong Howe. *Film Editor:* Warren Low. *Dialogue Director:* Jo Graham. *Assistant Director:* Lee Katz. *Art Director:* Carl Jules Weyl. *Special Effects by* Rex Wimpy. *Orchestrations by* Leo F. Forbstein. *Running time:* 93 minutes.

Cast

Stella Goodwin	Ida Lupino
Harold Goff	John Garfield
Jonah Goodwin	Thomas Mitchell
George Watkins	Eddie Albert
Olaf Knudsen	John Qualen
Igor Propotkin	George Tobias
Florence Goodwin	Aline MacMahon
Officer Magruder	Robert Homans
Sam Pepper	Bernard Gorcey
Eddie	Leo Gorcey
Boss	Ben Welden
Judge	Paul Harvey
District Attorney	Jerome Cowan
Caroline Pomponette	Odette Myrtil
Clerk	Murray Alper
Reporter	Charles Drake
Detective	Charles Wilson
Detective	Jack Mower
Bublitchki	Konstantin Sankar
Kibitzer	James Conlin
Dancer	Mayta Palmera
Morgue attendant	Herbert Heywood

14. ***Dangerously They Live*** (1942, Warner Bros.). *Directed by* Robert
Florey. *Produced by* Bryan Foy. *Associate Producer:* Ben Stoloff.
Screenplay by Marion Parsonnet. *Based on the novel* Remember Tomorrow
by Marion Parsonnet. *Director of Photography:* L. William O'Connell.
Film Editor: Les Guthrie. *Art Director:* Hugh Reticker. *Running time:* 71
minutes.

Cast

Dr. Michael Lewis	John Garfield
Jane	Nancy Coleman
Dr. Ingersoll	Raymond Massey
Mr. Goodwin	Moroni Olsen
Nurse Johnson	Lee Patrick
Steiner	Christian Rub
Mrs. Steiner	Ilka Gruning
Dr. Murdock	Roland Drew
Jarvis	Frank Reicher
Dawson	Esther Dale
Taxi driver	John Harmon
Eddie	Ben Welden
John	John Ridgely
John Dill	Cliff Clark
Gatekeeper	Arthur Aylesworth
Captain Strong	Matthew Boulton
Captain Hunter	Gavin Muir
Ralph Bryon	Frank M. Thomas
Carl	James Seay
Joe	Charles Drake
Miller	Murray Alper

15. ***Tortilla Flat*** (1942, Metro-Goldwyn-Mayer). *Directed by* Victor
Fleming. *Produced by* Sam Zimbalist. *Screenplay by* John Lee Mahin and
Benjamin Glazer. *Based on the novel by* John Steinbeck. *Director of
Photography:* Karl Freund. *Music by* Franz Waxman. *Film Editor:* James
E. Newcom. *Art Director:* Cedric Gibbons. *Special Effects by* Warren
Newcombe. *Musical Lyrics by* Frank Loesser. *Running time:* 105 minutes.

Cast

Pilon	Spencer Tracy
Dolores Sweets Ramirez	Hedy Lamarr
Danny	John Garfield
The Pirate	Frank Morgan
Pablo	Akim Tamiroff

Tito Ralph	Sheldon Leonard
Jose Maria Corcoran	John Qualen
Paul D. Cummings	Donald Meek
Mrs. Torrelli	Connie Gilchrist
Portagee Joe	Allen Jenkins
Father Ramon	Henry O'Neill
Mrs. Marellis	Mercedes Ruffino
Senora Teresina	Nina Campana
Mr. Brown	Arthur Space
Cesca	Betty Wells
Torrelli	Harry Burns

16. **Air Force** (1943, Warner Bros.–First National). *Directed by* Howard Hawks. *Produced by* Hal B. Wallis. *Original Screenplay by* Dudley Nichols. *Director of Photography:* James Wong Howe. *Music by* Franz Waxman. *Film Editor:* George Amy. *Dialogue Director:* William Faulkner. *Assistant Director:* Jack Sullivan. *Art Director:* John Hughes. *Special Effects by* Roy Davidson, Rex Wimpy, and H. P. Koenekamp. *Sound Recorder:* Oliver S. Garretson. *Orchestrations by* Leo F. Forbstein. *Aerial Photography by* Elmer Dyer and Charles Marshall. *Chief Pilot:* Paul Mantz. *Set Decoration by* Walter F. Tilford. *Running time:* 124 minutes.

Cast

Capt. Quincannon	John Ridgely
Sgt. Winocki	John Garfield
Sgt. White	Harry Carey
Lieut. Williams	Gig Young
Lieut. McMartin	Arthur Kennedy
Lieut. Hauser	Charles Drake
Cpl. Weinberg	George Tobias
Cpl. Peterson	Ward Wood
Pvt. Chester	Ray Montgomery
Lieut. Rader	James Brown
Maj. Mallory	Stanley Ridges
Colonel	Willard Robertson
Commanding Officer	Moroni Olsen
Sgt. Callahan	Edward Brophy
Lieut. Moran	Bill Crago
Susan McMartin	Faye Emerson
Maj. Daniels	Addison Richards
Maj. Bagley	James Flavin
Mary Quincannon	Ann Doran
Marine with dog	James Millican
Demolition Corporal	Murray Alper

Marine	Tom Neal
Control Officer	Warren Douglas
Sgt.	William Hopper
Copilot	Rand Brooks

17. *The Fallen Sparrow* (1943, RKO–Radio). *Directed by* Richard Wallace. *Produced by* Robert Fellows. *Screenplay by* Warren Duff. *Based on the novel by* Dorothy B. Hughes. *Director of Photography:* Nicholas Musuraca. *Music by* Roy Webb. *Film Editor:* Robert Wise. *Assistant Director:* Sam Ruman. *Art Director:* Albert S. D'Agostino and Mark-Lee Kirk. *Set Decorations by* Darrell Silvera and Harley Miller. *Gowns by* Edward Stevenson. *Special Effects by* Vernon L. Walker. *Sound Recorder:* Bailey Fesler. *Rerecorded by* James G. Stewart. *Orchestrations by* C. Bakaleinikoff. *Production Designed by* Van Nest Polglase. *Running time:* 94 minutes.

Cast

Kit (John McKittrick)	John Garfield
Toni Donne	Maureen O'Hara
Dr. Skaas	Walter Slezak
Whitney Parker	Martha O'Driscoll
Barby Taviton	Patricia Morison
Anton	John Banner
Inspector Tobin	John Miljan
Otto Skaas	Hugh Beaumont
Prince Francois de Namur	Sam Goldberg
Guest	Symona Boniface

18. *Show Business at War* (1943, 20th Century–Fox). Volume IX Issue 10 of the *March of Time. Directed by* Louis deRochement. *Produced by* the editors of *Time* magazine. *Running time:* 17 minutes.

Cast

As themselves: Eddie "Rochester" Anderson, Louis Armstrong, Jack Benny, Joe E. Brown, James Cagney, Bing Crosby, Michael Curtiz, Linda Darnell, Bette Davis, Olivia De Havilland, Marlene Dietrich, Irene Dunne, W. C. Fields, Errol Flynn, Clark Gable, John Garfield, Bert Glennon, Rita Hayworth, Bob Hope, Al Jolson, Brenda Joyce, Kay Kyser, Hedy Lamarr, Dorothy Lamour, Carole Landis, Anatole Litvak, Myrna Loy, Fred MacMurray, Victor Mature, the Mills Brothers, Tyrone Power, the Ritz Brothers, Mickey Rooney, Frank Sinatra, and others.

19. *Thank Your Lucky Stars* (1943, Warner Bros.–First National). *Directed by* David Butler. *Produced by* Mark Hellinger. *Screenplay by* Norman Panama, Melvin Frank, and James V. Kern. *Based on a story by* Everett Freeman and Arthur Schwartz. *Director of Photography:* Arthur Edeson. *Music and Lyrics by* Arthur Schwartz and Frank Loesser. *Film Editor:* Irene Morra. *Dialogue Director:* Herbert Farjean. *Assistant Director:* Phil Quinn. *Art Directors:* Anton Grot and Leo Kuter. *Gowns by* Milo Anderson. *Makeup Artist:* Perc Westmore. *Special Effects by* H. F. Koenekamp. *Sound Recorders:* Francis J. Scheid and Charles David Forrest. *Orchestrations by* Leo F. Forbstein. *Dances Created and Staged by* LeRoy Prinz. *Orchestral Arrangements by* Ray Heindorf. *Vocal Arrangements by* Dudley Chambers. *Musical Adaptation by* Heinz Roemheld. *Additional Orchestrations by* Mauric de Packh. *Running time:* 124 minutes.

Cast

Himself and Joe Simpson	Eddie Cantor
Pat Dixon	Joan Leslie
Tommy Randolph	Dennis Morgan
Farnsworth	Edward Everett Horton
Dr. Schlenna	S. Z. Sakall
Nurse Hamilton	Ruth Donnelly
Announcer	Don Wilson
Himself	Humphrey Bogart
Herself	Bette Davis
Herself	Olivia De Havilland
Himself	Errol Flynn
Himself	John Garfield
Herself	Ida Lupino
Herself	Ann Sheridan
Herself	Dinah Shore
Herself	Alexis Smith
Himself	Jack Carson
Himself	Alan Hale
Himself	George Tobias
Himself	David Butler
Himself	Mark Hellinger
Themselves	Spike Jones and His City Slickers
Barber	Henry Armetta
Bill	James Burke
Dr. Kirby	Paul Harvey
Ice Cold Katie	Rita Christiani
Gossip	Hattie McDaniel
Soldier	Willie Best

20. **Destination Tokyo** (1944, Warner Bros.). *Directed by* Delmer Daves. *Produced by* Jerry Wald. *Screenplay by* Delmer Daves and Albert Maltz. *Based on a story by* Steve Fisher. *Director of Photography:* Bert Glennon. *Music by* Franz Waxman. *Film Editor:* Christian Nyby. *Assistant Director:* Art Lueker. *Art Director:* Leo Kuter. *Set Decoration by* Walter Tilford. *Costumes by* Vladimir Barjansky. *Special Effects by* Lawrence Butler and Willard Van Enger. *Sound Recorder:* Robert B. Lee. *Orchestrations by* Leo F. Forbstein. *Narrated by* Lou Marcelle. *Technical Advisor:* Lt. Cmdr. Phillip Compson. *Running time:* 135 minutes.

Cast

Capt. Cassidy	Cary Grant
Wolf	John Garfield
Cookie	Alan Hale
Reserve Officer	John Ridgely
Tin Can	Dane Clark
Executive Officer	Warner Anderson
Pills	William Prince
The Kid	Robert Hutton
Dakota	Peter Whitney
Mike	Tom Tully
Mrs. Cassidy	Faye Emerson
Diving Officer	Warren Douglas
Sparks	John Forsythe
Ensign	John Alvin
Ensign	Ralph McColm
Torpedo Gunnery Officer	Bill Kennedy
C.O.	John Whitney
Quartermaster	William Challee
Yoyo	Whit Bissell
Toscanini	Maurice Murphy
Admiral	Pierre Watkin
Aide	Stephen Richards (Mark Stevens)
Hornet's Admiral	Cliff Clark
Debby Cassidy	Deborah Daves
Michael Cassidy	Michael Daves
Captain	Kirby Grant
Wolf's girl	Joy Barlowe
Tin Can's girl	Mary Landa
C.P.O.	Lane Chandler
Aide	Jack Mower

21. **Between Two Worlds** (1944, Warner Bros.). *Directed by* Edward A. Blatt. *Produced by* Mark Hellinger. *Screenplay by* Daniel Fuchs. *Based on the play* Outward Bound *by* Sutton Vane. *Director of Photography:* Carl Guthrie. *Music by* Erich Wolfgang Korngold. *Film Editor:* Rudy Fehr. *Dialogue Director:* Frederick De Cordova. *Assistant Director:* Elmer Decker. *Art Director:* Hugh Reticker. *Set Decoration by* Jack McConaghy. *Gowns by* Leah Rhodes. *Makeup by* Perc Westmore. *Sound Recorder:* Clare A. Riggs. *Orchestrations by* Leo F. Forbstein. *Running time:* 112 minutes.

Cast

Tom Prior	John Garfield
Henry	Paul Henreid
Thompson	Sydney Greenstreet
Ann	Eleanor Parker
Scrubby	Edmund Gwenn
Pete Musick	George Tobias
Lingley	George Coulouris
Maxine	Faye Emerson
Mrs. Midget	Sara Allgood
Rev. William Duke	Dennis King
Mr. Cliveden-Banks	Gilbert Emery
Mrs. Cliveden-Banks	Isobel Elsom
Dispatcher	Lester Matthews
Clerk	Pat O'Moore

22. **Hollywood Canteen** (1944, Warner Bros.–First National). *Directed by* Delmer Daves. *Produced by* Alex Gottlieb. *Original Screenplay by* Delmer Daves. *Director of Photography:* Bert Glennon. *Music by* Ray Heindorf. *Film Editor:* Christian Nyby. *Assistant Director:* Art Luker. *Art Director:* Leo Kuter. *Costumes by* Milo Anderson. *Makeup by* Perc Westmore. *Sound Recorders:* Oliver S. Garretson and Charles David Forrest. *Orchestrations by* Leo F. Forbstein. *Musical Numbers Created and Directed by* LeRoy Prinz. *Sets by* Casey Roberts. *Unit Manager:* Chuck Hanson. *Running time:* 124 minutes.

Cast

Joan	Joan Leslie
Slim	Robert Hutton
Sergeant	Dane Clark
Angela	Janis Paige
Mr. Brodel	Jonathan Hale
Mrs. Brodel	Barbara Brown

Soldier on Deck	Dick Erdman
Soldier on Deck	Stephen Richards (Mark Stevens)
Marine Sergeant	James Flavin
Dance Director	Eddie Marr
Director	Theodore Von Eltz
Captain	Ray Teal
Orchestra Leader	Rudolph Friml, Jr.
Tough Marine	George Turner
Themselves	The Andrews Sisters
Himself	Jack Benny
Himself	Joe E. Brown
Himself	Eddie Cantor
Himself	Jack Carson
Herself	Joan Crawford
Himself	Helmut Dantine
Herself	Bette Davis
Herself	Faye Emerson
Himself	Victor Francen
Himself	John Garfield
Himself	Sydney Greenstreet
Himself	Alan Hale
Himself	Peter Lorre
Herself	Ida Lupino
Himself	Dennis Morgan

Also: Eleanor Parker, John Ridgely, Roy Rogers, S. Z. Sakall, Zachary Scott, Alexis Smith, Craig Stevens, Barbara Stanwyck, Kitty Carlisle, Joseph Szigeti, Donald Woods, Jane Wyman, Julie Bishop, Tommy Dorsey, Carmen Cavallaro.

23. **Pride of the Marines** (1945, Warner Bros.). *Directed by* Delmer Daves. *Produced by* Jerry Wald. *Screenplay by* Albert Maltz. *Adapted by* Marvin Borowsky from a book by Roger Butterfield. *Director of Photography:* Peverall Marley. *Music by* Franz Waxman. *Film Editor:* Owen Marks. *Orchestrations by* Leo F. Forbstein and Leonid Raab. *Running time:* 120 minutes.

Cast

Al Schmid	John Garfield
Ruth Hartley	Eleanor Parker
Lee Diamond	Dane Clark
Jim Merchant	John Ridgely
Virginia Pfeiffer	Rosemary DeCamp
Ella Merchant	Ann Doran

Lucy Merchant	Ann Todd
Kebabian	Warren Douglas
Irish	Don McGuire
Tom	Tom D'Andrea
Doctor	Rory Mallinson
Ainslee	Stephen Richards (Mark Stevens)
Johnny Rivers	Anthony Caruso
Captain Burroughs	Moroni Olsen

Also: Dave Willock, John Sheridan, John Miles, John Campton, Lennie Bremen, and Michael Browne.

24. *The Postman Always Rings Twice* (1946, Metro-Goldwyn-Mayer). *Directed by* Tay Garnett. *Produced by* Carey Wilson. *Screenplay by* Harry Ruskin and Niven Busch. *Based on the novel by* James M. Cain. *Director of Photography:* Sidney Wagner. *Music by* George Basserman. *Film Editor:* George White. *Art Directors:* Cedric Gibbons and Randall Duell. *Orchestrations by* Ted Duncan. *Song by* Neil Moret and Richard Whiting. *Running time:* 113 minutes.

Cast

Cora Smith	Lana Turner
Frank Chambers	John Garfield
Nick Smith	Cecil Kellaway
Arthur Keats	Hume Cronyn
Kyle Sackett	Leon Ames
Madge Gorland	Audrey Totter
Ezra Liam Kennedy	Alan Reed
Blair	Jeff York
Doctor	Charles Williams
Willie	Cameron Grant
Ben	Wally Cassell
Judge	William Halligan
Judge	Morris Ankrum
Truckdriver	Garry Owen
Nurse	Dorothy Phillips
Doctor	Edward Earle
Picnic Manager	Byron Foulger
Matron	Sondra Morgan
Reporter	Dick Crockett
Bailiff	Frank Mayo
Customer	Betty Blythe
John X. McHugh	Joel Friedkin
Headwaiter	Jack Chefe

Telegraph Messenger	George Noisom
Snooty Woman	Virginia Randolph
Father McConnell	Tom Dillon
Warden	James Farley
Man	Paul Bradley

25. **Nobody Lives Forever** (1946, Warner Bros.–First National). *Directed by* Jean Negulesco. *Produced by* Robert Buckner. *Screenplay by* W. R. Burnett, *based on his novel* I Wasn't Born Yesterday. *Director of Photography:* Arthur Edeson. *Music by* Adolph Deutsch. *Film Editor:* Rudi Fehr. *Dialogue Director:* Herschel Daugherty. *Assistant Director:* Reginald Callow. *Art Director:* Hugh Reticker. *Set Decorations by* Casey Roberts. *Wardrobe by* Milo Anderson. *Makeup by* Perc Westmore. *Special Effects by* William McGann and Willard Van Enger. *Sound Recorder:* Dolph Thomas. *Orchestrations by* Jerome Moross. *Musical Director:* Leo F. Forbstein. *Running time:* 100 minutes.

Cast

Nick Blake	John Garfield
Gladys Halvorsen	Geraldine Fitzgerald
Pop Gruber	Walter Brennan
Toni	Faye Emerson
Doc Ganson	George Coulouris
Al Doyle	George Tobias
Chet King	Robert Shayne
Charles Manning	Richard Gaines
Shake Thomas	James Flavin
Windy Mather	Ralph Peters
Bellboy	Dick Erdman
Priest	William Edmunds
Orchestra Leader	Rudy Friml, Jr..
Counter Man	Grady Sutton

Also: Alex Havier, Ralph Dunn, and John Conte.

26. **Humoresque** (1946, Warner Bros.). *Directed by* Jean Negulesco. *Produced by* Jerry Wald. *Screenplay by* Clifford Odets and Zachary Gold. *Based on a story by* Fannie Hurst. *Director of Photography:* Ernest Haller. *Music by* Franz Waxman. *Film Editor:* Rudi Fehr. *Art Director:* Hugh Reticker. *Costumes by* Adrian. *Orchestrations by* Leo F. Forbstein. *Music Advisor:* Isaac Stern. *Running time:* 125 minutes.

Cast

Helen Wright	Joan Crawford
Paul Boray	John Garfield
Sid Jeffers	Oscar Levant
Rudy Boray	J. Carroll Naish
Gina	Joan Chandler
Phil Boray	Tom D'Andrea
Florence	Peggy Knudsen
Esther Boray	Ruth Nelson
Monte Loeffler	Craig Stevens
Victor Wright	Paul Cavanaugh
Bauer	Richard Gaines
Rozner	John Abbott
Paul, as a child	Bobby Blake
Phil, as a child	Tommy Cook
Eddie	Don McGuire
Hagerstrom	Fritz Leiber
Nightclub Singer	Peg LaCentra
Teddy	Richard Walsh

27. **Body and Soul** (1947, Enterprise–United Artists). *Directed by* Robert Rossen. *Produced by* Bob Roberts. *Screenplay by* Abraham Polonsky. *Director of Photography:* James Wong Howe. *Music by* Rudolph Polk and Hugo Friedhofer. *Film Editors:* Francis Lyon and Robert Parrish. *Assistant Director:* Robert Aldrich. *Art Directors:* Nathan Juran and Edward J. Boyle. *Costumes by* Marion Herward Keyes. *Song by* Johnny Green, Edward Heyman, Robert Sour, Frank Eyton. *Running time:* 104 minutes.

Cast

Charley Davis	John Garfield
Peg Born	Lilli Palmer
Alice	Hazel Brooks
Anna Davis	Anne Revere
Quinn	William Conrad
Shorty Polaski	Joseph Pevney
Ben Chaplin	Canada Lee
Roberts	Lloyd Goff (Gough)
David Davis	Art Smith
Arnold	James Burke
Irma	Virginia Gregg
Drummer	Peter Virgo
Prince	Joe Devlin
Grocer	Shimin Rushkin

Miss Tedd	Mary Currier
Dan	Milton Kibbee
Shelton	Tim Ryan
Jack Marlowe	Artie Dorrell
Victor	Cy Ring
Marine	Glen Lee
Referee	John Indrisano
Announcer	Dan Tobey
Doctor	Wheaton Chambers

28. **Gentleman's Agreement** (1947, 20th Century–Fox). *Directed by* Elia Kazan. *Produced by* Daryl F. Zanuck. *Screenplay by* Moss Hart. *Based on the novel by* Laura Z. Hobson. *Director of Photography:* Arthur Miller. *Music by* Alfred Newman. *Film Editor:* Harman Jones. *Art Directors:* Lyle Wheeler and Mark-Lee Kirk. *Running time:* 118 minutes.

Cast

Phil Green	Gregory Peck
Kathy	Dorothy McGuire
Dave	John Garfield
Anne	Celeste Holm
Mrs. Green	Anne Revere
Miss Wales	June Havoc
John Minify	Albert Dekker
Jane	Jane Wyatt
Tommy	Dean Stockwell
Dr. Craigie	Nicholas Joy
Professor Lieberman	Sam Jaffe
Personnel Manager	Harold Vermilyea
Bill Payson	Ransom M. Sherman
Hotel Manager	Roy Roberts
Mrs. Minify	Kathleen Lockhart
Bert McAnny	Curt Conway
Bill	John Newland
Weisman	Robert Warwick
Miss Miller	Louise Lorimer
Tingler	Howard Negley
Apartment Superintendent	Victor Kilian
Harry	Frank Wilcox
Maitre D'	Wilton Graff
Clerk	Morgan Farley
Ex-G.I. in Restaurant	Robert Karnes
2nd Ex-G.I.	Gene Nelson
Guest	Marion Marshall

Columnist	Mauritz Hugo
1st Woman	Olive Deering
2nd Woman	Jane Green
3rd Woman	Virginia Gregg
Elevator Starter	Jesse White

29. *Force of Evil* (1948, Enterprise–Metro-Goldwyn-Mayer). *Directed by* Abraham Polonsky. *Produced by* Bob Roberts. *Screenplay by* Abraham Polonsky and Ira Wolfert. *Based on the novel* Tucker's People *by* Ira Wolfert. *Director of Photography:* George Barnes. *Music by* David Raksin. *Film Editor:* Art Seid. *Dialogue Director:* Don Weis. *Assistant Director:* Robert Aldrich. *Art Director:* Richard Day. *Set Decorations by* Edward C. Boyle. *Makeup by* Gus Norin. *Sound Recorder:* Frank Webster. *Orchestrations by* Rudolph Polk. *Running time:* 78 minutes.

Cast

Joe Morse	John Garfield
Doris Lowry	Beatrice Pearson
Leo Morse	Thomas Gomez
Ben Tucker	Roy Roberts
Edna Tucker	Marie Windsor
Fred Bauer	Howland Chamberlain
Hobe Wheelock	Paul McVey
Juice	Jack Overman
Johnson	Tim Ryan
Mary	Barbara Woodell
Bunty	Raymond Largay
Wally	Stanley Prager
Frankie Tucker	Beau Bridges
Badgley	Allan Mathews
Egan	Barry Kelley
Ficco	Paul Fix
Mrs. Morse	Georgia Backus
Two and Two	Sid Tomack
Elevator Operator	Paul Frees
Policeman	Richard Reeves
Comptroller	Murray Alper

Note: Running time was cut from 88 minutes to 78 minutes, rendering Beau Bridges invisible, at least to this observer.

30. *We Were Strangers* (1949, Horizon-Columbia). *Directed by* John Huston. *Produced by* S. P. Eagle (Sam Spiegel). *Associate Producer:* Jules

Buck. *Screenplay by* Peter Viertel and John Huston. *Based on the "China Valdez" episode in Robert Sylvester's novel* Rough Sketch. *Director of Photography:* Russell Metty. *Music by* George Antheil. *Film Editor:* Al Clark. *Dialogue Director:* Gladys Hill. *Assistant Director:* Carl Hieke. *Art Director:* Cary Odell. *Set Decoration by* Louis Diage. *Costumes by* Jean Louis. *Hair Styles by* Larry Germain. *Special Effects by* Lawrence W. Butler. *Sound Recorder:* Lambert Day. *Orchestrations by* M. W. Stoloff. *Running time:* 106 minutes.

Cast

China Valdes	Jennifer Jones
Tony Fenner	John Garfield
Armando Ariete	Pedro Armendariz
Guillermo	Gilbert Roland
Chief	Ramon Novarro
Miguel	Wally Cassell
Ramon	David Bond
Toto	Jose Perez
Bank Manager	Morris Ankrum
Manolo	Tito Renaldo
Roberto	Paul Monte
Bombmaker	Leonard Strong
Rubio	Robert Tafur

31. *Jigsaw (aka Gun Moll).* (1949, Tower–United Artists). *Directed by* Fletcher Markle. *Produced by* Edward J. Danziger and Harry Lee Danziger. *Screenplay by* Fletcher Markle and Vincent McConnor. *Based on a story by* John Roeburt. *Director of Photography:* Don Malkames. *Music by* Robert W. Stringer. *Film Editor:* Robert Matthews. *Assistant Director:* Sal J. Scoppa, Jr. *Makeup by* Fred Ryle. *Special Effects by* William L. Nemeth. *Sound Recorder:* David M. Polak. *Running time:* 70 minutes.

Cast

Howard Malloy	Franchot Tone
Barbara Whitfield	Jean Wallace
Charles Riggs	Myron McCormick
Angelo Agostini	Marc Lawrence
Mrs. Hartley	Winifred Lenihan
Caroline Riggs	Betty Harper
Sigmund Kosterich	Hedley Rainnie
District Attorney Walker	Walter Vaughn
Knuckles	George Breen
Tommy Quigley	Robert Gist

Mrs. Borg	Hester Sondergaard
Pet Shop Owner	Luella Gear
Pemberton	Alexander Campbell
Waldron	Robert Noe
Nichols	Alexander Lockwood
Wylie	Ken Smith
Museum Guard	Alan Macateer
Warehouse Guard	Manuel Aparicio
Butler	Brainard Duffield

Unbilled Guest Stars

Woman in Nightclub	Marlene Dietrich
Man in Nightclub	Fletcher Markle
Waiter	Henry Fonda
Loafer	John Garfield
Secretary	Marsha Hunt
Columnist	Leonard Lyons
Bartender	Burgess Meredith

32. *Under My Skin* (1950, 20th Century-Fox). *Directed by* Jean Negulesco. *Produced by* Casey Robinson. *Screenplay by* Casey Robinson. *Based on the story* My Old Man *by* Ernest Hemingway. *Director of Photography:* Joseph La Shelle. *Music by* Daniele Amfitheatrof. *Film Editor:* Dorothy Spencer. *Art Directors:* Lyle Wheeler and Maurice Ransford. *Set Decoration by* Thomas Little and Walter M. Scott. *Costumes by* Charles Le Maire. *Makeup by* Ben Nye. *Special Effects by* Fred Sersen. *Sound Recorders:* George Leverett and Harry M. Leonard. *Orchestrations by* Maurice de Packh and Earle Hagen. *Songs by* Alfred Newman and Jacques Surmagne. *Running time:* 86 minutes.

Cast

Dan Butler	John Garfield
Paule Manet	Micheline Prelle
Louis Bork	Luther Adler
Joe	Orley Lindgren
George Gardner	Noel Drayton
Maurice	A. A. Merola
Rico	Ott George
Max	Paul Bryar
Henriette	Ann Codee
Bartender	Steve Geray
Rigoli	Joseph Warfield
Doctor	Eugene Borden

Nurse	Loulette Sablon
Detective	Alphonse Martell
Hotel Clerk	Ernesto Morelli
Express Man	Jean Del Val
Attendant	Hans Herbert
Flower Woman	Esther Zeitlin
Doorman	Maurice Brierre
Barman	Gordon Clark
Official	Frank Arnold
American Mother	Elizabeth Flournoy
Italian Officer	Mario Siletti
Porter	Guy Zanette
Gendarme	Andre Charise
Drake	Harry Martin
Girl in Cafe	Dusty Anderson Negulesco

33. **Difficult Years (Anni difficili)** (1950, Briguglio Films–Lopert Films). *Directed by* Luigi Zampa. *Produced by* Falco Laudati. *Screenplay by* Sergio Amidei, Vitaliano Brancati, Franco Evangelisti, Enrico Fulchignono. *Based on the novel by* Vitaliano Brancati. *English Narrative by* Arthur Miller. *Director of Photography:* Carlo Montevori. *Music by* Franco Casavola. *Running time:* 90 minutes.

Cast

Aldo Piscitello	Umberto Spadaro
Giovanni	Massimo Girotti
Rosina	Ave Ninchi
Elena	Odette Bedogni
Grandpa	Ernesto Almirante
The Twins	Di Stefano Brothers
Maria	Milly Vitale
The Baron	Enzo Biliotti
The Baron's Son	Carletto Sposito
The Fascist Minister	Loris Gizzi
The Pharmacist	Aldo Silvani
The American	Turi
Narrator	John Garfield

34. **The Breaking Point** (1950, Warner Bros.–First National). *Directed by* Michael Curtiz. *Produced by* Jerry Wald. *Screenplay by* Ranald McDougall. *Based on* To Have and Have Not *by* Ernest Hemingway. *Director of Photography:* Ted McCord. *Film Editor:* Alan Crosland, Jr. *Dialogue Director:* Edward Carrere. *Set Decoration by* George James

Hopkins. *Costumes by* Leah Rhodes. *Sound Recorder:* Leslie G. Hewitt. *Orchestrations by* Ray Heindorf. *Second Unit Director:* David C. Gardner. *Running time:* 97 minutes.

Cast

Harry Morgan	John Garfield
Leona Charles	Patricia Neal
Lucy Morgan	Phyllis Thaxter
Wesley Park	Juano Hernandez
Duncan	Wallace Ford
Rogers	Edmon Ryan
Hannagan	Ralph Dumke
Danny	Guy Thompson
Concho	William Campbell
Amelia Morgan	Sherry Jackson
Connie Morgan	Donna Jo Boyce
Mr. Sing	Victor Sen Yung
Macho	Peter Brocco
Gotch	John Doucette
Charlie	James Griffith
Dock Attendant	Norman Fields
Joseph Park	Juan Hernandez

35. *He Ran All the Way* (1951, Enterprise–United Artists). *Directed by* John Berry. *Produced by* Bob Roberts. *Associate Producer:* Paul Trivers. *Screenplay by* Hugo Butler and Guy Endore. *Based on the novel by* Sam Ross. *Director of Photography:* James Wong Howe. *Music by* Franz Waxman. *Film Editor:* Francis D. Lyon. *Assistant Director:* Emmett Emerson. *Art Director:* Harry Horner. *Running time:* 77 minutes.

Cast

Nick	John Garfield
Peg	Shelley Winters
Mr. Dobbs	Wallace Ford
Mrs. Dobbs	Selena Royle
Mrs. Robey	Gladys George
Al Molin	Norman Lloyd
Tommy Dobbs	Bobby Hyatt
Stan	Clancy Cooper

Appendix 2

Canada Lee Filmography

1. *Lifeboat* (1944, 20th Century–Fox). *Directed by* Alfred Hitchcock. *Produced by* Kenneth MacGowan. *Screenplay by* Jo Swerling. *Based on the story by* John Steinbeck. *Director of Photography:* Glen MacWilliams. *Music by* Hugo Friedhofer. *Music Director:* Emil Newman. *Editor:* Dorothy Spencer. *Art Directors:* James Basevi and Maurice Ransford. *Special Effects by* Fred Sersen. *Running time:* 96 minutes.

Cast

Connie Porter	Tallulah Bankhead
Gus	William Bendix
The German	Walter Slezak
Alice	Mary Anderson
Kovak	John Hodiak
Rittenhouse	Henry Hull
Mrs. Higgins	Heather Angel
Stanley Garrett	Hume Cronyn
Joe	Canada Lee
German Sailor	William Yetter, Jr.
Man in "Before and After" Ad	Alfred Hitchcock

2. ***Body and Soul*** (1947, Enterprise–United Artists). *Directed by* Robert Rossen. *Produced by* Bob Roberts. *Screenplay by* Abraham Polonsky. *Director of Photography:* James Wong Howe. *Music by* Rudolph Polk and Hugo Friedhofer. *Film Editors:* Francis Lyon and Robert Parrish. *Assistant Director:* Robert Aldrich. *Art Directors:* Nathan Juran and Edward J. Boyle. *Costumes by* Marion Herward Keyes. *Song by* Johnny Green, Edward Heyman, Robert Sour, and Frank Eyton. *Running time:* 104 minutes.

Cast

Charley Davis	John Garfield
Peg Born	Lilli Palmer

Alice	Hazel Brooks
Anna Davis	Anne Revere
Quinn	William Conrad
Shorty Polaski	Joseph Pevney
Ben Chaplin	Canada Lee
Roberts	Lloyd Goff (Gough)
David Davis	Art Smith
Arnold	James Burke
Irma	Virginia Gregg
Drummer	Peter Virgo
Prince	Joe Devlin
Grocer	Shimin Rushkin
Miss Tedd	Mary Currier
Dan	Milton Kibbee
Shelton	Tim Ryan
Jack Marlowe	Artie Dorrell
Victor	Cy Ring
Marine	Glen Lee
Referee	John Indrisano
Announcer	Dan Tobey
Doctor	Wheaton Chambers

3. *Lost Boundaries* (1949, De Rochemont Film Classics). *Directed by* Alfred L. Werker. *Produced by* Louis de Rochemont. *Screenplay by* Virginia Shaler, Eugene Ling, Charles A. Palmer, and Furland de Kay. *Based on an Article by* W. L. White. *Director of Photography:* William J. Miller. *Music by* Louis Applebaum. *Music Director:* Jack Shaindlin. *Editor:* David Kummins. *Art Director:* Herbert Andrew. *Music Lyrics by* Albert Johnston, Jr., Carleton Carpenter, and Herbert Taylor. *Running time:* 99 minutes.

Cast

Marcia Carter	Beatrice Pearson
Dr. Scott Carter	Mel Ferrer
Howard Carter	Richard Hylton
Shelley Carter	Susan Douglas
Lt. Thompson	Canada Lee
Rev. John Taylor	Rev. Robert Dunn
Mrs. Mitchell	Grace Coppin
Andy	Carleton Carpenter
Clint Adams	Seth Arnold
Mr. Mitchell	Wendell Holmes
Alvin Tupper	Parker Fennelly

Loren Tucker	Ralph Riggs
Arthur Cooper	William Greaves
Jesse Pridham	Rai Saunders
Janitor	Leigh Whipper
Dr. Walter Brackett	Morton Stevens
Dr. Cashman	Maurice Ellis
Mr. Bigelow	Alexander Campbell
Baggage Man	Edwin Cooper
Detective Staples	Royal Beal
Joan	Peggy Kimber
Dr. Howard	Emory Richardson
Mrs. Taylor	Patricia Quinn O'Hara
Nurse Richmond	Margaret Barker
Lt. Lacey	John Glendinning
George Turner	John Gerstad

Also: Peter Hobbs, Horace Mitchell, William G. Wendell, Lee Nugent, and Nancy Heye.

4. **Cry, the Beloved Country** (1951, LFP Lopert). *Directed by* Zoltan Korda. *Produced by* Alan Paton and Zoltan Korda. *Screenplay by* Alan Paton, *based on his novel. Director of Photography:* Robert Krasker. *Music by* R. Gallois-Montbrun. *Editor:* David Eady. *Music Director:* Dr. Hubert Clifford. *Running time:* 105 minutes.

Cast

Stephen Kumalo	Canada Lee
James Jarvis	Charles Carson
Rev. Maimangu	Sidney Poitier
Margaret Jarvis	Joyce Carey
John Kumalo	Edric Connor
Father Vincent	Geoffrey Keen
Mary	Vivien Clinton
Martens	Michael Goodliffe
Mrs. Kumalo	Albertina Temba
Absalom	Lionel Ngakane
Kumalo's Friend	Charles MacRae
Arthur Jarvis	Henry Blumenthal
Gertrude Kumalo	Ribbon Dhlamini
Matthew Kumalo	Cyril Kwaza
Father Thomas	Max Dhlamini
Father Tisa	Shayiaw Riba
Mrs. Lithebe	Evelyn Nayati
Gertrude's Child	Jsepo Gugusha

Taxi Driver	Reginald Ngcobo
Mrs. Ndela	Emily Pooe
Capt. Jaarsveldt	Bruce Meredith Smith
Farmer Smith	Bruce Anderson
Mary Jarvis	Berdine Grunewald
Harrison, Sr.	Cecil Cartwright
Harrison, Jr.	Andrew Kay
Young Man	Danie Adrewmah
1st Reporter	Clement McCallin
2nd Reporter	Michael Golden
Judge	Stanley Van Beers
Prison Warden	John Arnatt
Police Superintendent	Scott Harrold

Broadway Stage
Appearances of John Garfield

1. *Lost Boy* (a play in three acts by T. C. Upham). *Staged by* James Light. *Settings by* Walter Walden. *Produced by* Burton Harford. At the Mansfield Theatre. Opened on January 5, 1932, ran for 15 performances.

Cast

Joe Hebert	Edgar Barrier
Toivo	Mooney Diamond
Francis Demarco	Elisha Cook, Jr.
Aggie Demarco	Ann Thomas
Mrs. Demarco	Ruth Chorpenning
Mr. Demarco	George Colan
Mr. Gilkey	William Balfour
Gould	Ralph Chambers
Judge Donnelly	George Price
Dr. Stewart	Clyde Franklin
Court Clerk	Peter Robinson
Bill	Jules Garfield
Dick	Charles Berre
Albert	Richard Rosa
Mr. Bullock	Joseph Eggenton
Mrs. Hazelton	Carrie Weiler
Mr. Felch	Samuel Ferguson
Jimmy	Gilbert Squarey
Policeman	Alexander Smith

"Elisha Cook, Jr. gives a really stirring performance as young Francis. . . . Mr. Cook has mastered not only the psychology but the editorial truth of the character. *Lost Boy* is no exploitation of learned morbidity, but a candid statement of how things happen in this busy world" (Brooks Atkinson).

2. *Counsellor-at-Law* (a play in three acts and nine scenes by Elmer Rice). *Settings by* Raymond Sovey. *Staged and Produced by* the author. At the Plymouth Theatre. Opened on November 6, 1931.

Cast

Leslie Green	Constance McKay
Henry Susskind	Lester Salkow
Sarah Becker	Malka Kornstein
A Tall Man	Victor Wolfson
A Stout Man	Jack Collins
A Postman	Ned Glass
Zedorah Chapman	Gladys Feldman
Goldie Rindskopf	Angela Jacobs
Charles McFadden	J. Hammond Dailey
John P. Tedesco	Sam Bonnell
A Bootblack	William Vaughn
Regina Gordon	Anna Kostant
Herbert Howard Weinberg	Marvin Kline
Arthur Sandler	Conway Washburne
Lillian LaRue	Dorothy Dodge
An Errand Boy	Huddy Proctor
Roy Darwin	Jack Leslie
George Simon	Paul Muni
Cora Simon	Louise Prussing
A Woman	Jane Hamilton
Lena Simon	Jennie Moscowitz
Peter J. Malone	T. H. Manning
Johann Breitstein	John M. Qualen
David Simon	Ned Glass
Harry Becker	Martin Wolfson
Richard Dwight, Jr.	David Vivian
Dorothy Dwight	June Cox
Charles Francis Baird	Elmer Brown

"What Mr. Rice lacks as a showman, he supplies as a dramatist of the highest integrity in *Counsellor-at-Law*.... His portrait of George Simon is abundantly sympathetic. In the playing of this part, Mr. Muni is at the top of his form" (Brooks Atkinson).

Note: Garfield appeared in the Chicago production in the role of Henry Susskind, which played Chicago in the spring of 1932. When the play reopened on Broadway in September of 1932, Garfield was in the company as Henry Susskind. He was given featured billing in a cast that included Paul Muni, John Qualen, Martin Wolfson, and others from the original New York cast.

3. *Peace on Earth* (a play in three acts by George Sklar and Albert Maltz). *Staged by* Robert Sinclair and Michael Blankfort. *Settings by* Cleon Throckmorton. *Produced by* the Theatre Union as its initial offering. At the Civic Repertory Theatre. 106 West Fourteenth Street. Opened on November 29, 1933, ran for 126 performances; reopened on March 31, 1934, at the 44th Street Theatre; ran for 18 performances.

Cast

Laurie Owens	Julia Collin
Peter Owens	Robert Keith
Jo Owens	Ethel Latropidi
Walter McCracken	Clyde Franklin
Prof. Frank Anderson	Walter Vonnegut
Mary Bonner	Allace Carroll
Stephen Hamill	John Boruff
Bob Peters	Fred Herrick
Policeman	Jack Williams
Dean Walker	Charles Endale
Fred Miller	Victor Kilian
Primo	John Brown
Lena	Caroline Newcombe
Speed	Elliot Fisher
Mike	David Losan
Ann	Mara Tartar
Rose	Millicent Green
Ryan	Earl Ford
Flynn	Donald A. Black
Krauss	Frank Twodall
Max	John Boruff
Kemmerich	Jack Williams
Fanning	David Korman
Company Guard	Paul Stein
Henry Murdoch	James MacDonald
Dr. Carl Kelsey	John Brown
President Howard	Hallam Bosworth
Miss Ellen Bancroft	Caroline Newcombe
John Andrews	Alvin Dexter
Bishop Parkes	Thomas Coffin Cooke
Marjorie Howard	Allace Carroll
Bill Prentice	Frank Twodall

Note: Garfield was not billed during the initial run of 126 performances, but he did have a small part as a messenger. He was given billing in the revival of 18 performances in his dual role as the messenger and Bob Peters.

4. *Gold Eagle Guy* (a play in three acts by Melvin Levy). *Staged by* Lee Strasberg. *Settings by* Donald Oenslager. *Costumes by* Kay Morrison. *Dances Arranged by* Tamirio. *Produced by* the Group Theatre, in association with D. A. Doran, Jr. At the Morosco Theatre. Opened on November 28, 1934. Ran for 65 performances.

Cast

Macondray	Roman Bohnen
Adan Keane	Walter Coy
Guy Button	J. Edward Bromberg
Will Parrott	Morris Carnovsky
Emperor Norton	Luther Adler
Adah Menken	Stella Adler
Captain Roberts	Lewis Leverett
Ed Walker	Russell Collins
Jessie Sargent	Margaret Barker
Tang Sin	Luther Adler
Josiah	Clifford Odets
Lon Firth	Alexander Kirkland
Guy, Jr. (act 3)	Sanford Meisner
Okajima	Bob Lewis

"The material is engrossing, and Mr. Levy's half-admiring, half-amused point of view is full of relish; and the performance, staged with an imaginative use of acting levels, is one of the most interesting of the season. . . . J. Edward Bromberg's *Gold Eagle Guy* is solid, blunt, and resonant, and enkindled with the gleam of a man who likes what he is doing. As a knavish banker, Morris Carnovsky gives one of those fine-grained performances that keep acting high on the plane of art" (Brooks Atkinson).

Note: Garfield did not receive billing, but he did play dual roles as a sailor and as Mackay, both of which were small.

5. *Waiting for Lefty* (a play in six scenes, by Clifford Odets). *Directed by* Sanford Meisner and Clifford Odets. At the Civic Repertory Theatre. Opened on February 10, 1935.

Cast

Fatt	Morris Carnovsky
Joe	Art Smith
Edna	Ruth Nelson
Miller	Gerrit Kraber
Fayette	Morris Carnovsky
Irv	Walter Coy

Florrie	Phoebe Brand
Sid	Jules Garfield
Clayton	Russell Collins
Clancy	Elia Kazan
Gunman	David Korchmar
Henchman	Alan Baxter
Secretary	Paula Miller
Actor	William Challee
Grady	Morris Carnovsky
Dr. Barnes	Roman Bohnen
Dr. Benjamin	Luther Adler
Agate	J. E. Bromberg
A Man	Bob Lewis
Voices in the Audience	Herbert Ratner, Clifford Odets, Lewis Leverett

"Mr. Odets's saga, based on the New York taxi strike of last year, is clearly one of the most thorough, trenchant jobs in the school of revolutionary drama.... Incidentally, the progress of the revolutionary drama in New York City during the last two seasons is the most obvious recent development in our theatre.... In addition to the Theatre Union, there is the Artef band (Yiddish group).... Now, the Group Theatre gives its most slashing performance in a play about the taxi strike" (Brooks Atkinson).

Note: Waiting for Lefty had been playing weekends since January 5, 1935.

6. *Awake and Sing!* (a play in three acts by Clifford Odets). *Staged by* Harold Clurman. *Setting by* Boris Aronson. *Produced by* the Group Theatre. At the Belasco Theatre. Opened on February 19, 1935. Ran for 185 performances.

Cast

Myron Berger	Art Smith
Bessie Berger	Stella Adler
Jacob	Morris Carnovsky
Hennie Berger	Phoebe Brand
Ralph Berger	Jules Garfield
Schlosser	Roman Bohnen
Moe Axelrod	Luther Adler
Uncle Morty	J. E. Bromberg
Sam Feinschreiber	Sanford Meisner

"Jules Garfield plays the part of the boy with a splendid sense of character development.... As the daughter, Phoebe Brand gives her most attractive performance.... Although Harold Clurman's direction seems to this reviewer to be overwrought and shrill, no one can complain that it is lacking in conviction.... The pleasant news is that the Group Theatre has found a genuine writer among its own members and knows how to set his play to rattling on the boards" (Brooks Atkinson).
Note: Reopened on September 9, 1935, for 24 performances.

7. *Weep for the Virgins* (a play in three acts and seven scenes, by Nellise Child). *Staged by* Cheryl Crawford. *Settings by* Boris Aronson. *Produced by* the Group Theatre as its first offering of 1935-36 season. At the 46th St. Theatre. Opened on November 30, 1935, for nine performances.

Cast

Grandma Jobes	Eunice Stoddard
Homer Jobes	Art Smith
Oscar Sigsmund	J. E. Bromberg
Mr. Walters	Tony Kraber
Mrs. Bean	Margaret Barker
Ruby Jobes	Ruth Nelson
Violet Jobes	Phoebe Brand
Clarice Jobes	Paula Miller
Cecelia Jobes	Evelyn Varden
Mrs. Walters	Hildur Lanmark
Rita Elsbeth	Hilda Reis
Danny Stowe	Alexander Kirkland
Gladys Semp	Mildred Van Dorn
Piano Player	William Nichols
Hap Nichols	Jules Garfield
Peggy	Virginia Stevens
Belle	Marie Hunt
Nancy Kruger	Dorothy Patten
Mrs. Carsons	Margaret Barker
Sailors, waitresses, girls, wedding guests, fish butchers, etc.	Wilhelmina Barton, Mara Alexander, Natalie Harmon, Frances Hayes, Hal James, Robert Johnson, Victor Kraft, Edward Kogan

"Although the production includes an imaginative setting by Boris Aronson and several excellent bits of individual acting, it is difficult to understand what drew the Group Theatre into staging this script.... It is completely lacking in spontaneity ... but many of the individual parts are

extremely well played by actors who know how to create full-length characters—Art Smith, Ruth Nelson, J. E. Bromberg, Alexander Kirkland,
Jules Garfield, and Paula Miller" (Brooks Atkinson).

8. *The Case of Clyde Griffiths* (a dramatization of Theodore Dreiser's
An American Tragedy, by Erwin Placator and Lina Goldschmidt). *Settings
by* Watson Barratt. *Directed by* Lee Strasberg. *Produced by* the Group
Theatre and Milton Shubert. At the Ethel Barrymore Theatre. Opened on
March 13, 1936.

Cast

Speaker	Morris Carnovsky
Clyde Griffiths	Alexander Kirkland
Roberta Alden	Phoebe Brand
Sondra Finchley	Margaret Barker
Titus Alden	Art Smith
Mrs. Alden	Ruth Nelson
Emily Alden	Paula Miller
Samuel Griffiths	Roman Bohnen
Mrs. Samuel Griffiths	Virginia Stevens
Gilbert Griffiths	Walter Coy
Bella Griffiths	Kay Laughlin
Josiah Babe	Gerrit Kraber
Wiggham	Sanford Meisner
Working Men	Elia Kazan, Grover Burgess, William Challee, Jules Garfield, Anthony Ross
Working Girls	Eunice Stoddard, Ruth Nelson, Dorothy Patten, Paula Miller, Virginia Stevens, Helen Walpole, Kay Laughlin, Illah Lange
Orrin Short	Bob Lewis
Party Guests	Whitney Bourne, Beatrice Cole, Paul Morrison, Wendell Phillips, Jerome Thor
Doctor	Luther Adler
District Attorney	Lewis Leverett
Mrs. Asa Griffiths	Dorothy Patten

"*Case of Clyde Griffiths* sounds pretty silly when it is rattling the
skeleton of Karl Marx and accusing the audience of high treason and con-
spiracy. Between the story the play tells and the teaching shouted by the
Speaker there is a gap through which the validity of the drama escapes. . . .
The Speaker is Morris Carnovsky, who is the Group's finest actor" (Brooks
Atkinson).

9. *Johnny Johnson* (a "legend" in three acts and thirteen scenes by Paul Green with music by Kurt Weill). *Staged by* Lee Strasberg. *Settings by* Donald Oenslager. *Costumes by* Paul DuPont. At the Forty-Fourth Street Theatre. Opened on November 19, 1936. Ran for 68 performances.

Cast

The Mayor	Bob Lewis
Minny Belle Tompkins	Phoebe Brand
Grandpa Joe	Roman Bohnen
Johnny Johnson	Russell Collins
Anguish Howington	Grover Burgess
Captain Valentine	Sanford Meisner
Dr. McBray	Lee J. Cobb
Sergeant Jackson	Art Smith
Corporal George	Albert Van Dekker
Private Harwood	Tony Kraber
Private Kearns	Elia Kazan
A West Point Lieutenant	Joseph Pevney
An English Sergeant	Luther Adler
Johann Lang	Jules Garfield
A French Nurse	Paula Miller
A Doctor	Art Smith
A Sister	Ruth Nelson
Chief of the Allied Command	Morris Carnovsky

"It is the Group's most ambitious production. . . . Under Lee Strasberg's direction they have done an extraordinary job of dramatic expression. . . . As Johnny Johnson, Russell Collins gives a frank and manly portrait. . . . Morris Carnovsky gets hold of the part, all the comic nuances of the script reach the audience. . . . The Group Theatre has sponsored the first departure from polite mediocrity of the season" (Brooks Atkinson).

10. *Having Wonderful Time* (a comedy in three acts and nine scenes, by Arthur Kober). *Scenery by* Stewart Chaney. *Staged and Produced by* Marc Connelly. At the Lyceum Theatre. Opened on February 20, 1937. Ran for 132 performances.

Cast

Mac Finkle	B. D. Kranz
Gussie	Mona Conrad
Rosalind	Ann Thomas
Reba	Irene Winston
Tiny	Irving Israel

Maxine	Henrietta Kaye
Lois	Connie Lent
Sammy	Tony Kraber
Mrs. G.	Ann Brody
Hi	Mitchell Grayson
Sophie	Kay Loring
Itchy Flexner	Philip Van Zandt
Abe Tobias	Wolfe Barsell
Shmutz	Solen Burry
Barney	Edward Mann
Birdie	Helen Golden
Doc	Cornel Wilde
Eli	Shimin Rushkin
The Voice of Care-Free	William Swetland
Miriam Robbins	Muriel Campbell
Chick Kessler	Jules Garfield
Fay Fromkin	Janet Fox
Mr. G.	Hudey Block
Teddy Stern	Katherine Locke
Henrietta Brill	Louise Reichard
Charlie	Herbert Ratner
Joe	William Swetland
The Honeymooners	Herbert Vigran, Sandra Gould
Pinkie Aaronson	Sheldon Leonard
Kitty	Lily Winton
Sam Rappoport	Frank Gould

"Katherine Locke gives an extraordinarily beguiling portrait of a timid and inarticulate girl who is seething internally and behaving as though she were wordly wise. Jules Garfield has the sort of perceptions that make an admirable character of Chick Kessler, and he also knows how to convey them in the theatre.... Perfectly cast and sensitively acted under Marc Connelly's direction, *Having Wonderful Time* is not only amusing but tender, and a credit to the prevailing mood of good-will in the theatre" (Brooks Atkinson).

11. ***Golden Boy*** (a play in three acts and twelve scenes, by Clifford Odets). *Staged by* Harold Clurman. *Scenery by* Mordecai Gorelik. *Produced by* the Group Theatre. At the Belasco Theatre. Opened on November 4, 1937. Ran for 250 performances.

Cast

Tom Moody	Roman Bohnen
Lorna Moon	Frances Farmer

Joe Bonaparte	Luther Adler
Tokio	Art Smith
Mr. Carp	Lee J. Cobb
Siggie	Jules Garfield
Mr. Bonaparte	Morris Carnovsky
Anna	Phoebe Brand
Frank Bonaparte	John O'Malley
Roxy Gottlieb	Bob Lewis
Eddie Fuselli	Elia Kazan
Pepper White	Harry Bratsburg
Mickey	Michael Gordon
Call Boy	Bert Conway
Sam	Martin Ritt
Lewis	Howard Da Silva
Drake	Charles Crisp
Driscoll	Charles Niemeyer
Barker	Karl Malden

"Although Clifford Odets's *Golden Boy* has been a long time in the making, it is worth waiting for. As produced by the reunited Group Theatre, it is a hard-fisted piece of work about a prizefighter whose personal ambition turns into hatred of the world.... After writing all around it in the first act, Mr. Odets writes his way through the heart of it with the strength and gusto of a genuine artisan of the theatre" (Brooks Atkinson).

"*Golden Boy* offered some of the best character acting that I saw in New York, notably by Jules Garfield and Morris Carnovsky, as well as by Luther Adler in Harold Clurman's brilliant direction of a brilliant first act" (Ivor Brown—*London Observer*).

12. ***Heavenly Express*** (a fantasy in three acts by Albert Bein). *Staged by* Robert Lewis. *Settings and Costumes by* Boris Aronson. *Music Composed and Arranged by* Lehman Engel. *Produced by* Kermit Bloomgarden. At the National Theatre. Opened on April 18, 1940. Ran for 20 performances.

Cast

Tommy	Phil Brown
Stumpy	William Sands
Methuselah Mike	Art Smith
A Young Tramp	John Garfield
The Melancholy Bo	Curt Conway
"Bullhead" Anderson	Harry Bratsburg
Ed Peeto	Harry Carey
Dan	Randolph Wade

Shorty Bucker	Will Lee
Rocky Mountain Red	Phillip Loeb
Fred Norman	Russell Collins
Night Telegraph Operator	James O'Rear
Julio	Nicholas Conte
Betsy Graham	Aline MacMahon
Pat Borlie	Burl Ives
Andy Cameron	John O'Malley
Steve Corrigan	Jack Lambert
Scotty Thompson	Charles Thompson

"To say that *Heavenly Express* is too long, too sprawling, and underdeveloped in detail would doubtless be a sage observation, worthy the dignity of criticism. But matters of that sort are of academic interest only. For the important thing is that the characters are independent, original, earthy, and mad. For once, the theatre is truly imaginative. . . . As the Overland Kid, John Garfield gives an attractive, wholesome performance of a difficult role suspended halfway between realism and the supernatural. . . . Aline MacMahon is an actress by reason of her training, but she is also an artist by virtue of her perceptions. . . . The heroic part of the engineer is honestly, if too modestly played by Harry Carey" (Brooks Atkinson).

13. *Skipper Next to God* (a play in three acts by Jan De Hartog). *Staged by* Lee Strasberg. *Setting by* Boris Aronson. *Production Supervised by* Cheryl Crawford. *Presented by* the Experimental Theatre under the sponsorship of the American National Theatre and Academy. At Maxine Elliott's Theatre. Opened on January 4, 1948, ran for four performances. Reopened at the Playhouse Theatre on January 29, 1948. Ran for 93 performances.

Cast

Richters	Joseph Anthony
Henky	Robert White
Willemse	Si Oakland
Officer of South American Military Police	Carmen Costl
Meyer	John Becher
Joris Kuiper	John Garfield
South American Consul	Wallace Acton
Rabbi	Wolfe Barzell
First Jew	Michael Lewin
Second Jew	Peter Kass
Chief Davelaar	John Shellie

Bruinama	Jabez Gray
American Naval Officer	Richard Coogan
Dutch Naval Officer	Eugene Stuckmann
The Clergyman	Harry Irvine
Passengers	Florence Aquiso, Joe Bernard, Nola Chilton, Allan Frank, Frances Gaar, Ruth K. Hill, Bill Lazarus, John Marley, Edwin Ross, Paul Wilson

"Whatever its merits may be, Jan De Hartog's *Skipper Next to God* deserves to be produced. With the quixotic assistance of John Garfield, the Experimental Theatre produced it ... and did itself considerable honor.... Under Lee Strasberg's direction, the performance is thoroughly professional and above the usual standards of Experimental Theatre work.

"Mr. Garfield is an uncommonly enlightened actor who can appreciate the ethics of a part like the skipper who is trying to interpret God. He is well supported. There are excellent characterizations in all the parts.... *Skipper* lies somewhere on this side of perfection. But it is engrossing, high-minded, and intelligent, and worth the pains the Experimental Theatre has taken with it" (Brooks Atkinson).

14. **The Big Knife** (a play by Clifford Odets). *Staged by* Lee Strasberg. *Scenery by* Howard Bay. *Costumes by* Lucille Little. *Produced by* Dwight Deere Wiman. At the National Theatre. Opened on February 24, 1949. Ran for 108 performances.

Cast

Russell	Frank Wilson
Buddy Bliss	William Terry
Charlie Castle	John Garfield
Patty Benedict	Leona Powers
Marion Castle	Nancy Kelly
Nat Danzler	Reinhold Schunzel
Marcus Hoff	J. Edward Bromberg
Smiley Coy	Paul McGrath
Connie Bliss	Mary Patton
Hank Teagle	Theodore Newton
Dixie Evans	Joan McCracken
Frary	John McKee

"*The Big Knife* has the advantage of a sentient and pliant performance, directed by Lee Strasberg, and some excellent acting by a skillfully chosen cast. John Garfield and J. Edward Bromberg, both graduates of the Group Theatre, are uncommonly well matched — the warmth and moodiness of the star opposed to the heat and pompousness of the producer. That is the sort of balance Mr. Odets frequently achieves in the writing.

"As the troubled star, Mr. Garfield gives an interestingly moody performance that can be tremendously powerful at the crucial moment.... *The Big Knife* is an overwrought and meandering play.... There is a lot of distinguished art and craftsmanship in the play.... In its characters and episodes, it is a cheering reminder of Mr. Odets's uncommon theatre talents. But as Emerson remarked on looking at the stars, 'Why so hot, little man?' Under the stress of fiery emotions, Mr. Odets has overreached himself" (Brooks Atkinson).

15. *Peer Gynt* (a play in two acts and twelve scenes by Henrik Ibsen, in an American version by Paul Green, with musical score and direction by Lan Adomian). *Staged by* Lee Strasberg. *Choreography by* Valerie Bettis. *Setting and Lighting by* Donald Oenslager. *Costumes by* Rose Bogdanoff. *Near East Music by* Hillel and Aviva. *Music Conducted by* Eugene Keesmiak. *Revived by* Cheryl Crawford, in association with R. L. Stevens, under the sponsorship of the American National Theatre and Academy at the ANTA Playhouse. Opened on January 28, 1951. Ran for 32 performances.

Cast

Aase	Mildred Dunnock
Peer Gynt	John Garfield
An Elderly Man	Ray Gordon
An Elderly Woman	Ann Boley
Asiak	John Randolph
Solveig	Pearl Lang
Her Father	Joseph Anthony
Her Mother	Anne Hegira
A Buttonmolder	Karl Malden
Ingrid	Rebecca Darke
Her Father	Nehemiah Persoff
Her Mother	Peggy Meredith
Mada Moen	Mahlon Naili
His Father	Edward Binns
His Mother	Lisa Baker
The Master Cook	Ray Gordon
1st Herd Girl	Lucille Patton
2nd Herd Girl	Barbara Gaye
3rd Herd Girl	Beverlee Bozeman
A Greenclad Woman	Sherry Britton

The Troll King	Nehemiah Persoff
The Ugly Brat	Ed Horner
The Voice	John Randolph
The Flutist	Hillel
A Thief	Ray Gordon
A Healer	Ed Horner
A Singer	Aviva
Anitra	Sono Osato
Dr. Begriffenfeldt	Joseph Anthony
Hussein	Richard Purdy

"Give everybody all proper credit for trying to bring *Peer Gynt* to life at the ANTA Playhouse. For Ibsen's poetic classic is the sort of drama ANTA may well take out of the textbooks in its current series. And among those who have worked at the enterprise valiantly are John Garfield in the title role, Paul Green who made the American version, Donald Oenslager who has brilliantly designed the production, and Lee Strasberg who has staged the performance.... But, alas, the theatre is a cruel public medium. There is no reward in it for hard work if the product is nebulous or desultory" (Brooks Atkinson).

16. *Golden Boy* (a play in three acts and twelve scenes, by Clifford Odets). *Staged by* the author; *Revived by* the American National Theatre and Academy play series. *Managing Director:* Robert Whitehead. *Scenery, Lighting, and Costumes by* Paul Morrison. At the ANTA Playhouse. Opened on March 12, 1952. Ran for 55 performances.

Cast

Tom Moody	Art Smith
Lorna Moon	Bette Grayson
Joe Bonaparte	John Garfield
Tokio	William Hansen
Mr. Carp	Martin Greene
Siggie	Michael Lewin
Mr. Bonaparte	Lee J. Cobb
Anna	Peggy Meredith
Frank Bonaparte	Jack Klugman
Roxy Gottlieb	Rudy Bond
Eddie Fuselli	Joseph Wiseman
Pepper White	Arthur O'Connell
Mickey	Jack Warden
Call Boy	Sidney Kay
Sam	Gerald S. O'Loughlin
Lewis	Norman Brooks

Drake	Joe Bernard
Driscoll	Bert Conway
Barker	Tony Kraber

"*Golden Boy* is just as penetrating as it ever was. Perhaps the performance is even more overwhelming. For Mr. Odets has directed the revival of his own play, . . . and the acting is superb. Most of the players are old Group Theatre graduates, working again at one of their most memorable triumphs. For them, as well as for the public, the revival is worth-while. Mr. Odets never has said anything more pertinent, and the Group actors have never worked at anything more valid or decisive.

"Under Mr. Odets's direction the performance has coherence, solidity, and pace; and it brought the best out of the actors. Lee Cobb's kindly, sorrowing, courageous father; John Garfield's bombastic, nervous, callous prizefighter; Art Smith's shallow but human manager. . . . Although the writing is spare in the last act, the theatrical mood is devastating. No one is likely to forget the final scene. . . . Those stormy years of the old Group Theatre were not wasted; they have brought us one of the vital plays of this season" (Brooks Atkinson).

Appendix 4

New York Stage
Appearances of Canada Lee

1. *Stevedore* (a play by Paul Peters and George Sklar). *Staged by* Michael Blankfort. *Produced by* the Theatre Union. At the Civic Repertory Theatre in Fourteenth Street. Opened on October 1, 1934.

Cast

Jack Carter, Abbie Mitchell, Canada Lee, Thomas Coffin Cooke, Martin Wolfson, and Hilda Reis (subbing for the ill Millicent Green).

"The turbulent and exciting stuff of *Stevedore* returned last night with the reopening of Paul Peters's and George Sklar's fighting study in black and white. . . . Those who missed last April's liveliest theatrical bomb may make up for their negligence. . . . Its stormy and tearing rhythms are here again to be recaptured.

"A largely Negro cast, headed again by Jack Carter, paces swiftly through ten scenes which tell in terms of elemental struggle the war of black and white in almost any Southern seaport" (Brooks Atkinson).

Canada Lee replaced Rex Ingram who had appeared in the original April 1934 run.

2. *Sailor, Beware!* (a comedy in two acts and eight scenes, by Kenyon Nicholson and Charles Knox Robinson). *Staged by* Shepard Traube. *Revived by* the Harlem Players. *Presented by* Mr. Traube and Mack Hilliard. At the Lafayette Theatre, 131st Street and Seventh Avenue. Opened on May 6, 1935.

Cast

Mattie Matthews	Carrington Lewis
Flip Edwards	Paul N. Johnson
Spud Newton	Milton Williams
Barney Waters	James Dunmore

Pee Wee Moore	Henry Davis
Herb Marley	Canada Lee
Chester "Dynamite" Jones	Juano Hernandez
Lieut. Loomis, U.S.N.	Tom Moseley
Texas Patton	Reginald Fenderson
Ruby Keefer	Lulu King
Bernice Dooley	Dorothy Sinclair
Hazel De Fay	Florence Lee
Dode Bronson	Juanita Hall
Humpty Singer	Hayes Pryor
Louie	Frank Ross
Billie "Stonewall" Jackson	Christola Williams
Senor Gomez	Ken Renard
Jake Edwards	Frank Wilson

"Sailor, Beware! suits the Harlem Players. They selected the late comedy by Kenyon Nicholson and Charles Robinson for the opening bill at the Lafayette Theatre . . . and everyone who was present understood it completely.

"When white actors were playing it on Broadway last season, this marine 'variation of a familiar theme' seemed brisk enough to be thoroughly clear. . . . Harlem can absorb that sort of tomfoolery without self-consciousness. . . . In the tough Bruce MacFarlane part, Juano Hernandez is a handsome, strutting rooster. In the part that Audrey Christie played, Christola Williams is coy and languid" (Brooks Atkinson).

3. *Macbeth* (Shakespeare's play in three acts and eight scenes, arranged and staged by Orson Welles). *Costumes and Settings by* Nat Karson. *Lighting by* A. H. Feder. *Managing Producer:* John Houseman. *Produced by* the Negro Division of the Federal Theatre Project. At the Lafayette Theatre. Opened on April 14, 1936.

Cast

Duncan	Service Bell
Malcolm	Wardell Saunders
Macduff	Maurice Ellis
Banquo	Canada Lee
Macbeth	Jack Carter
Ross	Frank David
Lennox	Thomas Anderson
Siward	Archie Savage
First Murderer	George Nixon
Second Murderer	Kenneth Renwick

The Doctor	Lawrence Chenault
The Priest	Al Watts
First Messenger	Philandre Thomas
Second Messenger	J. B. Johnson
The Porter	J. Lewis Johnson
Seyton	Larri Lauria
A Lord	Charles Collins
First Captain	Lisle Grenidge
Second Captain	Gabriel Brown
First Chamberlain	Halle Howard
Second Chamberlain	William Cumberbatch
First Court Attendant	Albert McCoy
Second Court Attendant	George Thomas
First Page Boy	Viola Dean
Second Page Boy	Hilda French
Lady Macduff	Marie Young
Lady Macbeth	Edna Thomas
The Duchess	Alma Dickson
The Nurse	Virginia Girvin
Young Macduff	Bertram Holmes
Daughter to Macduff	Wanda Macy
Fleance	Carl Crawford
Hecate	Eric Burroughs
First Witch	Wilhelmina Williams
Second Witch	Josephine Williams
Third Witch	Zola King
Witch Doctor	Abdul

"Since the program announces *Macbeth* by William Shakespeare, it is fair to point out that the tragedy is written in verse and that it reveals the disintegration of a superior man who is infected with ambition. There is very little if any of that in the current Harlem festival" (Brooks Atkinson).

4. *One-Act Plays of the Sea* (a revival of four short plays by Eugene O'Neill). *Directed by* William Challee. *Scenery and Costumes by* Perry Watkins. *Produced by* the Federal Theatre Project at the Lafayette Theatre. Opened on October 29, 1937.

Cast — *Moon of the Caribbees*

Yank	Canada Lee
Jack	Joseph Pope Jones
Lamps	Oliver Foster
Chips	Walter Duke

Old Tom	Service Bell
Bella	Jacqueline Martin
Pearl	Rose Poindexter
First Mate	Edward Fleischer

In the Zone

Canada Lee did not appear in this play.

Cast — *Bound East for Cardiff*

Yank	Canada Lee
Driscoll	Lionel Monagas
Cocky	William Cumberbatch
Davis	Joseph Slocum
Scotty	Paul Johnson
Smitty	Wardell Saunders
The Captain	Thurman Jackson
First Mate	Edward Fleischer

The Long Voyage Home

Canada Lee did not appear in this play.

"The first play in the series, *The Moon of the Caribbees*, is loosely put together, and the Harlem actors, playing about three times too fast, cannot capture the languidly poetic spirit of this casual sketch of crew manners.... *Bound East for Cardiff* is at least intelligible.... They are fine plays, simple, vigorous, and warm-hearted, and they deserve a much more sensitive performance than the Negro actors have put together" (Brooks Atkinson).

5. *Brown Sugar* (a melodrama in three acts and seven scenes by Mrs. Bernie Angus). *Settings by* Cirker & Robbins. *Songs by* Haven Johnson. *Staged and Produced by* George Abbott. At the Biltmore Theatre. Opened on December 2, 1937.

Cast

Bartender	Richard Huey
Tom Warfield	T. Burton Smith
Trot	John T. L. Bunn
Lonny	Martin de C. Slade
Charlie	Ira Johnson
Ruby	Kathryn Lavall
Slim	Alvin Childress

Sam	Juano Hernandez
Rosalinda	Christola Williams
Sylvester	Richard McMyers
Tar	Paul Johnson
Musken	Eric Burroughs
Louella	Beulah E. Edmonds
Sarah	Ruby Elzy
Jeb	Bertram Holmes
Officer Leroy	Julian Miles
Man	Jimmy Waters
Rosco	Haven Johnson
Henry	Canada Lee
Lily May	Georgette Harvey
Butterfly	Butterfly McQueen
Walter	William Tinney
George	Allen Tinney
Stella	Beth Dixon
Cleo	Irene Hill
Pete Malley	John Shellie
First Mate	Ernest Rowan
Officer Kent	George W. Smith
O'Hara	George Fitzpatrick
McQuade	Fred Wallace

"Being a prudent fellow, George Abbott has not thrown the office safe into his production of Bernie Angus's *Brown Sugar*.... Mrs. Angus has written it with a studied avoidance of originality.... (Mr. Abbott's) production of *Brown Sugar* is as heavy-footed and loose-jointed as some of the WPA theatre routine activities in Harlem.... But credit him with appreciating the extraordinary artistry of a high-stepping little dusky creature with a piping voice who describes herself as Butterfly McQueen.... Butterfly has something on the ball" (Brooks Atkinson).

6. *Haiti* (a play in three acts by William Du Bois). *Staged by* Maurice Clark. *Scenery by* Perry Watkins. *Incidental Score by* Leonard de Paur. *Costumes Designed by* James Cochran. *Lighted by* Byron Webb. *Produced by* the Federal Theatre Project. At the Lafayette Theatre, 131st Street and Seventh Ave. Opened on March 2, 1938.

Cast

Toussaint L'Ouverture	Louis Sharp
Christophe	Rex Ingram
Jacques	Alvin Childress
Bertram	Canada Lee

Andre	Louis Smith
Guy	Frederic Gibson
Daughter	Zola King
Mother	Mary Barnes
First Woman	Jacqueline Ghant Martin
Old Man	J. Louis Johnson
Second Woman	Susie Sutton
Third Woman	Lulu King
Josef	Richard McCracken
Boule	Emile Hirsch
Duval	David Eaton
Phillipe	Alfred Allegro
Roche	Louis Polan
Boucher	William Sharon
Armand	William Greene
Jean	Byron Lane
LeClerc	Bernard Pate
Odette	Elena Karam
Pauline	Catherine Lawrence
Aimee	Lena Halsey
First Servant	Benny Tatnall
Second Servant	James Wright

"Any one in quest of excitement is respectfully directed to the Lafayette Theatre in Harlem, where William Du Bois's *Haiti* opened with a rumble of battle last evening.... Nothing so good has exploded in the midst of Harlem since the racy nights of *Macbeth*.

"Mr. Ingram has been a good actor for a long time. It is not very often that he finds a heroic part like that of Christophe.... Mr. Ingram gives a rattling good performance" (Brooks Atkinson).

7. *Mamba's Daughters* (a play in two acts and nine scenes by Dorothy and Du Bose Heyward). From the latter's novel of the same name. *Settings by* Perry Watkins (Assistant to Mr. Watkins: Rita Hassan). *Song "Lonesome Walls" Composed by* Jerome Kern *from the Lyrics by* Mr. Heyward. *Staged and Produced by* Guthrie McClintic. At the Empire Theatre. Opened on January 3, 1939.

Cast

Mamba	Georgette Harvey
Gardenia	Anne Brown
Tony	Jimmy Wright
Tessie	Dorothy Paul
Slim	Reginald Beane

Policeman	Bob Coogan
Another Policeman	John Rustad
Clerk of the Court	John Cornell
Prosecuting Attorney	Oliver Barbour
St. Julien de C. Wentworth	Jose Ferrer
The Judge	Harry Mastayer
Hagar	Ethel Waters
Davey	Al Stokes
Ned	Hayes Pryor
Mingo	Louis Sharp
Drayton	Canada Lee
Maum Vina	Ethel Purnello
Eva	Georgia Burke
Willie May	Helen Dowdy
Rev. Quintus Whaley	J. Rosamond Johnson
Gilly Bluton	Willie Bryant
Dolly	Alberta Hunter
Lissa (as child)	Joyce Miller
Martha (Eva's daughter)	Rena Mitchell
Lissa	Fredi Washington

"As the Heywards have retold the story for the theatre, *Mamba's Daughters* is a melodrama about elements of Negro life in South Carolina.... Although a good part of it is boldly and powerfully dramatic, it still has the shiftless style of a play at second-hand; and although Miss Waters plays with gleaming wholesomeness, she does not go very deep inside her part.... Fredi Washington beautifully plays the part of Hagar's talented daughter" (Brooks Atkinson).

8. *Mamba's Daughters.* At the Broadway Theatre. Opened on March 23, 1940.

Cast

Mamba	Georgia Burke
Policeman	Vincent Copeland
Clerk of the Court	John Kerr
Prosecuting Attorney	John O'Connor
St. Julien de C. Wentworth	Robert Thomsen
Judge	Barry Kelley
Hagar	Ethel Waters
Davey	Al Stokes
Ned	Wilson Bradley
Mingo	Louis Sharp
Drayton	Canada Lee

Maum Vina	Ethel Purnello
Eva	Edna Waters
Willie May	Laura Vaughns
Reverend Quintus Whaley	J. Rosamond Johnson
Gilly Bluton	Willie Bryant
Dolly	Alberta Hunter
Lissa (as child)	Charlotte-Ann Jack
Martha	Rena Mitchell
Gardenia	Maude Russell
Tony	Jimmy Wright
Lissa	Fredi Washington

"Although the intervening months have not taken the curse of fustian melodrama from the Dorothy and Du Bose Heyward saga of heroic, dim-witted Hagar, the production as a whole is more smoothly integrated and Miss Waters in the central role has a simple and eloquent grandeur" (Theodore Strauss).

9. **Big White Fog** (a play by Theodore Ward). *Staged by* Powell Lindsay. *Scenery and Lighting by* Perry Watkins. *Produced by* the Negro Playwrights Company. At the Lincoln Theatre, 135th Street and Lenox Avenue. Opened on October 22, 1940.

Cast

Ella Mason	Hilda Offley
Juanita Rogers	Maude Russell
Caroline Mason	Eileen Renard
Phillip Mason	Bertram Holmes
Mrs. Brooks	Louise Jackson
Lester Mason	Kelsey Pharr
Wanda Mason	Alma Forrest
Victor Mason	Canada Lee
Percy Mason	Roburte Dorce
Claudine Adams	Muriel Cook
Dan Rogers	Edward Fraction
Count Strawder	P. J. Sidney
Count Cotton	Andrew Walker
Brother Harper	Robert Creighton
Sister Gabrella	Trixie Smith
Bertha Reubel	Almeina Green
Nathan Piszer	Jerry Grebanier
Marx	Stanley Prager
Caroline	Valerie Black
Phillip	Carl Crawford

Bailiff	Stanley Prager
Police Sergeant	Lionel Monagas
Police Lieutenant	Ted Thurston

"As a drama of social significance Mr. Ward's play has the usual elements of the breed—monotony of tone and the regulation Communist finish. But within those boundaries *Big White Fog* is the best serious play of Negro authorship about race problems that this courier has happened to see.

"Canada Lee gives an excellent performance in the leading part. . . . Although this column cannot recommend *Big White Fog* as electric and fully resolved social drama, the Negro Playwrights Company has more ability than any other serious group that has tried to become established in Harlem" (Brooks Atkinson).

10. *Native Son* (a play in ten scenes without an intermission, dramatized by Paul Green and Richard Wright and derived from the latter's book of the same name). *Staged by* Orson Welles. *Settings by* James Morcom. *Production Supervised by* Jean Rosenthal. *Presented by* Mr. Welles and John Houseman, in association with Bern Bernard. At the St. James Theatre. Opened on March 24, 1941.

Cast

Bigger Thomas	Canada Lee
Hannah Thomas	Evelyn Ellis
Vera Thomas	Helen Martin
Buddy Thomas	Lloyd Warren
A Neighbor	Jacqueline Ghant Andre
Miss Emmett	Eileen Burns
Jack	J. Flashe Riley
Clara	Rena Mitchell
G. H. Rankin	Rodester Timmons
Gus Mitchell	Wardell Saunders
Ernie Jones	C. M. Bootsie Davis
Mr. Dalton	Erskine Sanford
Mrs. Dalton	Nell Harrison
Britten	Everett Sloane
Peggy	Frances Bavier
Mary Dalton	Anne Burr
Jan Erlone	Joseph Pevney
Buckley	Philip Bourneuf
Paul Max	Ray Collins
A Reporter	Paul Stewart
Judge	William Malone

Newspaper Men   John Berry, Stephen Roberts,
George Zorn, Don Roberts

"Out of Richard Wright's novel *Native Son,* Mr. Wright and Paul Green have written a powerful drama. Orson Welles has staged it with imagination and force. Those are the first things to be said about the overwhelming play . . . the biggest American drama of the season. . . . Mr. Welles picks up the bravura style of the Mercury Theatre where he left it two or three seasons ago. . . . In Canada Lee, the authors and producers have an actor for whom they should be devoutly thankful. . . . Mr. Lee catches the whole sequence of emotions from sullenness to fear to rebellion to relaxed acceptance of death; and he tosses in a personal quality of supple strength for good measure" (Brooks Atkinson).

11. *The Saroyan Theatre* (comprising two short plays, *Across the Board on Tomorrow Morning* and *Talking to You*). *Written, Directed and Produced by* William Saroyan. *Scenery by* Cleon Throckmorton. At the Belasco Theatre. Opened on August 17, 1942.

Cast — *Across the Board on Tomorrow Morning*

Harpist	Lois Bannerman
Thomas Piper	Canada Lee
Jim	Bill Challee
John Callaghan	Edward F. Nannary
Harry Mallory	Irving Morrow
Helen	Jane Jeffreys
Peggy	June Hayford
Lois	Carol Marcus
P. J. Pinkerton	Arthur Griffin
Pablo	C. Gilbert Advincula
Pancho	Sam Sotelo
Sammy	Larry Bolton
Rhinelander 2-8182	Lillian McGuinness
Fritz	Lewis Charles
A Poet	Maxwell Bodenheim*
Callaghan Mallory	William Prince

Reciting his own poem "Jazz Music."

Cast — *Talking to You*

The Dream Dancer	Lois Bannerman
The Crow	Peter Beauvais
The Tiger	Irving Morrow

Blackstone Boulevard	Canada Lee
The Deaf Boy	Jules Leni
Fancy Man	Lewis Charles
Maggie	Lillian McGuinness
The Midget	Andrew Ratoushoff

"*Across the Board on Tomorrow Morning* is a comic, spontaneous stage gambol that Mr. Saroyan has neglected to bring to life in the theatre. . . . With the exception of Lewis Charles as the wise-guy taxi driver, the performance is static and literal minded. . . . Canada Lee is honest and forceful . . . but with all respect to Mr. Lee's ability and sincerity, the serious point of view catches the play at its weakest point. . . . In *Talking to You*, Mr. Lee's personal magnetism and his forthright style of acting are of great value. . . . His scenes with the little deaf boy are extraordinarily true and disarming" (Brooks Atkinson).

12. *Native Son* (a revival of the Paul Green and Richard Wright dramatization of Mr. Wright's novel). *Staged by* Orson Welles. *Scenery by* James Morcom. *Presented by* Louis and George M. Brandt. At the Majestic Theatre. Opened on October 23, 1942.

Cast

Buckley, D.A.	Alexander Clark
Bigger Thomas	Canada Lee
Hannah Thomas	Evelyn Ellis
Vera Thomas	Helen Martin
Buddy Thomas	Rudolph Whitaker
Miss Emmett	Eileen Burns
Jack	Thomas Anderson
Clara	Rena Mitchell
G. H. Rankin	Rodester Timmons
Gus Mitchell	Wardell Saunders
Ernie Jones	C. M. Bootsie Davis
Mr. Dalton	Graham Velsey
Mrs. Dalton	Nell Harrison
Britten	Ralph Bell
Peggy	Frances Bavier
Mary Dalton	Anne Burr
Jan Erlone	Herbert Ratner
A Reporter	John Ireland
Judge	William Malone
Paul Max	John Berry

"Although Canada Lee gave a memorable performance when *Native Son* opened in March of last year, he is giving a triumphant performance in the revival. He has pulled the part taut and made it vibrant. He has grown in stature as an actor. . . . He is a superbly imaginative player. When he is on the stage he inhabits it. . . . Mr. Lee is certainly the best Negro actor of his time, as well as one of the best actors in this country. His head-long portrait of Bigger Thomas is the most vital piece of acting on the current stage" (Brooks Atkinson).

13. *South Pacific* (a play in three acts by Howard Rigsby and Dorothy Heyward, with incidental music by Paul Bowles). *Staged by* Lee Strasberg. *Setting by* Boris Aronson. *Production Supervised by* W. Horace Schmidlapp. *Presented by* David Lowe. At the Cort Theatre. Opened on December 29, 1943.

Cast

Sam Johnson	Canada Lee
Captain Dunlap	Wendell K. Phillips
Ruth	Wini Johnson
Daniel	Rudolph Whitaker
Limsol	Dan Johnson
Dr. John	Louis Sharp
The Littlest	Frank Wilson
Natives	Gordon Heath, Kate Deel, George Fisher, Ruby Dee
Native Children	Ledia Rosa, Gloria Robinson, Emanuel Gillard, James Reason, Clyde Goines

"Without question, *South Pacific* has many good qualities. . . . But judged strictly as an evening in the theatre, it does not entirely live up to the intentions. . . . In the plot lies most of the trouble. . . . It is garden-variety.

"In the leading role, Canada Lee gives a performance which always holds the interest. He does not play it as well as he did the tortured figure of *Native Son,* but the part is more loosely put together. Wini Johnson as the girl is beautiful, but her role often is a distraction from what should be the main part of the play. . . . A young boy, Rudolph Whitaker, obviously will grow up to displace both Mr. Lee and Paul Robeson as leading actors of the Negro race. *South Pacific* deserves credit for taking up a real theme; the regret is that it did not finish the job more successfully" (Lewis Nichols).

14. *Anna Lucasta* (a play in three acts by Philip Yordan). *Staged by* Harry Wagstaff Gribble. *Assisted by* Walter Thompson Ash. *Scenery by* Frederick Fox. *Costumes by* Paul DuPont. *Produced by* John Wildberg. At the Mansfield Theatre. Opened on August 30, 1944.

Cast

Katie	Theodora Smith
Stella	Rosette LeNoire
Theresa	Georgia Burke
Stanley	John Proctor
Frank	Frederick O'Neal
Joe	George Randol
Eddie	Hubert Henry
Noah	Alvin Childress
Blanche	Alice Childress
Officer	Emory Richardson
Anna	Hilda Simms
Danny	Canada Lee
Lester	John Tate
Rudolph	Earle Hyman

"While part of the play may be a bit talky, and purists might claim certain moments of confusion, no one will ever say anything bad about the acting. Hilda Simms, in the title role, is a beautiful young lady who also understands what can be done with a part. Frederick O'Neal, who was responsible for founding the American Negro Theatre, has a wonderful time as a hulking, pompous, faintly dim character.... Canada Lee, normally a star in his own right, [helps] out his friends this time ... acting in the way that made him a star.... And Alice Childress is drawing what must be the final picture of a glib, sardonic streetwalker" (Lewis Nichols).

15. *The Tempest* (a Shakespearean play as interpreted by Margaret Webster, based on a production idea by Eva Le Gallienne). *Scenery and Costumes Designed by* Motley. *Lighting by* Moe Hack. *Music Composed by* David Diamond. *Revived by* Cheryl Crawford. At the Alvin Theatre. Opened on January 25, 1945.

Cast

Shipmaster	Joseph Hardy
Boatswain	Steven Elliott
Alonzo, King of Naples	Philip Huston
Gonzalo	Paul Leyssac
Antonio, brother to Prospero	Berry Kroeger

Sebastian, Brother to Alonzo	Eugene Stuckmann
Prospero	Arnold Moss
Miranda, His Daughter	Frances Heflin
Ariel	Vera Zorina
Caliban	Canada Lee
Ferdinand, Prince of Naples	Vito Christi
Adrian, a lord	Jack Bostick
Trinculo, a jester	George Voskovec
Stephano, a butler	Jan Werich
Master of Ceremonies	Larry Evers
Dancer Spirits	Diana Sinclair
Mariners, Shapes, and Spirits	Steven Elliott, Larry Evers, Joseph Hardy, Norman Peck, Charlotte Keane, Diana Sinclair, Patricia Wheel

"As the local and completely official representative of the Bard, Margaret Webster has given New York another good production of Shakespeare. This Winter it is the *Tempest,* which is revived infrequently and offers more than its share of hazards to all but the very brave. Miss Webster has met the challenge in her own way. As Ariel she has cast Vera Zorina, a former dancer, and as Caliban, Canada Lee, a former prize-fighter, and around them she has built a production and an evening that is in the higher bracket.... Mr. Lee has a roar and a bellow and the frightening crouch of a Caliban about to spring, and he gives a realistic performance" (Lewis Nichols).

The Tempest was revived again in November of 1945 after having played on the road since its Broadway run early in 1945. Vera Zorina, Arnold Moss, and Canada Lee repeated in the three leading roles.

16. *On Whitman Avenue* (a play in two acts and four scenes by Maxine Wood). *Staged by* Margo Jones. *Setting and Lighting by* Donald Oenslager. *Lullaby Composed by* Paul Bowles. *Produced by* Canada Lee and Mark Marvin, in association with George McLain. At the Cort Theatre. Opened on May 8, 1946.

Cast

Johnnie Tilden	Martin Miller
Kate Tilden	Ernestine Barrier
Ed Tilden	Will Geer
Owen Bennett	Richard Williams
Gramp Bennett	Augustus Smith
Wini Bennett	Vivienne Baber
Bernie Lund	Kenneth Terry

Aurie Anderson	Hilda Vaughn
Cora Bennett	Abbie Mitchell
Toni Tilden	Miss Perry Wilson
David Bennett	Canada Lee
Jeff Hall	Philip Clarke
Belle Hall	Betty Greene Little
Walter Lund	Robert Simon
Ellen Lund	Jean Cleveland
Wilbur Reed	Stephen Roberts
Edna Reed	Joanna Albus

"The performance of *On Whitman Avenue* does not have the full purity of its heart. Maxine Wood is writing about the Negro and the White, and how an antagonistic relationship can and does affect both. She is not a practiced playwright, and the final treatment of a difficult theme has eluded her. It is easy to see why Canada Lee both cosponsored this drama, and is one of its leading players; but the fact remains that it is just not good theatre" (Lewis Nichols).

17. **The Duchess of Malfi** (a play in three acts by John Webster, adapted by W. H. Auden). *Staged by* George Ryland. *Incidental Music by* Benjamin Britten. *Arranged by* Ignatz Strasfogel. *Scenery by* Harry Bennett. *Costumes by* Miles White. *Revived by* Paul Czinner. At the Barrymore Theatre. Opened on September 25, 1946.

Cast

Ferdinand	Donald Eccles
The Cardinal	John Carradine
Giovanna	Elisabeth Bergner
Antonio Bologna	Whitfield Connor
Delio	Richard Newton
Daniel De Bosola	Canada Lee
Officers Attending on the Duchess	Ben Morse, Michael Bey, Lawrence Ryle
Ladies Attending on the Duchess	Robin Morse, Beth Holland, Diana Kemble
Cariola	Patricia Calvert
Old Lady	Michelette Burani
Roderigo	Rupert Pole
First Guard	William Layton
Second Guard	Frederic Downs
Julia	Sonia Sorel
Monk	Michael Ellis
Pilgrim	Jack Cook

Antonio's Son	Maurice Cavel
Antonio's Daughter	Kathleen Moran
Madmen: (1) Priest	Walter Peterson
(2) Lawyer	Robert Pike
(3) Astrologer	Frederic Downs
(4) Doctor	Guy Spauli

"Since the minor Elizabethan dramas are freely talked about and seldom performed, students of the theatre should be grateful for a chance to see what Webster looks like on the stage. In the performance staged by George Ryland, he looks tamer than one could wish.... Everyone knows that Miss Bergner is a very fine actress.... Here she adds an affecting development of character that gathers strength as it grows out of the beguiling opening scenes.

"Mr. Lee is playing in white face . . . but that is only an amusing detail by comparison with the intelligence, ease, and scope of Mr. Lee's acting as Bosola" (Brooks Atkinson).

18. *Set My People Free* (a play in three acts and ten scenes by Dorothy Heyward). *Staged by* Martin Ritt. *Produced by* the Theatre Guild. *Associate Producer:* Allyn Rice. *Scenery by* Ralph Alswang. *Costumes by* Ernest Schraps. *Choral Direction and Arrangements by* Joshua Lee. At the Hudson Theatre. Opened on November 3, 1948.

Cast

George	Canada Lee
Rose	Mildred Joanne Smith
Denmark	Juano Hernandez
Captain Wilson	Blaine Cordner
Phyllis	Marion Scanlon
Eliza	Gail Gladstone
Gullah Jack	Leigh Whipper
Trader Henri	Somer Alberg
Morris Brown	Frank Wilson
Patrolman	Tyler Carpenter
The Mauma	Bertha T. Powell
Pompey	Alonzo Bosan
Tina	Edith Atuka-Reid
Aneas	William Warfield
Pharaoh	William McDaniel
Benbow	Wanza L. King
Rachel	Fredye Marshall
Adam	Merritt Smith
Cuppy	Theodore Hines

Belletsie	Harry Bolden
Lot	Louis Sharp
Jemmy	George Dosher
Sinah	Musa Williams
Blanche	Uryice Leonardos
Peter Poyas	Earl Sydnor
Blackwood	Thomas Anderson
Ned Bennett	Earl Jones
Rolla Bennett	William Marshall
Monday Gell	Charles McRae
Perault Prioleau	John Bouie
Mingo Harth	Eric Burroughs
Blind Philip	Harold Des Verney
Frank Ferguson	Richard Silver
First Drummer	Samuel Brown
Second Drummer	Moses Mianns

"Dipping back into Negro lore of more than a century ago, Dorothy Heyward has come up with an interesting revolutionary drama.... Under Martin Ritt's competent direction, the drama is generally well acted.... Mr. Hernandez plays with intelligence and power.... Although this is not the biggest part Mr. Lee has had, it is one of the most difficult, and he is the actor who can make it intelligible and moving. The whole character rings with honesty" (Brooks Atkinson).

References

1. Larry Swindell, *Body and Soul: The Story of John Garfield* (New York: William Morrow and Company, 1975), pp. 1–2.
2. Ibid., p. 55.
3. Ibid., p. 64.
4. Ibid., p. 103.
5. Ibid., pp. 124–125.
6. Ibid., p. 150.
7. Ibid., pp. 159 & 162.
8. Rudy Behlmer, *Inside Warner Brothers (1935–1951)* (New York: Fireside Books, 1985), p. 250.
9. Swindell, p. 208.
10. Howard Gelman, *The Films of John Garfield* (Secaucus, New Jersey: Citadel Press, 1975), p. 14.
11. Behlmer, pp. 312–313.
12. Swindell, p. 232.
13. Victor S. Navasky, *Naming Names* (New York: Viking Press, 1980), p. VIII.
14. Swindell, pp. 263–264.
15. Ibid., p. 264.
16. Gelman, p. 36.
17. Ibid., p. 213.
18. Ibid.
19. Ibid., p. 9.
20. Ibid., p. 205.
21. Swindell, pp. 271–272.
22. Gelman, pp. 36 & 39.
23. James N. Beaver, *John Garfield: His Life and Films* (New York: A. S. Barnes and Company, 1978), p. 43.

Bibliography

Aylesworth, Thomas G. and John S. Bowman. *The World Almanac Who's Who of Film*. New York: Pharos Books, Bison Books, 1987.

Beaver, James N. *John Garfield: His Life and Films*. New York: A. S. Barnes, 1978.

Behlmer, Rudy. *Inside Warner Brothers (1935–1951)*. New York: Fireside Books, 1985.

Dickens, Homer. *The Films of James Cagney*. Secaucus, N.J.: Citadel Press, 1972.

_____. *The New York Times Directory of the Theater*. New York: New York Times Book Co., 1972.

Freedland, Michael. *The Warner Brothers*. London: Harrap Limited, 1983.

Gelman, Howard. *The Films of John Garfield*. Secaucus, N.J.: Citadel Press, 1975.

Katz, Ephraim. *The Film Encyclopedia*. New York: Putnam, 1979.

Morella, Joe and Edward Z. Epstein. *Rebels: The Rebel Hero in Films*. Secaucus, N.J.: Citadel Press, 1971.

Morris, George. *John Garfield*. New York: Jove, 1977.

Nash, Jay Robert and Stanley Ralph Ross. *The Motion Picture Guide*. Chicago: Cinebooks, 1987.

Navasky, Victor S. *Naming Names*. New York: Viking Press, 1980.

Okuda, Ted. *Grand National, Producers Releasing Corporation and Screen Guild/Lippert*. Jefferson, N.C.: McFarland, 1989.

Sennett, Ted. *Warner Brothers Presents*. Secaucus, N.J.: Castle Books, 1971.

Swindell, Larry. *Body and Soul: The Story of John Garfield*. New York: William Morrow, 1975.

Index

Numbers in **boldface** refer to pages with photographs.

Index

255

Wright, Richard 108, 232, 233, 234
Wrixon, Maris 186
Wyatt, Jane 168, 199
Wyler, William 51, 118
Wyman, Jane 195

Y

Yankee Doodle Dandy 25
Yordan, Philip 109, 236
York, Jeff 196
Young, Gig 61, **64,** 190
Young, J. Russell **70**
Young, Marie 226

Young, Walter 181
Young at Heart 173
Young Man with a Horn 79
Young Philadelphians 42

Z

Zampa, Luigi 203
Zanette, Guy 203
Zanuck, Daryl F. 123, 199
Zeitlin, Esther 203
Zinneman, Fred 174
Zorina, Vera 110, 237
Zorn, George 233